COLLINS
PRACTICAL DICTIONARY OF
HOUSEHOLD
HINTS

COLLINS

Commissioning Editor: Sarah Parr

Editor: Dorothy Darrell Ward

Contributing Editors: Barbara Croxford
Jill Blake
Mike Lawrence

Designers: Caroline Dewing
Val Heneghan

Illustrators: Anne Morrow
Lindsay Blow
Roy Flooks
Alicia Durdos
Andy Miles

Acknowledgements: We would like to thank the following
organizations for their special
contribution to the book:
Electrical Association for Women
Wallpaper Marketing Board

Designed and produced by
Marshall Cavendish Books Limited
58 Old Compton Street
LONDON W1V 5PA

Published by William Collins Sons & Co. Ltd.
London · Glasgow · Sydney · Auckland
Toronto · Johannesburg

First published 1982

ISBN 0 00 411636 4

Printed and bound by L.E.G.O., Vicenza, Italy

INTRODUCTION

Managing a household means that there are many occasions when you need to know – or have swift access to – information of the most diverse kind. From how to rewasher a tap, for example, to how to defrost the freezer, from how to administer basic first aid to how to plan tasty, inexpensive and nutrition-packed meals for the family.

Collins Practical Dictionary of Household Hints provides a reliable back-up for the harried householder. Its thirteen chapters are grouped in a most practical working order: beginning with the home (Home Decorating, Home Improvements, Home Repairs & Maintenance) and followed by more personal information such as Clothes Care and First Aid, ending with a special 'kitchen' section, including Food and Nutrition. Within each chapter all main entries are alphabetically arranged for easy reference and the emphasis throughout is on basic practical information presented in a straightforward readable way. A special 14-page fully cross-referenced index makes emergency use both feasible and easy. Specially noteworthy tips and hints to make life easier are starred as 'handy hints'; good advice on pitfalls to avoid or be careful of are given equal prominence as 'warnings'. And each chapter has been read and approved by experts.

Throughout the book the emphasis is on practicality, clarity and helpfulness. We feel sure that you will find our *Practical Dictionary* immensely helpful as a comprehensive, accurate reference volume for the whole family.

CONTENTS

CHAPTER 1

HOME DECORATION

Carpets • Curtains • Cushions
Floor coverings • Furniture • Lighting
Mirrors • Wallpaper

Blinds

Blinds make an economical alternative to curtains, and are particularly useful for dormer and similar windows which can be difficult to curtain.

Types of blind

Holland blinds Roller blinds made in linen-type fabric with a smooth, stiffened finish. Dust down to clean.

Insulated blinds These are pleated horizontal concertina blinds which cut heat loss by about a third and filter out the strong rays of the sun.

Paper blinds Inexpensive pleated paper blinds are obtainable in white and a range of colours. Dust regularly.

Roller blinds These can be bought in standard widths or made to measure. Standard widths, which may have to have roller, slat and fabric trimmed, come in sizes from 91cm (3ft) to 1.83m (6ft) wide and 1.83m (6ft) to 1.98m (6ft 6in) long. Ensure that the width you choose covers the window plus at least 5cm (2in) on each side.

Made-to-measure blinds can be matched with wallpaper and other furnishing fabrics. Wipe with a damp cloth.

Various styles of bottom trim include scallops, fringes and lacy edgings.

Roman blinds (sometimes called 'festooned' or Austrian shades) These are made to order and are expensive. When pulled up they form soft folds at the top of the window. They should be dry cleaned. Voile roman blinds – available by mail order – can be hand-washed.

Split bamboo blinds The cheapest ready-made blinds, they come in the same sizes as roller blinds. Clean with a soft brush and a damp cloth.

Venetian blinds The amount of light entering the room can be adjusted with these blinds; the slats can be slanted so that you can see out without being seen.

Slat widths vary from 2.5cm (1in) to 5cm (2in), and a wide range of pastel and strong colours is available. Two-tone blinds are white on the outside so the exterior of the house looks uniform, while inside the colours vary according to your colour schemes. Slat colours can also be mixed to create interesting visual effects. A new type of Venetian has been introduced which fits sloping windows, including skylights, and operates with remote control fittings. Wipe over with a damp cloth once a week. A special brush is available for cleaning them slat by slat. See also CLEANING THE HOUSE.

Vertical blinds Made of stiffened fabric upright slats linked at the bottom with a fine chain. They can be divided in the centre like a curtain, or drawn aside (when they take up very little space) and the slats can be rotated to let in light. They are expensive, but elegant over a large window.

Measuring for blinds

Take careful measurements, using a steel rule and when ordering, keep a copy of your order as a check. The width is normally calculated as the overall measurement with the brackets. The fabric is usually 4.5cm (1¾in) less than the total width. The fabric must cover the window recess or the glass, if you are fitting it inside the recess, by at least 5cm (2in) at the sides, top and bottom.

Carpets

There is a wide choice of carpeting available in various price ranges, so choosing can be confusing. If you want the best results from your investment you must choose the right quality for the area you want to carpet, taking into consideration the type of wear it will get.

 HANDY HINT

Choose the best possible quality you can afford for the areas with heavy 'traffic', such as the hallway, stairs and landing and main living rooms. Use lighter, cheaper grades for rooms which get less wear.

Types of carpet

The traditional types of carpet are woven. These are:

Axminster This is usually patterned, with an extensive choice of colours within the design. The pile yarn is seen on the surface and the backing is jute or hessian, sometimes strengthened by polypropylene. Different fibres and blends of fibres are used, but frequently Axminsters are made in an 80/20 wool/nylon mixture, and from Acrylic fibres.

Many different widths are available, including broadloom up to 5m (16ft 5in) wide. Axminsters can appear as carpet 'squares', with bound edges, rather like large rugs. The advantage with these is that they can be turned round to even out the wear.

Wilton This type of carpet is usually plain although some patterned Wiltons, with a restricted number of colour combinations, are produced. The carpet is close-textured with a velvet, close-looped or mixed cut-and-loop 'sculptured' pile. Any yarn not used on the face of the carpet is woven into the backing to add thickness and strength. The backing used is the same as for Axminster.

Different fibres and blends of fibres can be used, but usually Wiltons are made in 100 per cent wool or an 80/20 wool and nylon mixture.

Wilton carpet is woven in narrow widths, from 0.7m–1.8m (27in–6ft) wide, and widths are seamed to fit when fully fitted carpet is required. Wider widths (up to 3.6m or 12ft) are also available and can be bound to form a carpet 'square'.

The carpet industry has developed other techniques for making carpets. These include:

Tufted This is by far the most widely available and comes in many different effects, textures and fibres. Tufted carpets can be patterned or plain and widths can be from 1m–5m (3ft–16ft 5in). The tufts are needled into an already woven backing and anchored with an adhesive. Backings vary and can be hessian, latex or foam – a high-quality foam-backed tufted carpet can be laid without an underlay.

Bonded These are made face-to-face, just like a sandwich, with the 'filling' being the carpet pile, held between two specially treated woven backings. The carpet is sliced through the middle to make two carpets. All the carpet pile is on the surface, and can be in a wide range of lengths and textures from a shaggy effect to a close-cropped velour. The fibres can be traditional or synthetic or a mixture, and the carpets are usually plain. Broadloom widths (as with Axminster) are normally available.

Needlefelt or needlepunch A fibrous mass is needled by machine into a strong backing, creating a looped 'corduroy' or a dense felt pile. They are plain, mottled or printed, with a resin-coated or foam backing. The fibres are natural, synthetic or a blend, but usually this type of carpet is made from fibres, and broadloom widths are the norm.

Types of fibres

All these different types and styles of carpet can be made from a wide range of fibres, and blends of fibres.

Acrylics Have good resistance to flattening, but do not have such lasting qualities as wool and tend to show the dirt more.

Blended fibres These give, in proportion, the advantage of all the fibres used in the blend. For example, 80/20 per cent wool/nylon blend combines the soil resistance and resilience of wool with the hard-wearing characteristics of nylon. Many different fibres can be blended in carpet construction.

Cotton Has the advantage of being cheap; but although it washes easily, it flattens quickly and soils easily.

Nylon The hardest wearing fibre yet developed for carpets, but on its own it soils easily and can look scuffed and bedraggled very quickly. It can give a lustrous and luxurious look to a carpet. When nylon is added to other fibres, it increases the strength of the carpet.

Polyester A soft fibre, usually used in mini-shag and fluffy carpets. It has only moderate wear characteristics.

Polypropylene Often found in cord carpets. It provides moderate wear and appearance retention, is impervious to water and much used for backings.

Viscose rayon Inexpensive but does not wear well, and soils and flattens as badly as cotton.

Wool No complete substitute for wool has yet been found. A blend of the right kinds of wool will provide a hard-wearing, resilient carpet which shows soiling less than other fibres. But this special type of carpet wool is expensive and the wrong type of yarn makes a poor quality carpet. If you want wool, you will have to pay for it. A wool and nylon mixture in an 80/20 blend gives the very best performance.

Labelling for use

It is important to buy the right grade of carpet for your needs. Most pile carpets are classified as follows:

1 *Light domestic* for bedrooms and areas of light traffic.

2 *Medium domestic* or *light contract* for main bedrooms, medium traffic.

3 *General domestic* or *medium contract* for main living rooms, general traffic.

4 *Heavy domestic* or *general contract* for all heavy domestic situations, such as hallways and stairs.

5 *Heavy contract* for public buildings with heavy traffic.

6 *Luxury use* usually for a long pile carpet of quality better than category 3.

Carpet sizes

As carpet looms are not metric, widths are still calculated in feet (see REFERENCE TABLES).

For carpet cleaning and shampooing, see CLEANING·THE HOUSE – Carpet cleaning.

Laying carpets

This is not a particularly easy job and if you have an awkwardly shaped room or have bought expensive carpeting, it is better left to the professionals.

Underlay All carpets are improved by a good underlay of thick felt or canvas backed rubber. An underlay will make your carpets wear much better and provide added insulation. Foam and latex-backed carpets do not need an underlay.

Broadloom The easiest to lay as it comes in seven widths up to 4.57m (5yd) and avoids the necessity for seams in the middle of the room. It is, however, awkward to handle.

Foam rubber or latex-backed carpet This is easier to lay than secondary backed carpet and can simply be cut into shape and placed in position without securing the edges. Cut slightly larger, to allow for any irregularities in the wall, let the carpet fall into place and trim the edges with a Stanley knife.

'Strip' carpet Comes in widths of 69cm (2ft 3in) and 91cm (3ft) and is sold by the linear yard or metre. It is more economi-cal to lay in odd-shaped rooms with alcoves or recesses. The strips must be sewn together, using carpet thread, working from the back; or joined together from the back, using special adhesive carpet tape.

Securing the carpet

Using grippers These are strips of wood or metal with numerous small metal spikes projecting at an angle – they can be bought from hardware stores.

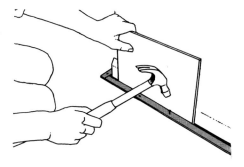

1 Nail or glue the grippers round the room, 6mm ($\frac{1}{4}$in) from the wall, spikes pointing up. Use hardboard to protect skirting board while hammering.

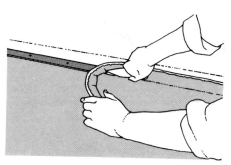

2 Lay the underlay so that it comes up against the grippers, staple in place or fix with latex-based adhesive.

3 Unroll the carpet, with the pile sweeping away from the window, and position it so that a margin of about 12mm ($\frac{1}{2}$in) overlaps on to the wall at each side.

4 Fix the carpet temporarily in one corner with a tack and stretch along one wall.

5 Fix over the gripper strip and stretch to the other side of the room.

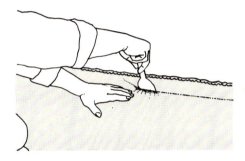

6 Push the carpet over the prongs of the gripper and into the gap between the gripper and the wall.

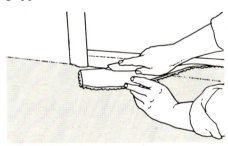

7 Trim the edges of the carpet and coat with latex adhesive if necessary to seal them and prevent fraying.

Turn and tack method

1 Lay the underlay leaving a gap of 4cm (1$\frac{1}{2}$in) all round.

2 Trim the carpet so that it is 4cm (1$\frac{1}{2}$in) larger than the room all round and seal the edges with latex adhesive.

3 Starting from one corner, turn in the margins and tack into position.

4 Stretch the carpet along one wall and then across the room.

5 Secure with 1.5–2cm ($\frac{1}{2}$–$\frac{3}{4}$in) tacks at 12cm (5in) intervals, using 2.5cm (1in) tacks at the corners.

Finishing off

Tape the exposed edge of the carpet at a doorway and tack to the floor or, preferably, fit a metal binder bar, so that it comes immediately under the door when closed. Fit the edge of the carpet inside the bar and secure by metal prongs, then hammer down the top of the bar to close it. Double binder bars can be bought to join two carpet edges.

 ★ **HANDY HINT** ★

A special tool is needed to stretch carpets. This can be obtained from hire specialists.

Some foam rubber and latex-backed carpets can be loose laid. In certain circumstances they can be stuck with double-sided tape or stapled to the subfloor.

Colour

Choosing your colours

You should always choose your colour scheme with your existing furnishings in mind.

HANDY HINT

If your curtains, upholstery or carpet are patterned, it is usually best to avoid a patterned wallpaper or the effect will be busy and cluttered.

If you can afford to buy new chairs or re-cover the old ones, and make new curtains, you will be able to achieve a well co-ordinated look. There are several ranges of matching fabrics, wall coverings and paints on the market which make this an easy task.

If, however, you have to make do with existing furnishings, you must build up your colour scheme round them. Select a colour in the pattern of your curtains, for example, or a different shade of the colour of your carpet.

Major surfaces Walls, curtains and ceiling. Choose the colour or pattern of the carpet first, then consider the ceiling and walls. A room should not have more than two or three main colours.

Making a colour board/plan Each colour you choose must be seen in relation to all the other colours, if you are to produce a successful decor and avoid drastic mistakes. It is a good idea to make up some kind of board/plan using swatches of fabric, paint charts and wall covering samples. Use coloured paper to add approximate colours for accessories.

 HANDY HINT

Look at your chart in the actual room, in daylight and artificial light before ordering anything.

Curtains

There are various points to bear in mind when choosing curtains, besides the all-over colour in relation to the room.

Choosing a fabric

Curtain material must hang well. Look at the fabric draped before you buy it and find out if it is washable or needs dry cleaning, whether it is shrink resistant and fade resistant.

Check that any pattern is printed correctly on the grain of the material.

Linings Lined curtains drape better, protect the fabric from light, dust and dirt, and provide some insulation. One type of lining has a metal finish which helps to prevent heat loss. They can also give windows a co-ordinated look from the outside.

 WARNING

The total width of the curtains must be at least one and a half times, preferably twice, the length of the curtain rail, plus enough for an overlap of about 20cm (8in).

Interlining This gives curtains extra body, helping them to drape better and showing off the fabric to its best advantage. Interlining fabrics are thick and fluffy and the extra weight means that you will need particularly strong curtain tracks or rods.

See also SOFT FURNISHINGS – Curtains.

Estimating quantities

Measure each individual window. To the length of the window, add about 30cm (1ft) for the hems at top and bottom. Short curtains should just clear the sill or any radiator under it.

Nets and *light materials* should be twice the width of the window. If you are choosing a *patterned fabric*, make sure you allow enough extra material to match the pattern when two lengths are joined together.

Curtain tracks

Here is a basic check list which may help you to choose curtain tracks.

● What is the track made of and what does it look like?

● Will it take a pelmet or valance?

● Can it take heavy curtains?

● Is it fixed to the wall, the window frame or to the ceiling?

● Can it bend to fit a bay window?

● Does it have overlap arms, which let the curtains hang one in front of the other where they meet in the centre?

● Do you need special runners or curtain hooks?

● Can you attach automatic or manual pulleys?

● What types of pleating can be used?

● Does it have pull-cord attachments?

Curtain rods and poles

You may want to fit a rod or pole which shows above the top of the curtain. The curtain is attached by traditional rings of wood or metal, depending on whether you choose a wood or metal rod. Metal rods are obtainable in various colours and finishes. The curtain can also hang from loops of material or from modern runners in grooves in the pole which look like traditional rings but run more smoothly and are attached to modern drawstring tapes.

Pelmets

The difference between a pelmet and a valance is that a valance is like a short unstiffened curtain, while a pelmet is flat, stiff and smooth. A valance is usually hung from a special rail on the curtain track.

Uses for pelmets and valances Their main purpose is to conceal the top of the curtain and the track, but the pelmet also has decorative value.

Proportions As a rough guide, the depth of a pelmet or valance for full length curtains should be about one-sixth of the length of the curtains. With short curtains you can allow 4cm (1½in) to every 30cm (1ft) of curtain length. The bottom edge of the pelmet or valance should be at least 2cm (¾in) below the upper window edge – lower if you have very shaped pelmets. To test the effect before you cut any fabric, make a template from newspaper or brown paper. Pin this to the top of the curtain to judge suitability and adjust if necessary.

Ready-made curtains

If you are not ready to try your hand at making your own, there are plenty of attractive ready-made curtains now available. These can be bought in varying lengths and widths and with a choice of pleating. They can also be matched with wallpaper and fabrics.

Cushions

Cushions, large and small and in all kinds of shapes, can help to brighten a room and pick out colours in your decor. Making your own cushions can save you money, but compare costs and prices before you start. A simple cushion may be cheaper to buy than to make, but if you want something special you may save money by making it yourself.

Fillings

Down This is the best and most expensive. Feather and down or feathers are light and resilient, but not as soft as down.

Foam fillings Latex and plastic shavings are cheap but lumpy. Latex and plastic foam sheeting can be cut to shape using a sharp craft knife, a hot-wire cutter obtainable from builders' merchants, or an electric carving knife.

 WARNING

Cover cushions filled with foam with a strong, flame-retardant fabric which allows air to pass through it, as some types of foam give off lethal fumes if they catch alight.

Kapok A soft, light, cotton-like fabric that is cheap but tends to become lumpy.

Synthetic fibre fillings Those such as Terylene and Dacron are soft, light, resilient and washable. This means that if your covers are washable you can wash the whole cushion at once. Old *nylon tights* cut into small strips, make a fairly satisfactory filling, but you do need a large quantity of them.

Inner covers If you are using down or feathers, you must use a down and feather-proof fabric for these. Use a washable fabric for synthetic fibres and any closely woven cotton fabric for other types of filling.

Making cushion covers

Cushion covers are not difficult to make and can add to the comfort and appearance of your rooms.

Inner covers Square covers look better if they are slightly rounded by cutting V-notches at the corners. If V-notches are cut on the outer curve of the wrong side of a *round cover* it will help the turnings to lie flat.

For feather and down cushions, stitch the seam twice, using a fine needle.

Outer covers *Openings* must be left so that the cushion can be removed and the cover cleaned. The simplest opening is slip-stitched by hand and unpicked for washing or cleaning.

Zips, strips of Velcro, press studs or popper tape are all satisfactory. Either allow extra material when cutting out, or use matching binding to neaten and strengthen the edges when using this type of fastening.

Floor coverings

The floor is an important element in a building and it receives harder wear than any other part of the home. Floor finishes have to stand up to the abrasive action of foot traffic, as well as having an attractive and durable appearance. In addition, floors often add quietness and warmth, need to be resistant to fading or staining and should be easy to clean. It is also advisable to have a non-slip surface.

Choosing your flooring

While the basic structure of the floor you have to cover may limit your choice, cost may also be a limiting factor, as may the sort of room and the amount of traffic, and the rest of the decor.

Cork tiling, for example, might look out of place with rich carpets, heavy traditional furniture and chintz curtains. On the other hand, a wood block floor will not look as good in a room furnished with cheap, modern furniture and cheap and cheerful blinds.

If you are flooring a kitchen, bear in mind the amount of time you spend on your feet there, and the spillage and splashes which inevitably happen. Choose a warm surface which can be easily cleaned, such as cork or flexible vinyl flooring.

Cork flooring

Cork must be laid over an absolutely smooth, flat surface or it will crack. On most floors this means laying a hardboard or flooring grade chipboard base before gluing the tiles into place. Cork tiles can be laid on a paper felt base. Tiles which are presealed are best for bathrooms and kitchens where some splashing is unavoidable.

When cutting cork flooring, undercut the tile edges very slightly for neat joins.

Replacing and repairing cork tiles When replacing a damaged tile, carefully scrape off all remnants of the old tile, paper and adhesive with a sharp chisel. Then line the space with fresh paper felt before inserting the new tile.

 ★   **HANDY HINT**   ★

If it is not possible to replace a damaged tile, a reasonable looking repair can be done by making a filler paste out of ground up cork of the correct colour mixed with epoxy resin adhesive. Fill the hole, press the filling well down, leave to dry and then sand flat and finish as required.

Linoleum and vinyl flooring

Both of these materials make practical and economical floor coverings. They are hard wearing, resilient, warm to the feet and easy to clean.

Linoleum This comes in various colours and patterns in sheet or tiled form. Better quality linoleum has inlaid, rather than surface printed, patterns that will not wear off.

Linoleum comes in 1.5mm ($\frac{1}{16}$in), 3mm ($\frac{1}{8}$in), 4.2mm ($\frac{1}{6}$in) and 5mm ($\frac{1}{5}$in) thicknesses, the last used mainly for tiles.

Sheet linoleum comes in a standard 1.8m (5ft 11in) width and tiles are made in 30cm (1ft) squares.

To create a patterned effect, different colours can be 'cut in' to form a design.

Vinyl Usually bought in sheet or tile form, with plain, patterned or embossed finishes. It comes in thicknesses from 1mm ($\frac{1}{25}$in) to 5mm ($\frac{1}{5}$in) and widths of

1.2m (about 4ft), 1.5m (4ft 11in), 2m (about 6ft 6in), 3.66mm (about 12ft) and 4m (13ft). Tiles can be bought in 22.5cm (8½in) up to 25cm (10in) and 30cm (1ft) squares and, in a limited range, in other shapes, such as rectangles.

Vinyl asbestos tiles are resistant to damp, but soften and indent at a lower temperature than ordinary vinyl. Felt-backed and cushioned vinyls are softer to the feet and deaden sounds.

Laying sheet linoleum or vinyl Loosen the roll and leave it in the room overnight, with the heat on, to make it more flexible and easier to handle.

1 Lay with the seams at right angles to the window, but not near a doorway, and line up the sheet under the thickness of the door, across the opening.

2 Fit so the sheets overlap each other by about 12mm (½in) with an extra 5cm (2in) turned up all round. Leave to settle, according to the manufacturer's instructions, before trimming to size.

3 Make a paper template to fit around any obstacles or projections, tape the template to the sheet and use it to cut a snug fit. Or use a special tool (available from do-it-yourself shops) which has adjustable 'needles' to record the shape.

4 Glue the floor under a join, butt the edges, matching the pattern carefully, and seal with a liquid cold sealant.

5 Finish cutting all material before applying adhesive according to manufacturer's instructions.

Laying linoleum or vinyl tiles

1 Mark the floor by stretching a length of string, coated with chalk, between centre points of opposite walls, and secure in position with drawing pins.

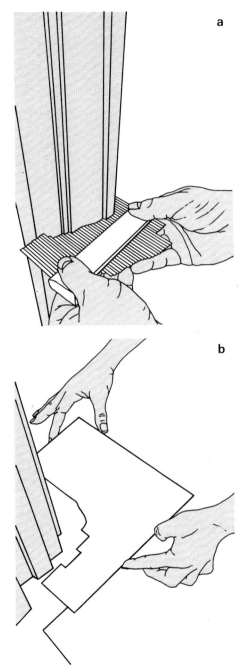

a

b

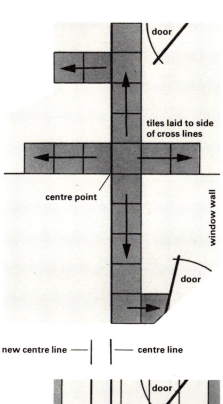

tiles laid to side of cross lines

centre point

window wall

door

door

new centre line — | | — centre line

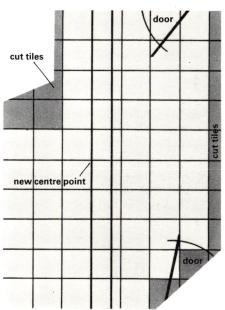

cut tiles

door

cut tiles

new centre point

door

2 Pluck the string at the centre, leaving a chalk line on the floor. Make a second line at right angles to the first, and use as a guide to setting out the tiles, working from the centre outwards.

3 Lay a row of tiles 'dry' against the marked lines to see how much space is left round the edges. If necessary, make another line parallel to the first, so that cut tiles at the edges will balance.

4 If you are using differently coloured tiles to make a pattern, lay these out dry to see the effect.

5 Using the correct adhesive, with a notched spreader, apply to an area about 1m (3ft 4in) square. Work up to the edge of the chalk lines but try to avoid covering them.

6 Warm the tiles to increase their flexibility, if necessary. Position the first tile carefully in the angle of the two marked lines, press down firmly, working from the centre to the edges.

7 Lay successive tiles in the same way, butting them against each other. Remove surplus adhesive immediately with a damp cloth.

8 Use a template for awkward and curved shapes (see Laying sheet lino-leum) and for edges where a full-sized tile is not needed. (Fig. **a** and **b**).

9 When the tiles are laid, sweep the floor, wipe with a damp cloth and apply the proprietary seal or polish recommended by the manufacturer.

Wood floors

There are various block, strip, mosaic and panel finishes which can be applied to a concrete or other sub-floor. They are usually made of hardwood, and are more expensive than plain floorboards, but give a more luxurious effect. They are most suitable for halls and reception rooms.

Wood block floors Usually made of hardwood, laid in a basket or herring-bone pattern; *wood mosaic* is thinner and cheaper than wood block, and comes in patterned panels, about 45cm (1ft 6in) square.

Parquet flooring Most expensive type of panel flooring, consisting of squares of decoratively arranged hardwoods, attached to a plywood base. The panels are glued and pinned to a smooth sub-floor.

Most types of parquet flooring need expert laying but there are self-adhesive ranges available for do-it-yourself enthusiasts.

Furniture – new

There are now so many types and ranges of furniture available that making a final choice can be difficult.

Be absolutely sure about what you are looking for and how much you are willing to pay, and shop around until you find what you want.

Take into consideration that you may have to pay cash at a discount store, and arrange your own transport from the store to the house which will add to the overall cost.

When buying new furniture, make sure that it carries the BSI kitemark and that the upholstery, where applicable, has the international Woolmark or Woolblend mark.

 ★ HANDY HINT ★

As well as measuring the space that you want your new furniture to fill, check that your doorways, stairs or passages are wide enough for it to pass through.

Checking new furniture

Cupboard doors These should open and close easily, hinges should not stick and handles and locks should be smooth and easy to use.

Drawers Check that they do not stick, move from side to side or jump off the runners.

Framework Check that this is rigid and cannot be rocked to and fro.

Joints Check that dovetails are neat and glued joints clean.

Tables Must be firm. Test drop-leaf or gate-leg tables carefully.

See what you are buying

Do not be afraid to look inside and underneath everything. You may find rough, badly finished wood, with perhaps sticky knots in it that have not been sealed properly. The bottoms of drawers may be thin and of poor quality or not securely fixed. Watch for veneer that is lifting or bentwood furniture that has split on the curve.

If you are buying upholstered furniture, check the cleanability, and the covering fabric, avoiding anything loosely woven. Look underneath to make sure the webbing and springs are not sagging.

Make sure that the upholstery fabric

and, preferably, the filling have been flameproofed.

If the piece of furniture is designed to be movable, test the runners or castors to make sure that they work smoothly.

When you consider that some of the items you buy may still be with you in 50 years, it is worth time and effort to be certain of buying something you like, that will last and even, as beautiful hardwoods do, improve with age.

Furniture – old

Knowing what to look for when buying old or antique furniture is a skill that takes time to acquire. Look for solid, well-made pieces and do not be put off by dirt or worn paintwork, provided the wood underneath is good.

Look particularly for furniture made before World War II, well made and strong.

What furniture to avoid

Avoid pieces made or fitted with:
● All synthetics, including plastic laminates, vinyl, acrylics, etc.
● Chipboard or hardboard.
● Plywoods.
● Blockboards faced with veneer.
● Pressed metal hinges and hardware fittings.
● Plated and/or lacquered metal parts.
● Rubber-shod castor wheels.
● Wire nails or cross-head screws.

Avoid furniture with several loose joints, panels with broad cracks in them or tide-marked wood which shows exposure to damp.

Avoid pieces with clumsy repairs, screws visibly placed, nailed patches, metal rods or wires. Most broken legs can be repaired or even replaced; but elaborate, curved legs which are badly broken and split will need professional attention. (See also REPAIRS AND MAINTENANCE – Furniture.)

 WARNING
Do keep a sharp look-out when buying old furniture for signs of attack by fungi or woodworm (see REPAIRS AND MAINTENANCE – Furniture).

Reviving old furniture

It is unlikely that the furniture you buy at an auction or in junk shops, etc. will be in first class condition. More likely it will be coated with many layers of paint, or black with grime, and will have to be cleaned or stripped and refinished.

With care and a fair amount of time, battered furniture can be turned into attractive, useful pieces. Some processes are difficult and should be tried on small areas first, or left to professional workmen. Once you have cleaned or stripped the piece, you will have a better idea of the quality of the wood it is made of, and you can decide which finish is best suited. (See also REPAIRS AND MAINTENANCE – Furniture.)

Finishing touches When you have completed the cleaning, stripping, painting or polishing processes it may be worth buying new hardware – handles, knobs, castors and so on – to make the piece of furniture look really good.

Handles and knobs can easily be replaced and it may be better to buy a new set rather than try to match existing oddments. Excellent reproduction metal hardware of this sort can be found in specialist shops.

Castors often work loose and re-drilling may weaken the legs. Therefore, completely re-fill the bottom of the leg, using matchsticks or dowel and PVA glue. When set and thoroughly dry, drill holes for the new castors.

Painting and decorating old furniture

If your piece of furniture is of poor quality or if your room needs extra colour, the best way of treating it, once it has been cleaned and stripped, may be to paint it. This provides a long-lasting finish with a wide choice of colours and is easy to change if you redecorate. Modern polyurethane and vinyl gloss paints are particularly tough and hard wearing.

By painting or staining odd bits of furniture – say a chest of drawers, a mirror-frame and an old table – the same colour, you can create a sense of unity, and the fact that the chairs may all be different is immaterial. Matching chair seats or cushions, new handles on drawers – choose the same pattern for each piece of furniture – all help to harmonise your scheme.

Using colours A stunning effect can be created by variations in shades, based on one or two colours. A chest with several drawers can, for instance, have the colour on the drawer fronts gra-duated from, say, deep orange at the bottom to pale yellow at the top. A plain wooden trunk or old fashioned blanket box can be stencilled in a contrasting colour.

Stencils Ready cut-out stencils can be bought in toy shops and from artists' suppliers. They may be somewhat limited in range, but can be combined and adapted to produce many different designs, or you can make your own, using special stencil shapes available from good stationers or art supply shops.

Use acrylic polymer paint, not too wet, with a stencilling or stippling brush, or paint pad or spray. Two brushes may be necessary, one for dark and one for light colours. Alternatively, use spray-on enamel paint.

 HANDY HINT

Acrylic polymer or spray-on enamel paints need not be cleaned off the stencil after you have finished sten-cilling, as they dry hard and will not run into other paints.

Indoor plants

Creative cultivation of plants can provide unlimited scope for the indoor gardener.

Choosing indoor plants

If you do not know much about plants, choose a hardy variety. It is disheartening to watch a prized, delicate specimen slowly fade and die.

Consider where and how you intend to display the plants and make sure those you choose will thrive in the position you have chosen.

Decide whether you need an upright or a bushy plant, a climber or a trailer or a plant with showy foliage. Flowering plants add colour often for only a relatively short period and evergreens are generally easier to care for.

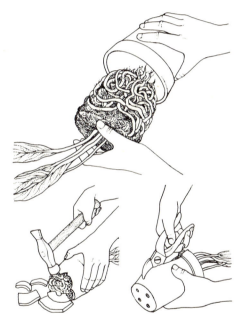

Repotting a plant

Holding your fingers around the base of the stem, turn the pot upside down and give it a sharp tap on the base.

If you have difficulty, don't try to prize it out as this may damage the roots. Break open a clay pot with a hammer. Use secateurs or scissors to cut open a plastic pot.

Care of house plants

Air Avoid draughts, but allow fresh air in mild or warm weather.

Cleaning Sponge glossy leaves with a soft, damp cloth; brush hairy leaves.

Food Feed plants during the growing season only.

Holiday care In winter it is probably enough to moisten the soil and move the plants away from windows. In summer you can invest in one of the numerous automatic watering systems now available, or the plants can be grouped together in a polythene bowl and covered with a large, clear polythene bag which is tied over them. Large pot plants can be placed on bricks or pebbles inside a polythene bowl. Fit a wick of cloth into the drainage hole of the pot and partially fill the container with water, so that the wick is covered not the roots.

Humidity Most plants except cacti appreciate occasional spraying with water.

Light Requirements vary. Signs of light deficiency are small, pale leaves and elongated stems.

Pests and diseases Healthy plants are more resistant to pests and diseases than neglected ones. The main pests to attack house plants are aphids, whitefly, black-fly and red spider mites which attack the undersides of young leaves and can be controlled with a proprietary spray; scale insects and mealy bugs which attack stems and joints can also be sprayed.

Mildew and rust Mildew is generally the result of overcrowding. With grey mould the affected parts must be cut off and burned. Rust, like mildew, can be treated with a fungicide. It is wise to ask for advice at your local garden shop, to find out which type of spray will suit your plant.

Repotting If the plant is growing very slowly and roots are appearing through the drainage hole, it needs repotting in a larger pot.

Soil Use a good potting compost for the best results.

Temperature Most plants prefer a steady temperature, but few live happily in really hot rooms.

Water More plants die from overwatering than underwatering. More water is needed during warm weather and the growing period. An occasional good watering is better than a daily dribble. If the soil in the pot feels dry, it is likely that the plant needs water. If the plant is drooping, it also needs water. Immerse the plant pots in water above their rims and leave until the bubbles stop rising, to make sure that the soil is thoroughly moistened, then remove and drain before replacing in position. If pots are standing in a container of gravel or pebbles, water can be given from below.

What went wrong?

Plants are not immortal and their life spans vary. Also it is normal for lower leaves to die and drop from time to time. As long as the plant looks healthy and puts out new leaves there should be no cause for alarm.

Some plants which have been forced, such as chrysanthemums and poinsettias, flower for quite a long time and then die back. It is probably best to regard them as long-lasting bunches of flowers and throw them away when the flowers are over, although poinsettias can be pruned, left to rest and repotted.

Some plants, such as cyclamen and azalea indica, can be planted out in the garden in the summer and brought back indoors in autumn. Others, such as hydrangeas, can be put out in the garden permanently.

There are, however, some danger signs which you should look for.

Brown tips to leaves Can be caused by overwatering, overfeeding, too much sun or gas fumes.

Dropping of buds and leaves Can mean overwatering, dry air or gas fumes, or can be caused by moving the plant.

Pale and spindly plants Generally indicates lack of food or light.

Slow growth May mean underfeeding or the plant may be pot bound, a naturally slow grower or in its rest period.

Variegated leaves going green Caused by lack of light.

Wilting May be caused by overheating, over- and underwatering.

Yellow leaves If they seem otherwise healthy this probably means an adverse reaction to lime, possibly from hard water. Try repotting and watering with rainwater. If yellow leaves wilt and drop, this usually indicates overwatering or a cold draught.

Lighting

However attractive your furnishing and colour scheme, the right lighting can make all the difference to the atmosphere and comfort of your home. It can also make a dramatic difference to the shape and style of a room. If a room is too tall, low-sited lights which direct illumination downwards and let little light out above, can direct the eye to the horizontal planes. White painted walls, washed with pools of light can create a sense of air and space. Properly used, lighting will enrich colours, complementing a dark decor or highlighting pretty pastel shades.

Types of lighting

A bare central bulb hanging high up in the middle of a room gives a flattening, dull light. The key to good and interesting lighting is variation in the light level in different parts of the room. There are four categories of lighting:
● Strong, localised light shining over an area for a definite purpose.
● Background or indirect lighting, which gives an overall light, such as a central ceiling light or a tall standard lamp.
● Reflected light which, shining from a basic source, reflects off a white or coloured surface to give a soft effect.
● Adjustable lighting, which includes spotlights and movable fitments, can be swivelled, dimmed, etc. to alter their effect.

Other sources of light Do not forget types of light other than electrical. Warmth, interest and a focal point can be created by the glow of a fire or by candles. If you do use candles, or other naked flames, position them in a safe place, away from draughts and out of reach of children.

Planning your lighting

Whether you are re-planning an old room or starting from scratch you must decide:
1 Plan your furniture positions and work out the necessary lighting in relation to them; you may need a lamp on a rise-and-fall fitting, for example, to pull down over the dining table; lamps on tables at each end of settees and bedside table lights.
2 Which types of light are most suitable for these functions.
3 Which type of fitting will give the required light.

Choosing the fittings

For a working light, the lamp should have a strong beam falling only on the desk or work table.

For a reading light, a table or standard lamp could be placed behind and to one side of an easy chair. This would require a wide shade and a crown-silvered bulb could be used.

For throwing sufficient light onto people engaged in conversation, a central pendant hanging low (just above head height) over a table where it would cast a wide pool of light would be suitable.

 ★ **HANDY HINT** ★
It is often worth while having some extra power points fitted in any room, not only to give more flexibility to your lighting pattern, but to avoid the danger of trailing flexes on the floor.

Mirrors

Mirrors are not only functional, they are popular from a design aspect. In many rooms, they not only provide decoration, but make the room look bigger and lighter because they reflect light and appear to double the size of the room.

Glass is the main material used for mirrors in the home. Sheets of mirror-glass can be cut into the shape and size required and for surface mounting, rather than framing, the edges of the glass must be polished. Holes for screws should be drilled by the glass cutter and the exact position of them specified when ordering. Clips can also be used for surface mounting.

Mirror tiles are available in sizes to match ceramic tiles, and in panels. Some mirror tiles and wall mirrors are available with self-adhesive pads for fixing. There is a type of aluminium foil sheeting available for installation in rooms where you may want to avoid condensation problems.

Mirrors for design effect

Mirrors will increase light in dim areas such as basements or halls. However, care must be taken in their use as it can be very confusing to have a room in which the walls are not well defined, and could even be dangerous. In a living room, mirrors can be very effective if used on a small wall or at the back of an alcove.

Large antique mirrors with intricately carved frames will complement a room furnished in the traditional style, and can sometimes be found in junk and antique shops. Damage to the reflecting surface of old mirrors can be put right by re-silvering, which is usually undertaken by large glassworks. Don't have a really valuable old mirror re-silvered as it will lose a lot of its value. An elaborate old picture frame can be cleaned, painted and fitted with a sheet of mirror glass cut to size, to make a handsome focal point in a room.

Painting

However your home is furnished and whatever your choice of decor, you are bound to have some areas – walls, ceilings or woodwork – which are painted and need repainting from time to time, or stripping and painting from scratch. Professional decorators are costly to employ and with a bit of know-how you can achieve professional results yourself at a fraction of the cost.

Preparation

Filling Before painting you may have to fill cracks and crevices in walls. Remove loose chips or pieces of unsound plaster, rake out cracks and use a filling knife to push plaster filler into the cracks. Allow to dry and smooth off the surface. Plaster filler can be bought ready mixed or as a powder to mix yourself. Larger holes must be filled with building plaster or sometimes old newspaper and filler can be combined. Woodwork can be filled in the same way, using a proprietary ready-mixed wood filler or an all-purpose filler.

Metal This must be primed. Manufacturers and do-it-yourself stores will advise which primers are right for which types of metal. Gloss-painted metal must be rubbed down in the same way as wood.

Painted surfaces Those surfaces in good condition need only a thorough wash with soap or detergent and water, or with a suitable solvent to remove grease and dirt. If the surface was gloss-painted, rub it down with fine glass-paper.

Peeling, lifting or blistered paint must be scraped or burnt back to a firm surface or, preferably, stripped completely.

★ **HANDY HINT** ★

If the surface was previously covered with a water-based, non-washable paint such as ceiling distemper or whitewash, remove the existing paint completely by scrubbing with water. Then proceed as though you were painting a newly plastered wall or cover with lining paper.

Papered surfaces If you want to paint walls which are papered, it is not always necessary to strip the paper first. Paint over a small trial area, to check the paper is colourfast and the paint will not soften the wallpaper paste. If you are using an oil-based paint, or if the pattern is not waterproof, the whole surface should be primed (sized) before applying the top coat.

Plaster New plaster must be thoroughly dried out before painting. Any white crystals should be rubbed off every week until they no longer appear. The walls can then be painted with a water-based paint. If the surface is very porous, thin the paint slightly, checking the manufacturer's instructions for proportions. Alternatively the plaster may be primed with an appropriate primer. Some new plaster, which is specially treated, can be papered over at once.

▲ **WARNING** ▲

Do not paint new plaster with totally waterproof, oil-based paint. Plaster contains alkaline salts which attack some of the ingredients in oil-based paints if the plaster is still damp. Oil-based paint on dry plaster should follow an alkali-resisting primer.

Stripping wallpaper If the paint will not take on wallpaper, or if the paper is in poor condition, it will have to be removed. The task is made a little easier if you use a proprietary wallpaper stripper. There is a new one which is specially formulated to strip paper which has been overpainted. If paper has been overpainted with gloss paint, you may need to hire a steam stripping machine.

For *non-washable paper*, brush warm water or water and stripper on to the surface, using a large, soft brush. Allow it to soak well into the surface and then scrape the paper off with a wide metal scraper.

Washable paper is a little more tricky.

The surface has to be scored first, using a wire brush or scraper, before soaking and scraping.

The surface of *vinyl* wall-covering can be removed by lifting a corner and peeling it away from the wall. This leaves a backing paper which provides an ideal surface for redecorating.

Woodwork New wood has to be treated carefully to ensure a tough lasting finish. Any knots should be sealed with a knotting preparation, based on shellac and obtainable from do-it-yourself and paint shops. To ensure a good seal, always apply the knotting for about 10mm (⅜in) all round the area of the knot.

★ **HANDY HINT** ★

Always treat knots in new wood; if left untreated they can break down a painted surface and leave bare, sticky patches.

The surface must next be primed with an appropriate sealer. All-in-one sealer/primer/undercoat paints seal the wood to prevent moisture getting into it. It also provides a firm anchor for the rest of the paint, and acts as an undercoat, masking blemishes and discoloured areas.

Old paint which is cracked, flaking or wrinkled should be removed. This may be done with a chemical paint stripper which is applied with a brush, so that the paint can then be lifted off with a scraper; or by using a blowtorch to burn the paint, which can then be scraped off. Do not remove more paint than is absolutely necessary, as it is a tedious task. If there are just odd flakes, scrape them away to a sound base and then rub down with glasspaper or steel wool to provide a suitable surface to anchor the new paint.

Choosing the right paint

Your choice will largely depend on the surface you are covering, the finish you want to obtain and the colours available. In some brands, colours can be mixed to your own specifications. Ease of application, quickness of drying and covering ability will also affect your choice. Bear in mind that some paints need at least two or three coats for an even finish, while for others one coat may be enough. Always check the manufacturer's instructions as to whether the particular paint has to be stirred or not, and what the appropriate solvent is for thinning the paint and cleaning brushes. Thixotropic or 'jelly' paints must not be stirred or they lose their special quality.

Metric can sizes	
5 litres	Roughly 1 gallon
2.5 litres	Roughly ½ gallon
1 litre	Roughly 1 quart
500ml	Roughly 1 pint
250ml	Roughly ½ pint

The table below indicates the approximate spreading capacity in square metres on non-porous surfaces.

Metric can size	primer (sq m)	gloss (sq m)	emulsion (sq m)
5 litres	60	75	90
2.5 litres	30	37	45
1 litre	12	15	18
500ml	6	7½	9
250ml	3	3½	4½

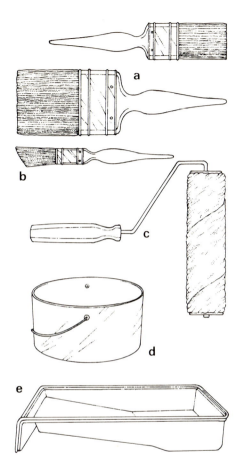

woodwork. Some oil-based paints can now be washed out of brushes with detergent and water.

Water-based paints These contain resins and additives which make them easy to apply and quite hard-wearing, as well as providing different finishes, from matt through satin to gloss.

If you are painting an uneven surface, it is generally advisable to use a matt finish as shiny finishes tend to exaggerate bumps in uneven surfaces.

Estimating the amount Covering power will vary according to brand of paint and the porosity and roughness of the surface.

Basic painting equipment

Brushes Used for wall and ceiling painting they are generally about 10 or 15cm (4 or 6in) wide (**a**). Do not use too wide a brush, as it will be heavy and tiring to use, although it covers the surface faster than a narrower one. You will also need a selection of smaller brushes to paint woodwork, get into corners and pick out lines between different areas. A slanted, flat brush, 2 or 3cm (¾ or 1¼in) wide (**b**), is useful when painting window frames.

Buy good quality brushes – they will last longer and hold the paint better.

Rollers These tend to use more paint than brushes, but make it easier to obtain an even finish, though it is often slightly stippled. Short-pile lambswool (**c**) or sheepskin rollers are suitable for all-round use, a longer lambswool for rough surfaces and mohair for applying oil-based and gloss paints to smooth surfaces. Foam rubber rollers are less

Primers and undercoats These may be necessary to give a good surface to which the top coat will adhere. Different types are available and a do-it-yourself store should be able to advise you as to what you need for any job.

Oil-based paints Generally more expensive than water-based ones, but they have better coverage and are more durable. They are now available in eggshell and silk finishes, are easily washable and some have the advantage of being suitable for both walls and

27

hard wearing and leave a rougher finish, but the sleeve is cheap to replace. They can be used with most paint and on most surfaces. Some rollers have hollow handles that can be fitted to poles for high work.

Paint pads Obtained in various sizes, these have a short synthetic pile on a foam backing. They are quick and easy to use and some have hollow handles that can be fitted to poles for high work.

Paint kettles and trays If you are using brushes, it is worth decanting some paint into a paint kettle – a small can with a handle that is wide enough to take your brush (**d**). This is more manageable than a full can of paint and polythene kettles are light and easy to clean. You should always strain the contents of a partly used can of paint through a mesh cut from nylon tights, to remove bits that could spoil the finish.

If you use a roller, you should have a specially designed sloping tray (**e**), slightly wider than the roller. If you are using a pad, special trays are obtainable, but any old baking tray will do, provided it is wide enough to take the pad.

Other equipment For preparing surfaces you will need scrapers (**f**), filling knives (**g**), sanding blocks (**h**) and glasspaper. You will also need brushes, a filling knife, buckets, sponges, and tools for removing and replacing fitments and fittings. A safe sturdy ladder is essential and for high ceilings you may also need a scaffolding board. You will also need plaster and wood fillers and may need chemical paint stripper, wallpaper stripper and plenty of white spirit. A blowtorch is an optional extra.

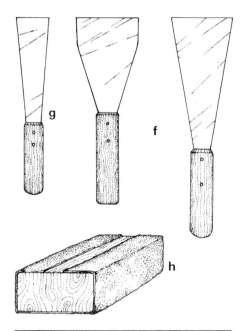

Painting – techniques

The aim when painting is to complete sections in continuous operations, so that one small area is not completely dry before you come to paint the adjacent area within the section. If you leave areas to dry for more than about 30 minutes, you may find that there is a mark between areas which will show after the job is completed.

Painting a ceiling

Start by cutting in the edges by drawing the brush sideways along the border between the ceiling and the wall.

Then, starting from a corner near the main window, work in 60cm (2ft) strips parallel to the window. This will help to prevent any streaks from showing.

Painting walls

Work round the room in 60cm (2ft) strips from ceiling to floor. Start each strip before the previous one has dried.

★ **HANDY HINT** ★

As you will probably have to leave the work at some stage before you have finished, it is sensible to end one day's work in a corner, where no joining line will show.

Painting windows

Before painting, check the condition of the putty holding the glass and replace if necessary (see REPAIRS AND MAINTENANCE – Glazing). Clean and strip all woodwork, as described.

When painting *casement windows*, start with the rebates (ridges inside the frame) and glazing bars; then top and bottom cross rails, then finally paint the sides.

When painting *sash windows* always thin the paint to prevent the window from sticking when dry. Push up the bottom sash and pull down the top one so that it comes below the bottom one by about 15cm (6in). Paint the bottom rail and vertical bars of the top sash as far as you can reach. Push down the bottom sash and push up the top one and paint both. Paint the frame and, when all the paint is dry, paint the runners. Do not paint the sash cords, or the window will not run freely. If you have to replace the sash cords take the opportunity of having the sashes out to paint them and the frame. To keep paint off glass, protect with a shield.

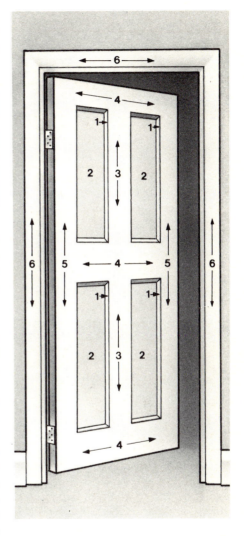

Painting panelled doors

1 Paint the mouldings around the panels.
2 Paint the panels themselves.
3 Paint the centre bars.
4 Paint the cross bars.
5 Paint the outer vertical edges.
6 Paint the door frame.

★ HANDY HINT ★

Stretch a thin piece of wire or smooth string across the top of your can of paint so that you can wipe your brush against it after dipping into the paint, and rest your brush on it during breaks in the work.

Cleaning painting equipment

Emulsion and water-based paints Wipe as much paint as possible off the brush, roller or pad first. Rinse the equipment under the cold tap and then wash in warm soapy water.

Oil-based paints Get as much paint as possible off the brushes first, then work them thoroughly in a jam jar or paint kettle with some white spirit. Next, wash them in soap and water and allow them to dry thoroughly before storing them.

Pictures

Pictures add character and individuality to a room. Not many people can boast of owning an Old Master, but a collection of small prints, carefully chosen and hung, can be most effective. A mixture of sizes hung on the same, preferably dark-coloured wall can change the appearance of a wide, dull wall space.

There is no need to feel that you must have all your pictures in the same type of frames; variety is the essence of success in this kind of picture hanging.

Picture rails

These can be painted either to blend with or to contrast with the colour of your walls. Large pictures look their best suspended from the rail by short chains attached to each top corner and hanging from picture hooks, carefully spaced on the rail so that the chains hang parallel to each other. You can highlight your favourite or most valuable painting by attaching a special 'highlighter' clip light to the top of the frame.

If they are of even size the tops of the pictures should be level. If they are a variety of sizes, uneven lines and different sizes can be very attractive if carefully planned.

★ HANDY HINT ★

If you are hanging a group of pictures, lay them out first on the floor so that you can get a good idea of their arrangement.

Room planning

When you decide to redecorate a room, you can take the opportunity to make changes not only in its appearance, but in the way it is used. Would you like to have a dining area in the kitchen? Could the dining room double as a study, or the bedroom as a sewing room? By careful planning you may be able to make some useful changes.

Making a plan

Buy some squared paper and draw an accurate scale plan of the room you are considering. Make the plan as large as you can, letting each square represent 1m (3ft). Next, measure the furniture that you wish to keep in the room. Draw the outlines on another piece of squared paper, to the same scale as the room plan. Shade these outlines with ink or pencil and cut them out. By moving these 'furniture patterns' about on your room plan, you can find out what alternatives you have when it comes to rearranging them.

Grouping and rearranging

If you are going to turn a room into a double-purpose one, group the furniture so that part of the room is devoted solely to the new use. For instance, in a dining room study, move the dining table from the centre of the room and install a desk and bookshelves at the end of the room furthest from the kitchen or the door. A room divider can be very successful in such cases. Make use of alcove space with a desk that has shelves or with a sewing machine table.

Traffic flows

One point you should bear in mind when reorganising a room, is to leave enough floor space to give access to various focal parts, such as the window, the fireplace, cupboards and so on. Nothing is more irritating and time-consuming than having to edge round furniture to get where you want to go – remember, too, when positioning the bed that it has to be made occasionally! Make sure that cupboard doors can open completely and that the door into the room swings freely.

★ **HANDY HINT** ★

Sometimes space can be saved by having the door re-hung so that it opens in the other direction.

Rugs

Rugs can give colour, warmth and softness if well-placed on cord, matting, vinyl or ceramic tiles or polished wood. They can break up a space visually and mark out different zones, and give protection to an area which receives a lot of wear.

Choosing a rug

Visit a number of shops before deciding on your rug or rugs. Some beautiful ethnic rugs are available and there is a wide choice of shapes and sizes in all kinds of fibre from wool to synthetics. Decide on the type and size you need for a room after the furniture arrangement has been fixed.

Types of rug

Chinese rugs Always softly coloured, they sometimes have a sculptured pile.
Flokatis Washable white wool rugs from Greece.
Indian rugs These are attractive and not expensive. *Numdahs* are made from brightly embroidered white felt. *Dhurries* are 100 per cent cotton in a flat weave and must, like *numdahs*, be dry cleaned. *Druggets* are heavier and more expensive, as they are made of pure wool or wool and cotton.

Long-pile, fluffy rugs Made in synthetic fibres, these rugs are excellent for bedrooms and bathrooms.

Oriental rugs These come from Persia, Afghanistan, Morocco, India and China. A good, wisely chosen oriental rug bought from a reputable dealer is likely to increase in value, whether new or second-hand. Machine-made imitations will not increase in value, but can look very attractive and colourful.

Washable cotton rugs These usually have a longish looped pile and are ideal for the bathroom (where they can be tailored to fit), the nursery and as bedside rugs. They can be washed in a washing-machine unless they are very large.

Rag rugs Can be made at home from folded or plaited strips of fabric, woven into ovals or circles. Short strips can be knotted into large-mesh canvas.

Rya rugs These have a long, shaggy pile and usually feature geometric motifs. Kits can be bought for Rya rugs.

Cleaning rugs

Most rugs can be shampooed (see CLEANING THE HOUSE – Carpet cleaning) but valuable oriental rugs must be professionally cleaned.

Slipping, curling or creeping rugs

Slipping Fit with a product that looks like rubberised fisherman's net; or glue or stitch a small piece of touch-and-close fastener, like Velcro, to the underside of the rug. With double-sided tape, join the corresponding piece of fastener to the floor to hold the rug in place.

Curling Curling corners can often be cured by applying latex adhesive to the underside. Stronger measures are to line the rug with underfelt or a double layer of hessian, using latex adhesive. Tack all over with a hammer to make sure the rug and backing are securely stuck together. If the rug has a really strong curl put a narrow wood batten under each end.

Creeping A special foam underlay will prevent rugs creeping when laid on carpets. The foam can be stuck directly over the whole of the back of the rug. Valuable rugs should simply be loose laid over the foam.

Wallpapering

Wallpapering is not a difficult task and with a little practice you will be able to achieve very professional results.

Choosing the wallcovering

Make sure that the paper you buy all comes from the same batch, and buy all you need at the same time. Check the number on individual rolls of paper to make sure they are from the same batch.

Embossed paper Has a more heavily textured surface. This can be printed with a pattern but is usually produced as a 'white' for overpainting. The best quality embossed wallcoverings consist of two layers of paper and hold the embossing when wet. *Anaglypta* and *Supaglypta* are particularly strong embossed papers. These and textured papers are painted over with emulsion or gloss paint to give a hard-wearing finish. Both are now widely used anywhere in the house.

Fabric can also be used as a wallcovering – there are paper-backed varieties available (see hessian and natural textures) which include felt wallcoverings, which are hung as paper, although they are quite difficult to handle because they are heavy. Fabric can also be stuck directly on to a good wall surface (paste the wall), but is difficult to remove and impossible to clean. Fabric is better fixed to walls by means of battens, or by a special track which is fastened to the outer edges of the wall and the fabric slipped between the two flanges in the track by means of a special 'shoehorn'-shaped tool. Either method means the fabric can be removed for cleaning, and can be combined with insulating material.

Flock wallcoverings These have a velvety texture and usually come in traditional patterns and stripes. The base material can be a paper or a vinyl, and some are ready-pasted. Care must be taken not to get paste on the flocked surface of paper-backed flocks.

Foamed polyethylene This is a new type of very light wallcovering sold under the brand name of Novamura. It is very light, tough and easy to hang, and warm to the touch. It is good for bathrooms and kitchens and can be hung on new plaster as it is porous and allows the wall to 'breathe'. The wall must be pasted and the wallcovering slid into position. It is easy to strip, since no backing is left on the walls.

Foil and metallic wallcoverings Made from a metalised plastic film on a paper backing. They are highly reflective and so create an illusion of space and light. Hang with a fungicidal paste, and do not put behind light switches and power points.

Friezes and borders These form a horizontal band of decoration and can be used with co-ordinating papers, plain textured papers or painted walls. They can be used to outline doors, walls, windows, fireplaces and other focal points. They usually need trimming before pasting (as ordinary paper) and hanging horizontally and/or vertically.

Hand-printed wallpapers These are very expensive and exclusive, and are printed by hand. They may not be colour-fast and the edges usually have to be trimmed before hanging. They are hung like ordinary wallpapers.

Hessian A coarsely-woven fabric which looks most attractive on walls as a background to pictures, etc. Hessian comes in two types – a paper-backed variety on a roll, which is hung like ordinary wallpaper, and a fabric sold by the yard/metre where it is usual to paste the wall and slide the hessian into position. Hessian comes in natural and a wide range of colours, but some tend to fade in bright sunlight. There are simulated hessian textures available in the vinyl and embossed wallpaper ranges.

Lining paper Comes in various grades and is used to cover poor surfaces, acting as a base for paint or for heavier papers.

Natural textures There are various wallcoverings in this category such as grass-cloth, silk wallcovering, sisal wallcovering, slivered cork, wool-weaves and wool-strands, as well as other fabric effects. These usually have a paper backing with the natural fibres stuck on the front. Care is needed in hanging, as paste must not get onto the textured surface. Some are sold by the yard/metre and others are sold by the roll.

Ordinary paper Made from paper similar to lining paper, but printed with a pattern. It can have a slightly embossed texture.

Ready-pasted coverings These are quick to hang and no paste is required. The adhesive is factory-coated on to the back of the paper and is activated by immersing each cut length of paper in a trough of water (supplied when you buy the paper). The paper is then hung in the normal way. It is a much wetter method than conventional pasting. Do not over-immerse ready-made wall-coverings – follow the manufacturer's instructions. These papers have a tough, washable finish.

Suede wallcoverings This is a velvety textured wallcovering made from thin suede (leather) bonded to a paper backing, which can be hung like paper, but care must be taken not to get paste on the front. There are many imitation suedes also available, which combine the qualities of suede texture with the easy-hang, easy-care properties of vinyls. Suede also appears as crushed suede with a slightly more crinkled texture.

Textured wallcoverings Particularly useful when you want to hide irregularities in the wall surface. They may contain wood chips which are mixed with the paper during manufacture. This paper can be pasted in the conventional way.

Vinyl coverings These are heavy-duty wall coverings. They can actually be scrubbed, making them a good choice for playrooms, hallways, doors and kitchens. There are also thicker, 'contoured' vinyl wallcoverings available, which often simulate ceramic tiles, wood cladding and other natural textures. These need a heavy-duty wallpaper paste containing fungicide, and the wall can be pasted rather than the back of the product, if preferred. These are ideal for use in kitchens and bathrooms and where there is a condensation problem.

Washable papers These papers have a spongeable surface and are suitable for kitchens or bathrooms. Clean with detergent and a damp cloth.

Wallcovering quantities chart

Standard wallpapers come in rolls approximately 10m long (11yds) by 53cm wide (1ft 9in). Many speciality wallcoverings are sold by the metre, or yard, and are usually much wider than the standard roll of paper, but widths vary according to type. Some hand-printed and imported wallpapers have different widths/lengths, so check with the supplier before ordering.

The chart will help you to work out the average quantity required if you are using the standard size roll.

Note You must also allow for pattern matching. If the paper has a large design you will need to buy extra rolls. Ask the retailer's advice, and it may be possible to have extra rolls on 'sale or return'.

Wallcovering quantities chart

WALLS Height from skirting	Distance around the room (doors and windows included)								
	9m 30′	10m 34′	12m 38′	13m 42′	14m 46′	15m 50′	16m 54′	17m 58′	18m 62′
2.15–2.30m 7′–7′ 6″	4	5	5	6	6	7	7	8	8
2.30–2.45m 7′ 6″–8′	5	5	6	6	7	7	8	8	9
2.45–2.60m 8′–8′ 6″	5	5	6	7	7	8	9	9	10
2.60–2.75m 8′ 6″–9′	5	5	6	7	7	8	9	9	10
2.75–2.90m 9′–9′ 6″	6	6	7	7	8	9	9	10	10
2.90–3.05m 9′ 6″–10′	6	6	7	8	8	9	10	10	11
3.05–3.20m 10′–10′ 6″	6	7	8	8	9	10	10	11	12

WALLS Height from skirting									
	19m 66′	21m 70′	22m 74′	23m 78′	24m 82′	26m 86′	27m 90′	28m 94′	30m 98′
2.15–2.30m 7′–7′ 6″	9	9	10	10	11	12	12	13	13
2.30–2.45m 7′ 6″–8′	9	10	10	11	11	12	13	13	14
2.45–2.60m 8′–8′ 6″	10	11	12	12	13	14	14	15	15
2.60–2.75m 8′ 6″–9′	10	11	12	12	13	14	14	15	15
2.75–2.90m 9′–9′ 6″	11	12	12	13	14	14	15	15	16
2.90–3.05m 9′ 6″–10′	12	12	13	14	14	15	16	16	17
3.05–3.20m 10′–10′ 6″	13	13	14	15	16	16	17	18	19

CEILINGS	To calculate the number of rolls required, work out the square area in metres and divide by five

Wallcovering symbols

Now the range of wallcoverings is so sophisticated, a chart of international performance symbols has been worked out. These are now appearing on the backs of the samples in wallcovering pattern books and on product labels, so look for the symbols when you shop.

Wallpapering equipment

Various basic tools are worth buying if you are going to do a lot of decorating. Good quality tools will last a lifetime.

Bucket You will need a bucket to make the paste in. Make sure it is wide enough to take your paste brush.

Knife A handyman's replaceable blade knife is useful for trimming, or use a safety razor blade with one edge stuck lengthways into an old cork. Single-edged safety razor blades are also good.

Metre rule This is useful for measuring walls and lengths of paper, and as a cutting guide.

Paperhanger's brush This is a wide, handleless brush used to smooth down the paper after it has been hung. A sponge may be used on washable and vinyl wallcoverings.

Paste brush Paste brushes are usually 15cm (6in) wide, with fairly soft bristles. A wide paint brush could be used instead.

Pasting table A folding table, 2m (about 6ft) long and slightly wider than the standard roll of paper, makes the task easier and if you are going to do a lot of decorating it is worthwhile buying one. A large table, which must be well protected with newspaper, can make a substitute.

Symbol	Meaning
	spongeable
	washable
	super-washable
	scrubbable
	sufficient light fastness
	good light fastness
	strippable
	peelable
	ready pasted
	paste-the-wall
	free match
	straight match
	offset match
$\frac{50}{25}$ cm	design repeat distance offset
	duplex
	co-ordinated fabric available
	direction of hanging
	reverse alternate lengths

Symbols by courtesy of the Wallpaper Marketing Board.

Pencil A soft pencil is used for marking the walls when using a plumbline and measuring and marking chimney breasts. When marking the ceiling, use coloured chalk to coat the string.

Plumbline This is a long piece of string with a weight attached. If you want to make your own plumbline, tie a nut to a long piece of string. It is essential to ensure that you hang the paper straight. For papering ceilings, a piece of string and two drawing pins are used to get a straight line to start from.

Scissors A pair of scissors with blades at least 28cm (11in) long is best for easy cutting. A smaller, sharp-pointed pair is needed for cutting round obstructions.

Seam roller This is used to run along the seams when you have hung two adjoining pieces of paper, to ensure that the edges are neatly stuck down.

Wallpaper paste Generally bought in powder form and mixed with cold water. For vinyls it is essential to use an adhesive containing a fungicide. Ask the stockist's advice on the right type of paste for the paper you choose, or follow the manufacturer's instructions.

Wallpapering techniques

Preparation

Previously papered walls must be stripped even if the existing wall covering seems firmly fixed (see Painting). After stripping, wash and fill the walls as for painting. *Emulsion-painted* walls can be papered over with no treatment other than washing down, but *gloss-painted* ones should first be rubbed over with fine abrasive paper to provide a roughened surface for the paper to bond to.

Using lining paper For the best wallpapering results, lining paper should first be hung *horizontally* not vertically, to avoid 'seam clashes', which make awkward ridges. Hanging paper horizontally is not easy. After pasting, fold the paper concertina-style, pasted sides together. Holding the paper in your left hand, place the paper end in a right hand corner of a wall, brushing the paper out with your right hand as you unravel it.

Leave some time for the paper to dry before hanging the heavier paper on top. In the case of heavy vinyl covering, use a paste containing a fungicide, and leave at least 24 hours.

Sizing If lining paper is not used and the walls are absorbent – unpainted or emulsioned – the whole area should be sized. Paint a diluted solution of wallpaper paste over the walls and leave to dry. Sizing helps positioning of paper.

Starting to paper the walls

If your paper has a small pattern, you should start by the window and work round the room in both directions, joining finally in a corner where any mismatching of pattern will not be too obvious. If you have chosen a paper with a large motif, particularly if this runs vertically, start hanging the paper with a length down the centre of the chimney breast and work outwards from there. Always use the plumbline when hanging the first length.

Using the plumbline Fix the free end of the string to the top of the wall about 50cm (20in) from one side of the window frame (or over the fireplace if you are using a large pattern). Mark at intervals the accurate vertical along the string line down to the floor. This is done so that once the first piece is hung vertically, all the others will follow correctly.

Cut a strip at least 10cm (4in) longer than the measured height of the room from skirting to ceiling or picture rail. There is less likelihood of mis-cutting if you cut only a few pieces at a time, carefully checking the edges of the strips together to make sure of a pattern match. You may find you have to waste quite an amount of paper at the head of each new strip.

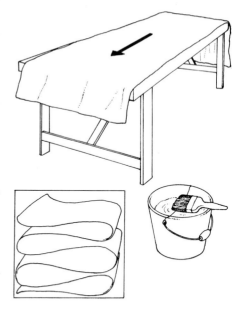

Pasting and hanging

Pasting Lay the first length of paper face down on the table, with one edge just overlapping. This prevents paste on the table getting on to the face of the next length. Apply paste evenly, with sweeping strokes down the middle and out to the overlapping edge. Move the paper so that the other edge overlaps and complete the pasting. Fold the pasted paper concertina style as you go, keeping pasted faces together. Keep the pasting table free of paste, by wiping over after each pasting.

Some heavy papers need to be left to allow the paste to soak in – check the manufacturer's instructions. In this case, one length of paper can be pasted and hung, still folded, over the step-ladder, while you are pasting the next length.

Hanging Fold the paper over your arm and climb the ladder to reach the area you are covering. Position the top of the paper against the ceiling or picture rail, allowing a small overlap for trimming. Make sure the vertical edge is against the pencilled guideline. Smooth down the centre of the paper with the paperhanger's brush and then, using sweeping strokes, brush from side to side in a herringbone pattern. When the top is firmly in position, unfold the bottom half and smooth that down too.

Make sure you have no major air bubbles showing before hanging the next piece of wallpaper. If you have, peel back the paper while still wet and repeat the process before the paste starts drying.

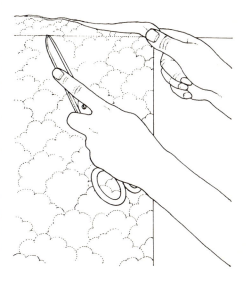

Trimming Mark the edge of the skirting board and ceiling or picture rail with the back of a pair of scissors. Peel the paper away from the wall and trim off along the marked line with a pair of scissors or a handyman's knife. Wipe off surplus paste on the ceiling or skirting board before it dries.

Follow the same procedure all the way round the room, making sure that all the edges are butted against one another and do not overlap. Except on embossed papers, after each sheet is pasted, run a seam roller down the join.

Special problems

Corners These are rarely true right angles or completely vertical. On internal or external corners, trim the paper so that about 4–5cm ($1\frac{1}{2}$–2in) will overlap round the corner. Paste and hang the trimmed strip, smoothing the overlap round the corner on to the next wall. With the plumbline, mark a vertical line on the next wall, as you have been doing on previous walls. Paste and hang this strip against the marked line and into the corner, to cover the overlap. The pattern will not match perfectly, but it should not be noticeable.

Doors When you reach a door, paste and hang a full width of paper, so that some of it overlaps the frame. Roughly cut out the shape of the door to within a few centimetres of the edge of the frame. Mark the position of the edge of the frame, using the back of a pair of scissors, then trim with a handyman's knife or scissors.

Paste a short strip over the wall on top of the door and repeat the process again down the other side.

Light switches and sockets If possible, tuck the paper behind the switch plate for a neat finish. Turn off the electricity at the mains. Unscrew the plate, hang the paper and trim a small hole. Tuck the paper in behind the switch plate, and only replace the plate when the paste is dry.

An alternative method is to paper over the switch and cut the paper away. After hanging the strip, locate the centre of the switch and make four diagonal cuts to the corners of the switch plate. Mark the position of the edge of the switch, trim and stick down the flaps.

Windows If your windows have frames similar to door frames, they can be treated in the same way. If you have to paper above and below the window, make sure that the edges of the strips

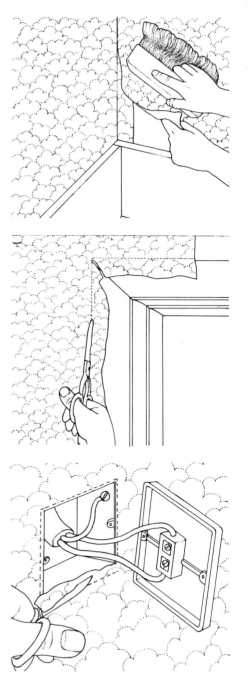

follow the same vertical line, so that the paper down the second side of the window is easy to hang. Trim the paper carefully if there is a protruding windowsill.

Recesses Papering into a recess round the window (or any other recess) is a little more tricky.

1 Hang the first window strip over the window recess.

2 Make a horizontal cut in the paper, up to the edge of the wall, a few milli-metres ($\frac{1}{4}$in) above the top of the recess.

3 Smooth the paper in place, sticking the paper round the corner. Mark and trim as usual, including the slight overlap at the top of the recess.

4 Hang the next length, carrying it round the corner and up to the top of the window.

5 Repeat this if necessary, and then hang the strip at the far end of the window strip. This should leave two small patches unpapered at the top of the window recess.

6 Cut small pieces to fill the two gaps, matching machine-cut edge to machine-cut edge where possible. Leave a 15mm ($\frac{5}{8}$in) overlap at the back and sides and a 2.5cm (1in) overlap at the front of the strip.

7 Paste in place and trim.

8 At the front, tear the overlap to leave a slightly ragged edge, which can be pasted over the paper on the wall to form a smooth joint.

Papering ceilings

This should be tackled *before* you paper the walls and is a considerably more difficult task. Do not try to hang a patterned or heavily embossed paper on a ceiling until you have had a great deal of experience. It is best to size the ceiling as described previously.

The paper is hung across the ceiling, parallel to the window wall.

Marking a straight line Cover a piece of thread with chalk and stretch it across the ceiling, holding it in place with a couple of drawing pins, so that it is parallel to the window wall. The line should be slightly less than 50cm (20in) from the edge of the ceiling. Twang the thread sharply so that it leaves a chalk line on the ceiling.

Cutting the paper Cut lengths of paper the width of the ceiling, allowing about 12cm (5in) for trimming.

Pasting Paste the paper as described for hanging wallpaper, but fold it concertina fashion as described for lining paper. By folding the paper like this, you can unfold and stick it a little at a time.

Hanging the paper Using a roll of unused paper to support the folded and pasted length, position one end against the wall and along the chalk guide line. Gradu-ally move along, brushing out the paper as you go. At the end, trim off the surplus in the usual way. If you are going to paper the walls, leave an overlap of a few millimetres ($\frac{1}{4}$in) which can be covered by the wallpaper.

Ceiling rose Paper up to the rose, cut a star pattern, pull through the light flex and then brush round the rose and trim.

You may find it easier to work by arranging a platform between two step ladders, so that you can cover the room width without having to get down.

CHAPTER 2

HOME IMPROVEMENTS

Attic and basement conversions•Bathrooms
Dimmer switches•Improvement grants
Shelving•Showers•Tiles

Attic conversions

If you have a growing family that is bursting out of your present home, you may well be considering moving house. This can be costly and an alternative answer to your problem could be to convert your attic into another room.

Regulations

Plans must be presented to your local building authority and planning permission and Building Regulations approval obtained before work is started. It is as well to check the regulations right from the start as they affect various aspects of your plan.

Ceiling height In Britain it is required to be not less than 2.3m (7½ft) over at least half the area of the room (this area has to be measured at 1.5m – 4ft 11in – above floor level). If this is a difficulty, the insertion of a dormer window could help.

Fire precautions You may have to install fireproof, self-closing doors.

Stairs There are regulations on the width and gradient of stairs and details of banisters, treads, widths and risers.

Windows Regulations also govern size, opening and position of windows.

Obtaining advice Consult the local authority building inspector or building surveyor. The Department of Planning may be able to help with paperwork and drawings.

Neighbours As a matter of courtesy, tell neighbours of your plans well ahead of time.

Calling in the experts

Attic conversions are not a job for amateurs and do-it-yourself enthusiasts. First, have existing joists, beams and load-bearing walls surveyed to make sure that they are strong enough.

Architects If you engage an architect he will deal with the whole project – plans, consents, drawings and specifications, tenders and builders – and he will supervise the actual work. Commissioning an architect will add to the cost, but will take many problems off your hands.

Builders A local builder may offer to obtain the consents and should include his charge for this in his estimate. You will have to supervise the work yourself.

 WARNING

Specialist loft conversion and home extension companies exist; always make sure that any company you employ is reputable – there are many unreliable outfits around.

Choosing a staircase

Always bearing in mind local regulations there is a choice between close-tread stairs (which can have storage cupboards built in beneath them), open plan stairs (which give a light, modern effect but can be dangerous for the very young or the very old), and spiral staircases (which take up more room than they appear to and are very expensive). However, spiral staircases can be bought ready-made. Space can be saved by having a staircase of two adjoining flights, either parallel or at right angles, depending on the shape of the space available.

Choosing windows

Dormer windows help to give extra ceiling room. Inverted dormers, that is dormers cut back into the roof, can give a small balcony, which must be very carefully waterproofed. Sloping windows (skylights) also need particular care in weatherproofing. They can be screened by roller or Venetian blinds running on cords down the sides, or sandwiched between the panes of double-glazing units. (See also Double glazing.)

Windows in existing gables are the simplest to install.

Basement conversions

With imagination, careful planning and some work, the dreariest basement can be turned into useful new living space.

Structural alterations

You may need re-wiring, new plumbing and heating and you must consider the ventilation and drainage.

Can you get more light into the room? Possibilities include enlarging a window or adding a new one; white paint on the wall facing the window, to reflect light; removing anything that blocks light and even, in town houses, having pavement lights put in.

Building regulations are:
- Minimum ceiling height of 2.3m (7½ft)
- Adequate damp proofing.
- An open space extending at least 3.7m (about 12ft) out from one of the external walls.
- Some form of ventilation directly linked to the open air.

There are further regulations covering knocking down of walls or chimney breast and Building Regulations approval is needed for any structural changes. Consult your local authority's building inspector.

Damp proofing

One technique is to fit bitumen-impregnated lathing to the internal walls, but this involves removing skirting boards and plaster and eventually replastering the wall. Another technique is the 'osmosis' method where wires are inserted into the wall and charged electrically to 'frighten away' the damp. This is, however, very definitely a job for expert contractors.

Preservative-treated battens can be fixed to the face of the existing plaster and covered with insulating plasterboard.

You will probably find it easier and more satisfactory to call in a builder for such jobs.

Decorating

You can be as unconventional as you like in the decoration of your basement. Sound *brick walls* can be left as they are or look marvellous if whitewashed or painted with gloss paint. *Timber or plastic laminate* imitations look warm and welcoming. If using *real timber* have it treated with wood preservative against damp. *Cork tiles* for walls and floor might also be a good choice.

Whatever you want or need in your basement, the secret of success is to plan carefully, get all the necessary permissions straightened out and use your imagination.

Bathrooms

If you want to make major alterations to your bathroom you will almost certainly need professional help. The installation of baths, basins, showers and WCs is subject to strict regulations to ensure safety and hygiene. The local authority should be consulted before any major changes are put in hand.

Safety

● There must be no open electrical sockets in a bathroom, except for a safety socket for an electric razor.
● All switches must be outside the room or fitted with pull cords.
● Gas water heaters must be professionally installed and certified safe.
● There must be adequate ventilation (0.4sq m/about 4sq ft) of window space or some form of mechanical ventilation.
● Toilets must be separated from kitchens or food stores by a ventilated lobby.
● It is sensible to see that plumbing and other services are reasonably accessible in case of blockages or leaks; and to fit isolating valves in the water supply to fittings, to make tap rewashering easier. (See REPAIRS AND MAINTENANCE – Tap rewashering.)

Baths

If your bath is damaged or otherwise unsatisfactory, you will find a large choice of replacements: enamelled cast iron, acrylic and vitreous enamelled pressed steel. Vitreous enamelled pressed steel is the cheapest and cast iron baths most expensive. All are available in a wide range of colours.

The standard size of an ordinary bath is 170×75cm (5ft 7in $\times$ 2ft 6in) (outside measurements) with a rim height of 50–60cm (1ft 8in–2ft). Small sizes go down to 135×68cm (4ft 6in $\times$ 2ft 3in) to fit into cramped spaces, and in the luxury category, much bigger baths are available in unusual shapes.

Ready-made bath side panels are available in colours matching or toning with the bath. A cheaper alternative is to build a light framework of 5×5cm wood covered in plastic laminate or sealed and painted hardboard.

Extra basins; bidets

An extra basin can be incorporated into a vanity unit if you have the wall space. Remember that providing a water supply does not present a problem, but that getting rid of waste water might not be so easy.

Installation of a bidet is not difficult, provided you have free wall space. Your water authority can advise you on what regulations apply as regards plumbing and water supply – particularly important for bidets with rising sprays.

Heating

Unless you have central heating, an oil-filled electric radiator or towel rail will provide gentle background heat, while an infra-red heater mounted on the wall will boost the temperature quickly. *Never* use a portable heater of any kind.

Lighting

Good general background lighting can be supplemented by extra light at the hand basin or mirror. Some form of strip light – tungsten or fluorescent – is ideal, but make sure it is long enough to provide even brightness for shaving or making-up. Some strip fittings incorporate shaver sockets.

Reflecting mirrors can increase the light and can be made of mirrored tiles of silvered acrylic sheeting, which resists steaming.

To prevent ordinary mirrors steaming up, treat them occasionally with an anti-mist fluid.

Decoration and floor covering

Choose a good vinyl wallcovering and paint woodwork with washable matt or silk-finish paint which resists condensation better than gloss.

Floors should be covered with a material which will not rot or hold water. Synthetic carpeting or carpet squares, cork tiles and sheet flooring are all satisfactory (see HOME DECORATION – Floor coverings).

 ★ HANDY HINT ★

It is possible to buy modernising kits for old taps, which consist of new plastic tops and, sometimes, parts to replace the interior mechanism.

Bedrooms

Most bedrooms are essentially simple, peaceful rooms that need little in the way of structural additions, with the possible exception of built-in wardrobes.

Built-in furniture

If the room has a chimney breast with alcoves on each side of it, these are ideal for built-in cupboards. If the alcoves are shallow, the cupboards can be built out and, if the fireplace is not in use, a shallow dressing-table space with a mirror and strip lighting can be built into the centre.

Building-in furniture does require skill and patience and you might be well advised to seek help from a local carpenter to build the units, which you can then paint yourself.

Built-in furniture kits, which are very simple to assemble, can be purchased, but make sure the dimensions are suitable for your space.

Though purpose-built suites are quite expensive, inexpensive whitewood units, bought unpainted in the correct sizes to fit the space, are much cheaper and equally useful.

The whitewood departments of large stores have an excellent range of units and give catalogues listing dimensions, so that you can plan carefully before buying. The units, when installed, can then be decorated to match the room.

Bedheads A built-in bedhead can incorporate storage cupboards at each side, shelves and strip lighting.

Cloakrooms

The word cloakroom can cover anything from a cupboard to hang your coat to a sumptuous mini-bathroom. However, it is more likely to be a small room near the front door that serves as an extra lavatory.

Rules and regulations

Planning permission must be obtained before altering the appearance of your house by building a cloakroom extension; you may also find that your rates would be increased.

Building Regulations approval will also be needed from the local authority, especially if you are altering drains – that is, the soil pipe from a lavatory – or putting in a basin.

Possible sites

Building regulations forbid any room containing a lavatory to open off a kitchen or living room.

The hall This is the traditional place for a cloakroom and is excellent when coat storage is important.

The larder In older houses, there is often a ground floor walk-in larder. Because of the necessity for ventilation, this is always on an outside wall and converts admirably to a cloakroom.

The landing Tall, narrow, terraced town houses frequently have generous half-landings. A cloakroom made here is reasonably near the front door, but will probably block out a certain amount of outside light.

Under the stairs Whether or not you put a lavatory in an understair cloakroom depends on the difficulty and expense of installing a soil pipe. However, the space might convert well to a small shower room (see Showers), providing your water pressure is adequate.

Space needed

A lavatory needs an area approximately 80cm (about 2ft 8in) wide by 1.3m (4ft 3in) deep. Of this last measurement, 60cm (about 2ft) is activity space – the amount of room you need to be comfortable and move around.

★ **HANDY HINT** ★

While full standing height is needed in the activity space, the lavatory itself can be sited under a slope, such as under the stairs, which may help to save space.

An average-sized washbasin requires an area approximately 100cm (about 3ft 4in) wide by 110cm (about 3ft 8in) deep, of which 70cm (about 2ft 4in) is activity space. However, with a small cloakroom-type basin, these dimensions can overlap – they will not be needed simultaneously. Thus an area of 80cm (2ft 8in) by 160cm (5ft 3in) would be just about big enough for a cloakroom containing a small basin and lavatory.

Plumbing

The quietest type of lavatory is the kind with a siphonic cistern. Some lavatories can be cantilevered out from the wall, which makes for ease of cleaning and looks good. Another way of achieving a neat finish is to build the rear part of the lavatory (soil pipe, duct and cistern) into a wall-to-wall section of fitted cupboard.

A wall-hung basin is the cheapest and easiest to install. A vanity unit can be bought ready-made or be custom-built. A really small basin can be installed if it is needed just for washing hands. The most economical type is the triangular, corner basin. Wall-mounted taps leave the basin free, make cleaning easier and looks elegant.

Ventilation

Building regulations stipulate that any window must open to the outside by an amount equal to one-twentieth of the floor space.

For an internal cloakroom, a ducted extractor fan giving at least three changes of air per hour is required, and it must be connected directly to the outside air. Siting the fan as far away as possible from the head of the duct, and using anti-vibration fan-mountings, will cut the noise problem.

Cupboards

Cupboards are something everybody always seems to need more of. Older houses are often generously supplied, but modern homes tend to be less well equipped.

Planning sizes

Consider carefully the size and shape of cupboards needed in each location.

 HANDY HINT
Usually, shallow cupboards are better than deep ones in which things at the back get lost or forgotten.

Depth For general storage, 60cm (2ft) deep is a comfortable maximum. Cupboards for stacked plates are most convenient if about 30cm (1ft) deep, while those for canned goods need only be 15cm (6in).

For hanging clothes you need about 50cm (1ft 8in). (See also CLOTHES CARE.)

Width and height This largely depends on the space available. Floor-standing cupboards with working surfaces are generally 91cm (3ft), but this height can be adjusted by cutting down or building up the plinths on which they stand. When fitting new cupboards take into consideration the height of any equipment you have, such as a dishwasher or washing machine, so that you can create a continuous working surface.

If you tend to store things on top of cupboards it is probably best to box in the top to the ceiling – particularly if the articles stored there are seldom used. However, a ceiling height cupboard is more obtrusive than two lower ones that have the same storage capacity.

New cupboards

Built-in cupboards look better than free-standing ones, but are expensive if put in professionally. A self-assembly kit, or building them in yourself, should be within the scope of most do-it-yourself amateurs.

Low cupboards can be built in below bay windows to double as window seats.

There are three types to buy new: whitewood ready-assembled units, self assembly kits and shelving systems which include cupboards.

Whitewood These come in a range of sizes with interior fittings available to suit different purposes. They come unfinished and usually need a light sanding with fine glasspaper before painting or varnishing.

They can be built in to give the effect of a storage wall, by using plywood infill panels above and extending the sides where necessary. As this means fitting the ply very accurately to the line of walls which may not be completely plumb, you may find it worth while to get a carpenter or joiner to fit them professionally for you.

Self-assembly kits These are ideal for covering a whole wall, or part of one. They come as free-standing units, wardrobe fronts or sliding walls. Though often designed for bedrooms, they can be put anywhere if suitably finished.

When designing a storage wall from free-standing units, plan for a few gaps, spanned with shelving or a worktop or bedhead, to give lightness.

Free-standing units are made in laminated chipboard, whitewood or solid pine. They are the most expensive of the self-assembly kits, but can be taken down and rebuilt if you move. Installation is fairly easy, but make sure they are absolutely level – insert wedges underneath if necessary.

Wardrobe fronts are much cheaper because they are just what they are called – fronts only. You only buy the minimum number of dividing panels, so there is no doubling up of side panels as there is when you put two free-standing units side by side.

Sliding wall units are best for filling an awkward length of wall, as you can order them to the exact size you want. A new cantilevered type is available with ceiling-hung doors.

Damp problems

No matter what age your house may be, it can be affected by damp for many different reasons. Failure to eliminate the cause can lead to rot in structural timbers and expensive major repair jobs. See also REPAIRS AND MAINTENANCE – Dry and wet rot.

Condensation

This happens most often when warm air is subjected to a drop in temperature and is most troublesome on windows or cold external walls in steamy rooms like bathrooms and kitchens (see also Bathrooms).

How to recognise trouble You have a condensation problem if paint lifts where putty joins the glass on the lower horizontals of window frames; wallpaper peels or streaks and runs, or discoloured patches appear on walls.

Typical places to look for condensation damage are above baths and cookers, and along window bars and sills.

Where paint has lifted away from wood or metal, scrape some off to see whether or not the surface underneath is still dry. Rust or white powder (found on aluminium sometimes) or spongy, soft fibres of wood, indicate that water has got under the paint.

Controlling condensation

● Cut down vapour production – i.e. do not leave water boiling for long periods and try to keep tap water to 60°C (140°F).
● Try to keep the house warm.
● Insulate vulnerable surfaces like water pipes, and clad walls and ceilings with insulating materials.
● Ventilate at times when condensation is likely to occur, ideally by having through ventilation with an efficient extractor fan.

HANDY HINT

Efficient, purpose-built, whole-house heating is the best method of combating condensation as the inside walls are kept warmer and the air is at its maximum water-carrying ability (see Heating).

Insulation on inner walls should be backed by an aluminium, polythene or gloss paint vapour check. In the case of solid walls, waterproofing can be applied to the outside.

Some insulants, like cork or close-celled foam, need no vapour check but mineral fibre boards or quilts, wood fibre boards and similar insulants really should have one.

Unless you are an experienced do-it-yourselfer you may find it wise to consult a professional before spending money on cladding and insulating materials which may be wrong for your particular problem.

Sheeted roofs

Sun lounges and similar buildings often have roofs constructed from single sheets of asbestos cement, metal or transparent plastic; these are particularly liable to condensation. Insulating one of these sheet roofs is a job for a professional builder.

Rising damp

The symptoms of rising damp are damaged decorations inside, or an obvious damp patch spreading up the wall from floor level. In severe cases, the damp can set up rot in floors and timbers.

Nowadays all houses are built with a damp-proof course (dpc) which prevents moisture from the earth from rising above it. However, if yours is an older house it may have been built without a damp course, or the dpc may have deteriorated.

Earth, rubble and debris piled up against a wall will form a 'bridge' over the damp course and must be cleared away so that the brickwork can dry out. To be extra safe, you can paint the bottom 30cm (1ft) or thereabouts of the wall with a proprietary water-proofer. When replacing the soil, after the waterproofer has dried, leave at least 15cm (6in) clear space below the damp-proof course.

If the damp-proof course has deteriorated, or if there never was one, you should seek professional help with regard to having one installed. This is an expensive process, so get several quotations and when the work has been done you should have a guarantee of 25 years or so.

 ★ HANDY HINT ★

When a damp-proof course has been installed, it is reasonable to wait for a month or so before paying, to make sure the treatment is working.

Damp on a solid floor

When the floor is damp all over, it is probably caused by rising damp. It is possible to combat this by painting on a proprietary sealing compound which dries to form a waterproof skin, but if it seems serious, call in an expert.

In modern or converted houses, central heating pipes are sometimes laid in a concrete floor. If you have an isolated patch of damp near a radiator, suspect a leaking pipe. The concrete will have to be cut out, the system drained, and the damaged pipe replaced and tested before re-laying the floor.

Damp on a suspended floor

Leaking pipes apart, dampness on a suspended wood floor is often caused by blocked ventilation bricks. Clear the soil away from the airbricks and unclog all the holes with a meat skewer or something similar. If the floor is very damp, check the floorboards and joists for rot.

Damp patches on walls

These often appear on external walls which are exposed to the prevailing wind. Look for obvious signs of damage such as cracks. If the wall appears to be all right, check the guttering. Even a blockage of leaves can cause water to pour onto and penetrate a wall. The wall may need to be re-pointed outside with mortar.

Damp patches round windows

A damaged seal between window frame and brickwork allows rainwater to penetrate and, if neglected, may lead to rotting woodwork.

From the outside, scrape out any loose mortar and fill the gaps with waterproof mastic. At the same time, check the putty holding the glass and renew if necessary; check the panes themselves and also the windowsill. If this is cracked, moisture will eventually seep through the wall. Regular painting safeguards frames and sills from rot.

Dampness on a chimney breast

Damp patches on a blocked-up chimney breast may be due to insufficient ventilation in the chimney. An airbrick in the wall could cure the trouble. In old houses with wide chimneys, rain and damp could be penetrating from above and the chimney should be capped.

Alternatively, the metal flashing between chimney and roof may be at fault but this requires expert attention.

Damp on ceilings

This is usually the result of a missing roof tile or leaking skylight. If you cannot check the condition of the slates or tiles from the ground, go up into the loft and look for indications of where the damp may be entering. Water coming through a skylight may be the result of damaged putty, cracked glass or deteriorated metal sealing strip (flashing) round the window. Flexible bitumen strips can be moulded round the frame to form a completely waterproof join.

Look out, too, for leaks in pipework in the loft, or between ground and first floor, and repair if found. Other sources of leaks are faulty flashings round the chimney stack and joins between a wall and a flat roof or built-on extension. Flat roofs are notoriously prone to leaks and should have a slight slope to drain them, but subsidence and bad workmanship often make them really flat so that they retain water.

Damp in basements

Damp-proofing basement walls is a difficult and costly business. One treatment is to coat the earth-retaining walls with bitumen, but there is a possibility that dampness building up behind may eventually push the bitumen away from the brickwork.

More thorough and expensive is 'tanking' – asphalting the walls and building up a second wall to sandwich the asphalt and the outer wall. An alternative is to cover the outer wall with a waterproofed rendering and then build a second wall about 5cm (2in) away, fitting ventilation grilles in the new wall and rendering with waterproofed cement. Provided the floor of

the basement has been damp-proofed, the new wall will not need a damp-proof course.

Dimmer switches

Dimmer switches are used to control the amount of light put out by a ceiling or wall fitting or lamp. You adjust the level of brightness by turning a small dial or rotary knob which is fitted in place of the usual on/off switch.

You can buy wall-mounted one-way and two-way dimmer switches to replace conventional ones, and also dimming controls for lamps. dimmer switches for fluorescent lighting are not very widely available.

★ **HANDY HINT** ★

Before buying, check an identical demonstration model in the shop to see that it dims the light evenly, with a good range of brightness levels, and avoid those which go jerkily from very bright to very dim.

A two-way conventional switch must be replaced with a two-way dimmer switch.

Fixing a switch

The easiest type of dimmer switch to fit is the lamp dimmer which is fitted into the bulb socket or inserted in the flex of a lamp. Some are a combination of dimmer unit and adaptor and go on the end of the flex, instead of a conventional plug.

Replacing wall-mounted switches with dimmers can be fairly easily done by anyone experienced in simple electrical work.

● First check the dimmer has clear instructions which you understand fully.

● Turn off the electricity at the mains.

● Remove the old switch and, ideally, disconnect one wire at a time and connect each one immediately with the relevant terminal in the new switch.

Doors, exterior

The front door of any house not only indicates the way in, but gives a first impression of the house and its occupants.

Use the original door whenever possible, especially with older houses; if you need to have a new door, choose a style compatible with the architecture.

Types of wooden front door

Hardwood doors Those made from teak, mahogany or oak are the most expensive. To show off the wood grain, give the door a few coats of exterior grade polyurethane varnish.

Softwood doors These are usually deal frames with plywood panels and are relatively inexpensive. They are best primed and painted with good quality gloss paint.

Glazed doors

If you are considering a glazed door, take into account the amount of light in the hallway, your privacy and warmth requirements, and also the question of security-glazed panels which are easily broken by burglars.

Frosted or patterned glass gives more privacy than plain glass, but if the panels are low enough to be accidentally kicked, fallen against or broken into, choose toughened or wired glass.

Back and side doors

Styles tend to be simpler than for a front door. If a door opens off the kitchen, glass panels will make the room seem larger and lighter.

A back door made like a stable door, which divides widthways, can be opened at the top during warm weather to let in fresh air but keep toddlers safe from straying. Make sure that both pieces can be locked.

Doors, interior

Most older houses were built with attractive solid, panelled doors inside, but unfortunately until about 10 years ago these doors were considered old-fashioned dust traps and were replaced with plain flush doors.

In some cases, you may find that the original panelled doors were covered with a sheet of thin plywood or hardboard nailed over the panels. If you have doors like this but would prefer the original doors back, it is fairly easy to prise off the covering and reveal the panels underneath.

Panels and substitutes

If you want to replace flush doors with

panelled doors, there is a wide range to choose from. Unfortunately, solid panelled doors are very expensive, especially if you are thinking of fitting them throughout the house. Cheaper, passable imitations have a softwood frame with a hardboard covering, moulded to look like panels. Once they have been primed and painted they look fine, but are no substitute if you want a natural wood finish.

Much cheaper are the doors with softwood frames and flat plywood surfaces, and cheapest of all are doors with softwood frames covered with a sheet of hardboard, but these are easily damaged. A chance knock with a piece of furniture can make a hole that is very difficult to repair.

Glazed doors Inside the home, glazed doors will make the most of light to brighten a gloomy room or let light from a sunny room into a dark hallway. Small glass panes are less likely to break than larger areas: these should be made of toughened glass. Perspex panels can be used instead of glass for extra safety, but they are more expensive.

Doors with a difference

If space is a problem, or if you have several doors opening into a cramped hallway, folding or sliding doors may help.

Folding doors Made in various plastic finishes over a metal frame (which folds away like a concertina and runs from an overhead track); or as narrow, louvred wooden panels, hinged together, which are more trouble to open and close than ordinary doors, but are useful for shutting off a kitchen from a dining area or dividing up a large, open-plan living room.

Patio doors An expanse of sliding glass door, though it enhances a sunny and attractive outlook, has its dangers. One is that, with such a large area, people (especially children) may not realise it is there and may walk or run into the glass.

Toughened glass is essential, but expensive. Another point to consider is the heat loss through such a large expanse of glass, which could turn the room into an ice-box in winter. Double-glazing of patio doors is a must.

Sliding doors These require a stretch of wall, to take the runners, that is at least as wide as the door itself.

Swing doors A swing door can solve the problem of carrying a loaded tray from kitchen to dining-room, but has its disadvantages. Space is needed on either side of the doorway so that the door can swing fully both ways. You must also be careful not to swing the door into an unsuspecting person on the other side. Glazed upper panels prevent such collisions. If space is limited, two narrow, louvred doors look good and need less swing space.

Double glazing

Double glazing is an effective way of cutting down heat losses through windows and glazed doors, although you should not expect it to cut fuel bills dramatically. In an average-sized house, 10 to 15 per cent of the heat loss goes through glazed areas; double glazing will at best halve the heat lost, and so could reduce fuel bills by between 5 and 7½ per cent.

Double glazing to reduce noise is always effected with secondary glazing units because, for optimum noise reduction, the panes need to be separated by at least 10cm (4in) and preferably more. In addition, the sides, top and bottom of the air space between such panes should be lined with sound-absorbent acoustic tiles, to improve the insulation further. There are grants available to help with double glazing costs for those who live near airports and motorways. Check your local authority for details.

Types of double glazing

Sealed units This is the most efficient form of double glazing: it consists of two panes of glass separated by a hermetically-sealed spacer strip. This

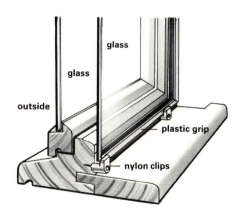

A clip and frame arrangement is an ideal low-cost solution for the secondary glazing of individual panes and small fixed windows.

unit replaces the existing pane of glass in the window frame, and it is important to choose the right type for your frames.

The standard sealed unit needs a deep rebate, and if yours are not deep enough to take such a unit (which may be the best part of an inch thick) you will have to fit what is known as a stepped unit instead. Such sealed units should have an air gap of at least 12mm (½in) to give really effective insulation. In addition, they should be of toughened glass, particularly if they are installed in doors.

Secondary units The alternative way of double-glazing windows and doors is to leave the existing glass in position and to fit a second pane of glass on the inside to trap an insulating layer of still air between the two panes. These secondary panes can be fixed to the window frame, hinged to it or mounted in a sliding track. In the last two cases they can then be opened for ventilation and cleaning.

Such secondary systems can be professionally installed, although this is likely to be expensive on a whole-house scale. There are also a great many do-it-yourself secondary double-glazing systems on the market, consisting of mouldings, fittings, track and so on: you have to supply the glass. However, if carefully installed, these can be just as effective as professional systems, and offer a much cheaper alternative. Fitting them is well within the scope of the average do-it-yourselfer, as no great skill is required to assemble and fit the panels.

The most important consideration with both professional and do-it-yourself secondary glazing installations, is efficient draughtproofing of the existing window and the secondary units. If the air space between the panes is ventilated, the insulation benefits are almost completely lost.

Exterior decorating

Weatherwise, autumn is probably the best time for outside decorating, though you may have to wait a little to let the overnight damp dry off. Spring is an alternative time.

If you prefer to pay for a professional painter to do the job for you, obtain several estimates and make sure you know exactly what they cover.

Preparation

As with interior decoration, it is necessary to clean down and repair before you start painting. Points you should watch for are:

● Broken or crumbling brickwork.
● Cracks in stucco, cement or roughcast walls.
● Damaged seals between window frames and brickwork.
● Choked or defective gutters and downpipes.
● Decayed and rotting woodwork.
● Blocked or defective airbricks and ventilators.
● Rusty metalwork.
● Cracked, loose or missing putty from windows.

All these must be attended to before painting starts (see REPAIRS AND MAINTENANCE).

Painting

● Thoroughly clean woodwork before painting commences. On exterior doors you should remove handles, knockers, etc. to give a clear surface.
● Strip off old paint that is cracked or peeling with a proprietary paint stripper or a blow lamp. Wash down and, when dry, apply an exterior wood primer, followed by an undercoat and a coat, or preferably two, of high quality gloss paint. Rub down with fine glasspaper between coats.
● Metal gutters and downpipes should be cleaned with a wire brush, rubbed down and immediately given a coat of metal primer followed by two coats of undercoat before the top coat of gloss is applied.
● Do not paint plastic pipes.

 HANDY HINT
Make up a strong bleach solution and apply to all mould and plant growth to destroy it – wash off bleach with water. Protect skin from bleach by wearing rubber gloves.

Rough-cast walls

Special masonry paints are available for this type of surface, giving a thick, waterproof surface. Most of these paints should be applied thickly and dabbed on rather than brushed into the surface; a long-pile roller is very effective. Manufacturers' instructions will indicate their covering capacity, but this is generally about half that of ordinary paints (see HOME DECORATION – Painting).

WARNING

It is dangerous to lean sideways from a ladder, so if you are covering a wide surface, such as a wall, you will find it safer and more efficient to hire or even buy an easily erected scaffolding kit.

Extractor fans

In order to keep the air in your home fresh, a simple airbrick or window-mounted ventilator may not be enough, particularly in steamy rooms.

The simplest fans can be fitted into a window or wall, and have a switch or pull cord which simultaneously opens the shutters over the fan (which prevent draughts when closed) and turns on the electrically operated fan blades.

Window models are generally the easiest to fit. Some fans are ducted so that they can be fitted to the ceiling and pass air out through ductwork to the loft; others can be fitted into an airbrick in a flat roof or roof lights.

Most fans are designed so that they can either take in or extract air. In order to obtain the best ventilation, they should be fitted on the wall or ceiling furthest from the door, so that air circulates round the room. Sizes vary from about 15cm (6in) in diameter for bathroom or lavatory, through 25cm (10in) for kitchens to about 30cm (1ft) for larger rooms.

If you are fitting a fan into a window or skylight, consult a glazier about the weight and type of glass to be used and get him to cut the hole in the glass. Specially designed fans can be fitted into double-glazed windows. If you have sealed-unit double glazing, consult the manufacturer about fitting a fan.

Ventilators for internal rooms

Some homes are designed with bathrooms and lavatories with no exterior walls, so that some form of ducted ventilation is essential (this is a statutory requirement). This is particularly common in cases where large houses have been converted into flats.

Controls for ducted extractor fans are usually linked to the lighting, so that the fan comes on with the lights and goes on ventilating the room for a set period after the light has been switched off. It is also possible to fit timed controllers to ducted or non-ducted ventilators, so that the air is cleared regularly.

Flooring

The floor receives harder wear than any other part of the house, so it is particularly important to maintain it in good condition and to replace and improve when necessary.

Wooden flooring

Wooden floorboards can curl, due to the effects of drying out, leaving ridges at the joints between boards. There is a possibility that, even with a thick, resilient underlay, the unevenness will show on the surface after a time. It may be possible to sand down the ridges using a mechanical sander, but it is likely also to need a sub-floor of 3–4mm (about ⅛in) plywood, hardboard or flooring-grade chipboard, nailed to the floorboards before laying carpets or other floor coverings.

Old wood-block floors can also wear unevenly and may therefore need similar treatment.

Loose boards These should be nailed down to the joints and all nailheads punched below the surface of the floor. Remove all nails used to fix previous floor coverings.

WARNING

Do check that there are no pipes or electric cables running near the boards before nailing them down.

Blemishes and cracks Small dents and cracks along the grain of the wood can be filled with plastic filler. A more attractive filler can be made by mixing sawdust with cellulose-based wallpaper adhesive.

Badly damaged boards Cut them out, piece in a matching section of similar wood, and nail to the nearest joist at each end. If the boards are tongued and grooved, it is necessary to cut through the tongue of the damaged board to release it, and to cut off the tongue of the replacement board.

Sanded and sealed boards

These are not so much a floor covering as a form of processing wooden floors. They are a popular, satisfying choice since they are warm-looking, easily

maintained and the only costs normally involved are machine hire and sealing material.

Not all floorboards lend themselves to sanding and sealing. Do not attempt floors with gaps unless you can plug the gaps efficiently. Likewise, boards rotted from damp or dry rot are not suitable – loose or damaged boards should be replaced before the work begins.

Sand the surface with a sanding machine and finally rub down with a fine grade of glasspaper, working right into the corners and angles. Seal with a few coats of polyurethane sealer, rubbing down between each coat, followed by two or more coats of wax polish. Remove dust carefully with a cloth soaked in white spirit between coats of sealer and work in a clean atmosphere. If the boards are uneven in colour or too pale, stain them with a stain recommended by the manufacturer of the sealer.

WARNING

The very fine wood dust produced by floor sanding is dangerously flammable, which is why sanders have dust bags. Always wear a mask when floor sanding, and seal the inside of the room door with masking tape and open the window. Always dispose of the dust outside the house.

Sheet flooring

Vinyl sheeting is the modern version of linoleum. It does not look dramatically different from lino but is more flexible and comes in both cushioned and single gauge. It is marketed in a great variety of colours and patterns, is extremely easy to lay and is also hard wearing.

Plywood sheeting is also now available in simulated traditional wood-block floor patterns. It looks impressive, is very durable and can be used on both wooden and solid floors. Do not use it in areas of prolonged dampness, such as a bathroom.

Floor tiles

Floor tiles are practical and visually appealing, particularly in areas which require regular cleaning. Cork and vinyl tiles are soft underfoot, while ceramic and quarry tiles give a crisp, clean feel to a room.

Cork tiles These are warm underfoot, hard wearing and easy to clean. They come in two types – plastic faced and natural (the former are more expensive and tend to look shinier but wipe clean more easily; the latter, which are finished with a flexible lacquer, need polishing from time to time).

Ceramic tiles They are hard-wearing, easy to clean and are unaffected by prolonged exposure to sunlight or steam. They are cold to stand on, however, and they can be rather brittle, so dropped dishes are more likely to shatter than on vinyl or cork. Ceramic tiles need a base of blockboard or plywood for the best support.

Quarry tiles These are thicker than ceramic tiles but wear even better. They are warmer in tone, and are therefore a good option for kitchens or storerooms where a subtle, warmer effect is pre-ferred. Like ceramic tiles, however, they can be cold underfoot.

Quarry tiles are firmest when laid on concrete screed. This makes them more of an effort to lay than other coverings, and restricts them to concrete floors – but their permanence and efficiency do make them worth the effort. For the best results, use quarry tiles in conjunction with matting or rugs, making sure that the rugs have a non-slip backing.

1 Lay on a level, smooth concrete floor if an underlay is not required. Use a bolster to remove surface flaws.
2 Use the recommended adhesive and fix a small area of tile at a time. Remove adhesive squeezed up between tiles before it sets.
3 Use a steel rule, heavy-duty handyman's knife and a cutting board when you trim sheet or individual tiling.
4 Take special care when cutting tiles to fit architraves and other awkward obstacles. A card template or special tool is useful.

Heating

Choosing a heating system will depend on the size and type of house or flat, and whether storage space is available for solid fuel or oil. Good insulation is important to make any heating system work economically.

Central heating

There are four types of central heating and it is best to consider which would suit your purposes before investing in any system.

Full central heating All living areas of the house are heated to a required temperature.

Background central heating The kind of heating that warms every room but not enough for comfortable living, and has to be boosted with extra heating in particular areas.

Partial central heating Systems which are restricted to some parts of a house only.

Selective central heating The kind of system which is connected through the house but can only adequately heat a few rooms at a time. The householder decides which areas to heat or leave unheated at any particular time.

Choice of fuel

Apart from personal preference, which fuel you use for central heating may depend on the facilities you have for a flue. Solid fuel and oil systems as well as some gas boilers, need to have a conventional flue. This may either use an existing chimney which, in old houses, has to be fitted with a stainless steel liner or may be attached to an outside wall. If this is impracticable, your choice has to be electricity or a balanced-flue gas boiler, which exhausts its combustion gas through a small flue in the wall on which it is mounted.

Systems

Once you have chosen the kind of fuel that is best for your home, decide what type of system you want.

Ducted warm-air These systems run on gas, oil or electricity and are usually installed when a house is built. They can be difficult to put in later. Hot air is circulated through the house by a fan through ducts to grilles in the floor or skirting boards, and returns through grilles over the doors. In spite of filtering, strong smells tend to be blown around the house.

Gas convector heaters Individual convector heaters throughout the house are thermostatically controlled by a central automatic clock. The heaters work by warming air passing through them. They are economical to run – just turn them on when you need them – and take up little space.

Balanced flue convectors can be fitted wherever there is an outside wall and are useful in buildings which may be unoccupied in very cold weather, as there is no danger of their freezing up.

Metrication of copper pipes

Copper pipe used for plumbing and central heating is now described by its outside diameter in mm instead of its inside diameter in inches. So 15mm pipe has replaced the old $\frac{1}{2}$in size, 22mm has replaced $\frac{3}{4}$in pipe and 28mm has replaced 1in pipe. Compression fittings in 15 and 28mm sizes will fit old imperial-sized pipe, but 22mm fittings need a special adaptor if they are to fit $\frac{3}{4}$in pipe. Capillary fittings in metric sizes will not fit imperial-sized pipe, but special adaptors are available in the various sizes. Threaded pipe fittings, such as those connecting pipe to radiators and boilers, are still sized in inches.

Hot-water The invention of an almost silent pump for domestic use has led to an increase in hot-water central heating systems.

The pipes through which the water is pumped to the radiators can be small-bore 12 to 18mm ($\frac{1}{2}$–$\frac{3}{4}$in) or micro-bore less than 12mm ($\frac{1}{2}$in).

Heat is provided by a boiler which can be fired by gas, oil or solid fuel. There is also an electric heater, which is not strictly a boiler. These systems are easily installed and controlled and help to prevent the plumbing freezing up in cold weather.

Storage radiators These are popular forms of electric heating, which run off cut-price electricity at night. Some have a fan fitted to discharge heat more quickly, while some can have a mid-day boost. Before buying storage radiators, obtain all the information you can from your electricity board about different tariffs and running costs, as well as electricity consumption of the different models.

Underfloor heating The heating elements are embedded into a solid floor, so this form of heating can only be installed in new houses or if floors are being resurfaced. If anything goes wrong with underfloor heating, the floor has to be dug up.

Radiators

Panel radiators Available in standard heights from 30 to 75cm (1–2$\frac{1}{2}$ft) and in standard lengths up to 4m (about 13ft). Larger sizes can be made to order.

Panel radiators can come in double or triple panelled versions, to increase the

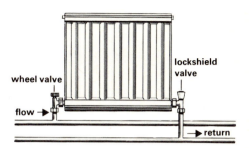

Wheel valves control day-to-day adjustments; lockshield valves balance water flow and, once set, should not be moved. A thermostatic device may be fitted to the wheel valve.

amount of convected air output. Panel radiators usually have a surface temperature below 80°C (176°F).

Convector radiators These usually produce more heat, size for size, than the panel type. Air entering these radiators passes over a hot pipe and rises through a grille or vent in the top of the panel. Fan-assisted convectors are also available, but can be noisy and uncomfortably warm if you are near when the fan is on.

Skirting heating This is a continuous strip of convecting radiator fixed round the walls of a room in place of a skirting board. It is unobtrusive and allows for a more flexible furniture arrangements, but it is not very efficient in high ceilinged rooms.

Installation costs

Installation costs must be compared with running costs. For example, storage radiators are cheaper to install but more expensive to run than a hot-water central heating system. Solid fuel installations are usually the cheapest to run but can be expensive to install.

The least expensive hot-water systems are those sold as package deals providing a boiler, piping and a certain number of radiators for a fixed price – but your house must fit the system, otherwise it is better to have one specially designed.

Insulation Must be counted as part of the initial outlay, and is vital if you are to use central heating economically and get the best results (see Insulation.)

Maintenance

It is advisable to take up the maintenance contracts offered by installation firms and fuel industries. Check the contract to make sure exactly what it covers.

Keep cisterns and storage tanks in good repair and run the system occasionally for a few minutes during the summer, to check the pump.

★ **HANDY HINT** ★

Do bleed radiators and turn valves as far as they will go each way, once or twice a year.

Sweep the flueway in a solid fuel boiler during the summer and leave the boiler empty with the door open when not in use.

Heating – water

If central heating is installed in your home, it is likely that at least part of your hot water will be supplied by the heating system. If this is not the case, or if your central heating system does not supply hot water during the summer months, there are various alternatives which you can consider.

Electricity

Immersion heater Can supply all your hot water, or merely be used for water heating in summertime, when the boiler is off. The heater must be fitted with a thermostat – a temperature of 60°C (140°F) is generally high enough – and the storage tank must be well lagged to conserve heat.

Sink heaters Although they heat water quickly, if continuous hot water is required sink heaters are slow and expensive to run.

Storage heaters These heat the water to about 60°C (140°F) and store it until needed. They are generally only suitable for a fairly small house without a long pipe-run. In a larger house, separate heaters could be installed for the bathroom and kitchen.

Gas

Boilers An independent boiler can be fitted, but needs its own flue. Some types are able to produce hot water quickly enough for any number of baths one after another. These have several heat settings.

Multipoint heaters These provide a continuous supply of hot water as soon as they are turned on, but the water temperature is sometimes difficult to adjust and maintain. They will supply taps in kitchen, bath and basin. Some models require a flue.

Instantaneous heaters Can be fitted over a sink and supply warm, hot or boiling water. They do not require a flue.

Oil

An independent boiler can be fully automatic and incorporate a time clock and thermostat if required.

Solid fuel

Supplies hot water in various ways:
● An independent boiler with an enclosed fire-box and a circular water jacket.
● A curved water jacket fitted round the back boiler of an open fire, which is capable of burning continuously.
● Most of the heavy, insulated cookers which use solid fuel to heat ovens and boiling plates, will also heat water for a tank of 140 litres (30 gallons) or so.
● Some multifuel-burning stoves will heat water, with the addition of a water-heating kit which is an optional extra. This may be used to supply hot water for washing up or, if the tank has a thermostat, for baths.

Insulation and draught proofing

In every home, heat is constantly escaping through doors, windows, roof, walls and floor. Proper insulation will make your home more comfortable.

Draught-proofing

This is the most cost-effective element of insulation, as it is cheap and easy to install. Draughts account for about 15 per cent of the total heat loss.

Foam strips These are easy to fix, but are not durable. They are fixed by pressing the sticky backing round door or window frames. The door or window, when closed, compresses the foam and forms the seal.

Overflow pipes They can be covered with special hinged flaps to stop the draught that often blows through them.

Plastic and metal strips Usually made of sprung bronze, aluminium or vinyl, they are pinned to the frame so that the flap stands away from the frame and on closing the door, a seal is formed. They are much more effective than foam.

It is also possible to get strips with flexible rubber inserts, which are fixed to the door jamb and are compressed when the door is closed.

Under-door draught excluders The simplest excluders are flexible plastic or plastic, aluminium or wood strips with rubber, nylon, felt or brush insert. The strip is pinned to the bottom of the door so that the insert is against the threshold when the door is shut.

It is also possible to fit an excluder consisting of an aluminium strip housing an arched piece of vinyl, to the threshold itself.

Some metal excluders come in two parts, one attached to the door and the other to the threshold, while others have a loose section which rises to clear floor coverings when you open the door.

Loft insulation

Up to 25 per cent of heat loss is through the loft. Insulating is easy to do yourself with a choice of two reasonably cheap methods.

Glass fibre or mineral wool quilts These are placed in the spaces between the joists. Start at one side of the loft and work across to the other. Leave a space at the edge under the eaves so that there is adequate ventilation in the loft.

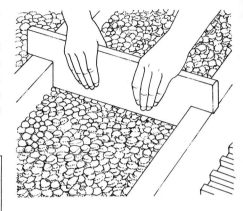

★ HANDY HINT ★

You can get grants from your local authority towards the cost of insulating uninsulated lofts.

As far as possible, take the material under any electrical wires or pipes so that they remain accessible for maintenance or repair.

Joists are usually spaced at 40mm (1ft 4in) intervals. The material is made to convenient widths so that the edges lap up against the sides of the joists. You must have a layer at least 7.5cm (3in) thick for efficient insulation, and up to 12.5cm (5in) is cost-effective if you have central heating.

Loose fill granules This is the alternative filler, made of vermiculite or mineral wool pellets. They come in large bags and are simply poured between the joists and leveled, using a T-shaped plywood spreader (see illustration above). You will need a layer at least 10cm (4in) thick.

A broom is useful to push the material into inaccessible corners under the eaves. The loose fill granules are easier to use than quilts in a loft with joists at irregular intervals or awkwardly shaped areas.

WARNING

These insulating materials can cause irritation to skin and nostrils, so wear gloves and a handkerchief as a face mask while working.

Trapdoor Do not forget to cover the trapdoor with a layer of mineral wool or glass fibre.

Water tanks and plumbing In lofts these should also be insulated, once you have cut down the amount of heat loss, to prevent freeze-ups. Wrap the sides and top of the cold water tank with mineral wool, but *do not* insulate underneath. (If the cold water tank has no lid, make a hardboard cover on a simple frame.) Heat can then rise from below to prevent the tank from freezing. Pipework should be wrapped in mineral wool or felt bandages, taped at intervals, or you can use foam plastic or expanded polysytrene tubes for straight lengths, with extra bandages round bends and joints.

Walls

Some 35 per cent of the total heat loss is through walls, which are difficult to insulate.

Cavity walls These are insulated by ureaformaldehyde foam, mineral wool or polystyrene pellets. All are installed the same way, through holes in the outer part of the wall, and are a job for professional contractors. The whole operation takes less than a day on most houses.

Solid walls These are the most difficult parts of a house to insulate. The inner faces of all external walls are insulated using dry lining methods, which entail fixing an extra insulating layer to the wall. This can be *fibreboard*, usually called *insulating* board or softboard; or *composite insulating board*, consisting of a plastic insulating foam used as a backing for plasterboard or layered in a sandwich construction. These should be mounted on battens, but *closed-cell foams* can be directly stuck on to walls with adhesives.

 HANDY HINT

If the solid wall is being insulated on the inside by a method which incorporates the use of battens (eg wood cladding, insulation board etc.), loose roof insulating material can be put down behind the cladding for extra protection.

Mineral fibre mats Efficient insulators, but must be mounted on battens and will protrude into the room by anything up to 10cm (4in).

Floors

Gaps between floorboards and under the skirting boards should be sealed. (See Flooring.)

A good quality underlay beneath a fitted carpet does much to reduce draughts.

Gaps below skirting can be blocked with quadrant moulding, which is obtainable from timber merchants and do-it-yourself stores. This is pinned and glued to the skirting board with its lower edge pressing against the floor. You can improve the draught proofing by sticking foam draught excluder to the bottom edge of the moulding before pinning it into place. (See also Double glazing.)

Improvement grants

If you buy a house built before 1961 which is structurally sound but needs some basic amenities installed, such as a bathroom or inside lavatory, or important repairs done, your local authority may be prepared to help you with a grant.

The following basic conditions apply throughout the United Kingdom.

Types of grant

Improvement grants, intermediate grants, special grants and repair grants are only given to improve houses built *before* 1961 and are not available for a holiday or second home, or to enlarge a modern house. Your local authority will help you to decide which type is best for your needs.

Grants are not given to install central heating unless, for example, a large, old house is being converted into self-contained flats.

Who can apply? Anyone can apply for a local authority grant provided that the applicant owns or is buying the freehold, or has a lease with at least five years to run.

Improvement grants

As well as improving an old house or converting a large house into flats, these grants might be given for the conversion of a basically sound building, such as a barn into a home, or for enlarging a kitchen.

Installing a damp course, providing adequate ventilation and windows, a new staircase, bathroom, inside lavatory and kitchen sink are all eligible for grant aid.

Such a grant can also cover repairs and replacements if at least half the grant is to be used for actual improvements.

If there is a registered disabled person in the house, a grant may also be available for installing special facilities such as a lift, downstairs lavatory, a special bath or slopes for a wheelchair.

Rateable value Improvement grants are only awarded for houses which are *below* a certain rateable value. Check with your local authority for details and for grants available for flats.

Amounts awarded Maximum amounts vary but in most cases a grant would cover up to 50 per cent of the estimated costs, going up to 60 per cent in an area designated as a general improvement area. In certain cases of hardship it could go up to as much as 90 per cent. In every case the balance must be paid by the applicant for the grant.

Other grants

Intermediate and special grants cover the installation of basic amenities: hot and cold water, inside lavatory, bathroom, wash basin and kitchen sink. Provided that you fulfil certain basic requirements, a local authority cannot refuse you an intermediate grant.

Special grants are given in houses occupied by several families, and have to be applied for by the landlord.

Repair grants are for general structural repairs rather than installation of amenities and can cover between 60 and 90 per cent of the cost of the repairs. Such grants are likely to be given to people who only have a low income, pensioners, etc.

Basic requirements

When the work is finished, the council will expect the house to be fit to be lived in for at least 30 years. Basic requirements are:

● A bath or shower (preferably in a bathroom), a washbasin, a kitchen sink, an indoor lavatory and hot and cold water for sinks and baths.

● The house should be free of damp, adequately lighted and ventilated in every room, with adequate provision for artificial lighting and power points for other appliances.

● Proper drainage and places for dustbins, structural stability and a convenient internal layout.

● Proper facilities for heating the home, storing fuel if used, and for preparing and cooking food.

Applying for a grant

First decide what needs to be done, then visit the appropriate council department for an informal chat. You will be given the relevant form and must send in the estimated cost of the work, with any plans you have drawn up.

You will have to sign a certificate saying you will be living in the house for five years following the completion of the work or, in the case of a second home, that it is to become your main home within a year of work being finished.

Approval and payment

Do not start on any work until you have received formal approval of the grant from the council. Grant approval is not the same as consent under the building regulations, or planning permission.

Timing This varies from area to area, but it will be about three months from your application to approval.

When the money is available Depending on the extent and size of the job, the money is paid either when the finished work is approved. Sometimes the council will pay in instalments, as each stage is completed.

Loans The council will sometimes pay for your share of the costs, charging interest on the loan and postponing the repayment of the capital for an agreed period.

Breaking the agreement

If you sell a house for which you have received a grant before the five years is up, or if you use it as a second home, the council has the right to demand the repayment of part or all of the grant plus interest.

Shelving

All houses need shelving, for books, precious ornaments and storing all manner of things.

Dimensions and fixings

The distance between supports depends
on the material you use for the shelves.
The table shows recommended spans.

Strengthening shelving If you want to
build shelves marginally longer than the
recommended spans (for example,
across an alcove), battens can be fixed
along the backs of the shelves, or to the
front of the shelves, flush with them or
slightly recessed. For extra support, a
corner block can be fitted under the shelf
and pinned and glued to the batten. It is
advisable to add extra brackets to
shelves which are longer than 1.1m (3ft
8in).

Depth of shelves Shelves intended for
storage should be quite narrow as deep
ones make it difficult to reach things
stored at the back. A 15cm (6in) shelf
will take a double row of standard cans
in the larder; a 30cm (1ft) deep shelf is
ample for large crockery and 45–50cm
(1ft 6in–1ft 8in) for general storage.

Shelves for standard paperbacks need
to be no more than 13cm (5in) deep,
while average hardbacks need about
20cm (8in); but if you have a lot of large
books you will have to adjust this.

For pot plants, ornaments and so on,
shelves can be anything from 15–30cm
(6–12in) deep and for stereo systems and
records you will need 45cm (1ft 6in) or
more.

Distance between shelves This depends
on the height of the tallest object that
you wish to store. Allow at least 2cm
($\frac{3}{4}$in) more than the height of your tallest
book.

Fixing techniques Bear in mind that your
shelves, however strong the supports

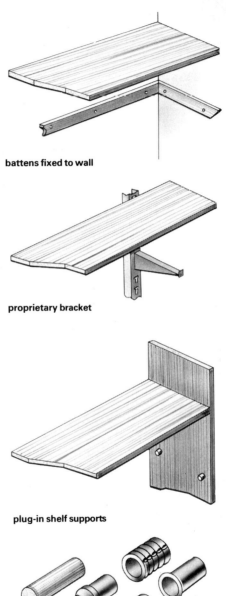

battens fixed to wall

proprietary bracket

plug-in shelf supports

types of plug

Recommended spans for selected materials

Material	Suitable thickness	Maximum span	Notes
Chipboard	15–20mm ($\frac{5}{8}$–$\frac{3}{4}$in)	40cm (1ft 4in)	Cheap, but not strong
Veneered, laminated chipboard	12mm ($\frac{1}{2}$in) 18mm ($\frac{3}{4}$in) 25mm (1in)	40cm (1ft 4in) 60cm (2ft) 75cm (2$\frac{1}{2}$ft)	Better looking and stronger than plain chipboard.
Blockboard	12mm ($\frac{1}{2}$in) 18mm ($\frac{3}{4}$in) 25mm (1in)	45cm (1ft 6in) 80cm (2ft 8in) 100cm (3ft 4in)	Core must run lengthwise for maximum strength. Both sides must have matching finish to prevent warping.
Plywood	12mm ($\frac{1}{2}$in)	45cm (1ft 6in)	Majority of plies must have grain running lengthwise. Both sides must have matching finish to prevent warping.
Timber	16mm ($\frac{5}{8}$in) 22m ($\frac{7}{8}$in) 28mm (1$\frac{1}{8}$in)	50cm (1ft 8in) 90cm (3ft) 105cm (3ft 6in)	Greatest spans can be achieved with solid timber.
Glass	12mm ($\frac{1}{2}$in)	90cm (3ft)	Must have polished edges. Needs special brackets.

are, will only be as strong as the wall fixing. Solid walls can be drilled and plugged with plastic or fibre wall plugs ready for screws. In general the longer the screw, the firmer the fixing. The minimum recommended are No. 8 screws, 5cm (2in) long. Use a masonry bit in a power tool or, for hand drilling, use a club hammer and jumper – an ordinary hand drill is not tough enough to make adequate holes in concrete, brickwork and stonework.

Systems with brackets

The simplest type of shelf support is a metal bracket with holes for screwing to shelf and wall. Plain brackets are unattractive, but there are other designs in wood, plastic, cast iron and so on, which can become part of your decor.

Adjustable brackets There are several bracket systems on the market, consisting of metal uprights with a vertical channel or slotted strip fixed to the wall to hold the brackets. The slotted systems can usually only be fitted with supports at 2–3cm ($\frac{3}{4}$–1$\frac{1}{4}$in) intervals. Other systems are infinitely adjustable as to height and look less industrial than the slotted type.

As a general guide, brackets should be at least three-quarters of the depth of the shelf, positioned one quarter of the way in from each end in the case of shelves supported by only two brackets. If materials permit (see Table) they may be less obtrusive if they are fixed at the sides of an alcove.

In some cases, the brackets are designed to form book ends, in which case the uprights have to be positioned at the ends of the shelves. This type is suitable for systems mounted on flat walls rather than in alcoves. To help hide brackets, a lip can be attached to the front of the shelf.

To fit these shelves flush against the wall, you will need to cut out a small section of the shelf with a tenon saw.

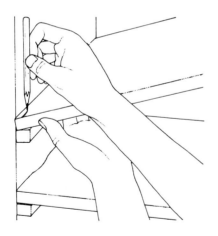

Saw shelf to just over required width. Position shelf in alcove, front edge forward. Run a soft pencil vertically along inside edge of alcove to transfer any irregularities from wall to shelf. Saw along pencil line to achieve an exact fit. Repeat other end.

Shelving attached to uprights

There is less leverage on the support if the shelving can be attached at each end to upright panels or the sides of alcoves. **Permanent fixings in alcoves** The simplest method of fixing is to screw battens to the walls and rest the shelves on these. Less obtrusive is an L-shaped metal support, screwed to the wall along its length. The shelf can simply be rested on this, as on a batten, or the end thickness of the shelf can have a groove cut into it, so that the support can be slid into it. Use a strip slightly shorter than the width of the shelf and stop the groove a few centimetres from the front, if you are using solid timber.

Adjustable fixings to uprights Proprietary metal strips with slots or holes can be attached to alcove walls or upright end panels, and take inconspicuous shelf supports. Alternatively, two rows of holes can be drilled down each upright to take commercially produced studs or wooden dowelling supports.

Supporting the uprights These need to be fixed to the wall to prevent toppling and swaying. The simplest method is to use mirror plates.

Proprietary systems There are many adaptable systems where shelves are attached to ladder-like uprights of metal or wood, which often need no extra fixing to steady them against the wall.

Showers

A shower uses far less hot water than a bath. It is also quicker and, some people claim, it gets you cleaner. An average bathful needs about 140 litres (about 30 gallons) of water, but a shower of ordinary duration uses about 20 litres (4½ gallons), thus making a considerable fuel saving.

Showers take up far less space than a bath. If you need an extra bathroom but do not have the room, a shower cabinet makes a satisfactory solution.

Types of shower

Showers range from portable units which work on the stirrup-pump principle to sophisticated impulse showers which offer a rapidly alternating sequence of hot and cold jets to refresh and stimulate the skin. Showers can be fitted to the existing hot and cold water system in the bath, or can be separate with their own cubicle.

The cheapest and simplest devices are those which can be attached to the hot and cold taps and are fitted into holder brackets screwed to the wall. Next are mixer taps, replacing standard bath taps and providing a tap/shower option. There are also instantaneous showers, run off the cold water supply and heated by electricity. These can have thermostatic controls. In general, thermostatically controlled showers are recommended to avoid possible scalding.

Units built into a wall so that all you see is nozzle and control taps, should have easy access to the feed pipework – perhaps by a removable panel tiled or otherwise surfaced to match the wall.

Water supply

Instantaneous showers use water from the cold main pipe and should be professionally fitted.

Most showers are designed to operate from the bathroom hot and cold supply pipes which deliver approximately the same pressure as they both get their pressure from the cold water cistern in the loft.

The shower design normally caters for variations between hot and cold supplies of up to four or five to one, to allow for alterations in flow ratios caused by other taps in the house being turned on.

 WARNING

A shower connected to an indirect tank-supplied hot feed and a direct mains-pressure cold one, cannot give satisfactory control, even with thermostatic mixing units.

Head of water There must be an adequate difference in height between the cold tank in the loft and the shower spray on a lower level. There can be water head problems even in a bathroom underneath the feed tank unless there is a head of at least 1m (3ft 3in) – preferably 1.2m (about 4ft).

A pressurised feed tank can be installed or the existing tank raised.

Pipe runs These should be kept as short as possible by choosing a site near the existing pipes, either in the bathroom or, if possible, in an adjacent room, either beside or below.

Waste pipes must be joined either to existing waste runs, or led outside separately.

Installing showers is best left to the

professional, except for the simple hose-to-spray-head type.

Shower surrounds

Telephone box type shower cubicles are easy to fit on landings or even in bedrooms, provided you have a site which offers an adequate fall for the waste pipe. Care must also be taken to prevent splashing or overflowing of the water on to wood floors, carpets and so on.

The shower surround must be waterproof. Tiles are the most satisfactory solution, but alternatives include plastic laminate, acrylic plastic panels and even well-sealed wood. All must be carried well above the shower itself and joints sealed with a proprietary caulking compound, especially the areas round the bath.

★ **HANDY HINT** ★

Shower trays or baths used for showers should be non-slip, and you should fix a handle on the wall nearby for support.

Tiles and tiling

Types of tile

Wall tiles These are medium-glazed, and available in a wide range of plain colours and an almost limitless number of patterns. Such tiles are usually square and come in three sizes – 10cm (4in) square, 15cm (6in) square and 20cm (8in) square. Rectangular tiles,

20×10cm (8×4in), 20cm (8in) square are also available.

There is also a range of interlocking tiles in various shapes, and tiny mosaic tiles on a fabric mesh backing.

Square wall tiles come in three types: the field tile with a glazed surface and unglazed, square edges and tiles with one or two edges rounded off and glazed.

Floor tiles Come in both plain and patterned varieties, but are thicker than wall tiles. There is also a range of interlocking floor tiles available.

Quarry tiles are unglazed, self-coloured floor tiles that are particularly hard-wearing. They are usually square and come in sizes from 7·5cm (3in) up to 23cm (9in) square. The common colours are buff, red, brown and black. They can be bought in three types, as wall tiles, and special skirting tiles to match can also be obtained.

Ceramic quadrant tiles are sold for filling the gaps between baths and the adjacent wall surface. They come in packs containing enough to edge three sides of the bath and consist of straight pieces, internal corner pieces and rounded end pieces. They are stuck in place with flexible adhesive.

Surfaces for tiling

Tiles can be fixed to most sound, level surfaces. Wallpaper must be removed as well as flaky paint, and flexible boards must be securely fixed to battens.

Tools and adhesives

You will need:
A tape measure

A notched spreader
A large filling knife
A tile cutter
A pair of pincers for nibbling irregular shapes
A carborundum stone for smoothing cut edges
A straight edge
A spirit level and a plumbline

Tile adhesives are widely sold in ready-mixed form. The supplier of the tiles will recommend the best adhesive for you to use.

Estimating quantities

Measure the length and width of the area to be tiled and divide each measurement by the size of the tile you intend to use; multiply the two figures together. Be careful to count the number of special tiles you need to finish off edges and corners and allow a margin for breakage or faulty cutting.

Half-tiling a wall Measure down from where the top row of tiles will come and mark the position of the lowest row of full tiles with a batten pinned lightly to the wall.

Next mark the centre of the area to be tiled and use a spirit level or plumbline to draw a vertical line on the wall at that point. Check what size of cut tile will be needed at each end and if this is less than 2.5cm (1in) wide, shift the centre line to give a whole tile in one corner and a wider cut one in the other.

Start tiling from the batten upwards, checking that the rows of tiles are horizontal and finish off the top with a row of round-edged tiles. Then turn your attention to cut tiles.

Cutting tiles

Simply place the tile on a flat surface and score the glaze along the cutting line with the tile cutter. Then put the tile over your straight edge and use firm hand pressure to snap it neatly along the scored line.

Awkward shapes should be scored and the waste area nibbled away with pincers.

Measure each cut tile individually and remember to allow for the spacer lugs in your calculations.

Grouting

Allow tiles to set for about 24 hours before filling the gaps between them with grout. Rub the mixture well into the gaps with a sponge and wipe off excess when it has begun to dry.

It is recommended that you run a piece of dowel or a moistened finger along each line of grout to give a smooth finish and leave to dry. Wipe with a soft, dry cloth when the grout has fully hardened.

Floors Tiles can be laid on solid or timber floors, but not if they are rough or uneven. A floor-levelling compound can be used on solid floors, but it is best to seek professional advice before tiling on a wood floor. If you are contemplating using floor tiles upstairs, the floor joists must be checked to make sure they can take the weight.

The method of setting out is the same as for linoleum and vinyl tiles (see HOME DECORATION – Floor coverings) and tiles are cut and grouted as above.

CHAPTER 3

REPAIRS AND MAINTENANCE

Chimneys•Cisterns•Dry and wet rot
Furniture•Fuses•Glazing•Metals
Types of tools•Windows

ABC of tools

For home repairs and maintenance you will need a tool kit. You can start off with the bare minimum needed to get you out of trouble, and from there on you can buy what you need as the jobs come up.

▲ WARNING ▲

Do not economise by buying cheap tools – they can be dangerous.

Store cutting tools separately, with blades covered; small tools in a metal box and larger ones in a wooden box or a canvas tool bag in a dry place.

Basic tool kit list

Bradawl For making small pilot holes for screws in wood **(a)**.

Chisels One 12mm ($\frac{1}{2}$in) and one 25mm (1in) wide with bevel edge for making simple joints, cutting out a recess **(b)**.

Drill A small hand drill and drill bits of various sizes including masonry drill bits, sizes No. 12 and 8. It is well worth investing later in a power drill.

File A metal file, or a 'Surform' type with replaceable blades **(c)**.

Hammer Choose a medium-weight claw type one with a comfortable handle. Check the feel and stability before buying **(d)**.

Handyman's knife These have interchangeable blades for cutting different materials. Choose one with a retractable blade **(e)**.

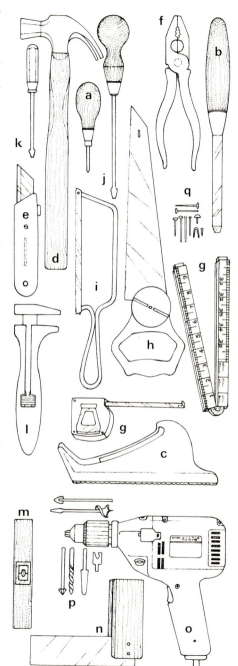

Pliers For gripping and cutting through thick wire or cable. Buy a pair with insulated handles so you can use them for electrical jobs too **(f)**.

Rule A 1m (3ft) folding type or steel tape with locking catch **(g)**.

Saw Choose a general purpose saw with adjustable handle and replaceable blade **(h)**. A *tenon saw* is also needed if you intend doing a lot of woodwork. For cutting metal, use a *junior hacksaw* with a replaceable blade **(i)**.

Screwdrivers You need at least three:
● One about 25cm (10in) long for dealing with large screws in wood **(j)**.
● One medium size for the same sort of work. The blade width should be the same size as the slot of the average screw (gauge 8 or 10).
● One small insulated screwdriver for minor electrical jobs **(k)**.
● You may also need a special screwdriver for 'Pozidriv' cross-headed screws.

Spanner An adjustable one, at least 25cm (10in) long **(l)**.

Spirit level Buy a small one with a bubble in both planes, to check vertically as well as horizontally. Fix it to a batten if a longer length is needed **(m)**.

Try square or carpenter's square For marking off and checking exact right angles **(n)**.

Vice A clamp-on vice is not absolutely necessary, but does help in holding wood firmly while working.

Wire cutters and strippers With adjustable blades, for electrical wires.

Workbench A small folding one is useful if you intend doing many do-it-yourself projects.

Power drills

These make drilling fast and easy. A one- or two-speed drill will do most jobs, but a hammer-action drill is necessary for drilling masonry and concrete **(o)**.

Drill accessories save time and labour. They include all kinds of bits, saws, sanders, wire brushes and polishers **(p)**.

Nails, screws and bolts

A selection of basic nails, screws and bolts is a necessary adjunct to any good tool kit **(q)**.

Adhesives and glues

As there are so many types of adhesives and glues now on the market, it is essential to know which one is most suitable for your particular purpose.

Basic types

Clear adhesives These cope with small repairs, such as mending an earring or simple craftwork.

The joins will be reasonably strong, but will not stand up to the tough water and heat conditions in a dishwasher or a hot oven. They give a transparent join.

Contact adhesives These are usually used for sticking sheet materials (plastic laminate, cork tiles, fabrics according to type).

They have about the same resistance to water and heat. Some types allow a brief period for repositioning before the bonding begins.

Epoxy resins These make the toughest of all joins and resist heat and moisture

Adhesives chart

In this chart, letters refer to groups of adhesives and numbers to notes. Where two letters are given without a note, either group of adhesives can be used.

To stick to	Fabric	Glass, pottery	Wood, hardboard	Leather	Rubber	Metal	Foil	Paper, card	Plastics	Foam polystyrene	Stone, concrete
Fabric	B	DE7	B1 DE27	B	B1 DEG27	DE7	DE17	B	A DE57	B	B1 DE27
Glass, pottery	DE7	F	DE1 F2	F	F	F	DE	DE	DE5	B1	F
Wood, hardboard	B1 DE27	DE1 F2	AC_6 F4	DE	F4	F	B1 DE2	AB	DE5	B1 A2	F
Leather	B	F	DE	B1 DE2	DE1 G2	F	DE1	B1 DE2	DE5	B1 G2	F
Rubber	B1 DEG27	F	F4	DE1 G2	B1 DE2	F	DE1	DE1 G2	DE5	B1 G2	F
Metal	DE7	F	F	F	F	F	DE1 F2	DE	DE5	F	F
Foil	DE17	DE	B1 DE2	DE1	DE1	DE1 F2	B1 D2	B	DE5	B	B1 DE2
Paper, card	B	DE	AB	B1 DE2	DE1 G2	DE	B	B1 A2[3]	A DE5	B	B1 DE2
Plastics	A DE57	DE5	DE5	DE5	DE5	DE5	DE5	A DE5	A DE5	B	DE
Foam polystyrene	B	B1	B1 A2	B1 G2	B1 G2	F	B	B	B	B	F
Stone, concrete	B1 DE27	F	F	F	F	F	B1 DE2	B1 DE2	DE	F	F

KEY		NOTES	
A	PVA adhesives	1	For light duty only
B	Latex adhesives	2	For heavy duty
C	Animal glue	3	For light work
D	General purpose clear adhesives	4	For outdoor woodwork
E	Contact adhesives	5	For acrylics, solid polystyrene
F	Epoxy resins	6	For balsa and light craft woodwork
G	Rubber adhesives	7	Liable to stain – use lightly

very well, but are not very successful for plastic. They come in two tubes; a resin and a chemical hardener, which are mixed together. Some of them take up to three days to reach maximum bond strength, but this can be speeded up by putting the glued item in an airing cupboard.

★   **HANDY HINT**   ★

Awkward items can be held together with sticky tape or Plasticine while setting.

Airlocks

These are caused by air trapped in the tops of bends in water pipes and in the tops of radiators. They may stop the flow of water through pipes which depend on the siphon effect and, therefore, have to be completely full of water.

Airlocks in radiators

An airlock in a hot water radiator results in the radiator becoming noticeably cooler than the others in the system, and also cooler than its supply pipes, so it is easy to spot.

A radiator has a bleed valve in one top corner. This is a small, square-ended stub set in a short, round tube. You should have a key provided to fit this, but if not you can get one at an ironmonger's.

To bleed off the air Wearing rubber gloves, hold a cloth or jug under the bleed valve and unscrew the valve a short way. As soon as the slight hissing of air stops and water appears, shut off the valve.

All radiators should be bled in this way when the heating is turned on after a long period of inactivity. Frequent airlocks show that something is wrong with the system, which should then be checked professionally.

Airlocks in taps

1 To remedy an airlock in the hot tap, first block the overflow pipe which leads up to the cold water tank from the hot water cylinder. This is an open-ended pipe finishing in the air above the cistern. Make the block airtight by folding a strong polythene bag into several thicknesses and binding it over the end of the pipe with string.

2 Turn on a hot tap anywhere but the kitchen sink and leave on.

3 Go to the sink and connect the outlets of the hot and cold taps with a short length of hose and a couple of hose clips.

4 Turn both taps on. The pressure in the

direct cold-water supply should drive the airlock back around the loop and, when you disconnect the hose, water should start to flow. If it doesn't, try leaving a different hot tap on. If this fails, call a plumber.

Chimneys

Chimneys may be built either at the same time as the house, or added later. Chimneys or flues are necessary for all types of fuel-burning appliance.

Ensuring the chimney is airtight

To get a good draught, the chimney must be airtight and of a suitable height.

★ HANDY HINT ★

Check the draught in a chimney by lighting a piece of paper at the base of the chimney and see if it flares up satisfactorily.

Sealing the walls of the chimney To make the chimney completely airtight, it may be necessary to re-line it. Check with an expert that your chimney has been properly lined throughout its length, according to building regulations.

Outside the house, check that the chimney stack is not leaning and that the brickwork is sound. If this means going on the roof, get help from the experts.

Obvious leaks in the chimney can be checked by using smoke pellets or a smoke bomb available from builders' merchants. Light the pellets or bomb in the fireplace or boiler and hold a sheet of metal or newspaper over the mouth of the fireplace. Ask someone to check if smoke emerges in any parts of the house. If it does, you need expert help.

Sweeping the chimney

Clean soot from around the lower part of your chimney once a week, using a hearth brush. If you burn wood, have the chimney swept two or three times a year, as wood makes more soot than other fuels.

Most chimney sweeps now use traditional brushes, plus a modern suction cleaner, which eliminates much of the mess, but ask him if the carpet or furniture, etc. should be covered.

See also HOME IMPROVEMENTS – Damp problems.

China

It is often possible to repair broken china at home, but valuable pieces should be repaired professionally.

Cleaning

For a good repair, broken edges must be entirely free of dirt, grease and any previous adhesive. Clean off dirt with a sponge or toothbrush, scrape old glue off carefully with a sharp knife and wipe the edges with a clean rag dipped in methylated spirit.

Hot water and detergent will remove embedded dirt and some old glue, methylated spirit or carbon tetrachloride will remove grease, and hot water with a little bleach in it should get rid of stains. Bad stains may need neat bleach or hydrogen peroxide – clean cracks this way, too. For stubborn adhesives, use pure acetone or, to get rid of epoxy adhesives, you might need to use paint stripper. Finally rinse and leave to dry for some hours.

Getting a good join

Simple breaks Spread one edge of china thinly with adhesive mixed with artist's white pigment. Bring the two edges together, press firmly and stick strips of adhesive tape or wetted brown paper gumstrip across the join at right angles on both sides, back and front. Pull across tightly and use as many strips as necessary to achieve a perfect join.

When the join has set, use warm water to loosen the gumstrip if necessary. Remove any excess adhesive with a razor blade or methylated spirits.

Multiple breaks Work out the order in which the pieces should be put together, starting with two that join easily. Glue and gumstrip together. Deal with the remaining pieces, making sure that all fit together before the adhesive finally sets.

Cracks Prise the crack open as far as possible without breaking, using a thin blade. Work in the adhesive with a penknife and press the edges together, applying gumstrip as usual.

When the glue has set, peel off the gumstrip and put the piece into really hot water to test the join before using it. Finally, dry carefully and then rub the join with fine glasspaper.

Filling in chips Use either a resin filler or epoxy resin adhesive and titanium dioxide kneaded together to make a stiff putty. Clean surfaces and pat the filler into shape to fill the gap or hole. Use Plasticine underneath to prevent the filler from sagging.

Cisterns

In most households there are at least two types of cistern – the cold water storage cistern and the lavatory cistern. Many houses with central heating have a third one which tops up the radiators and domestic hot water system.

Leaks

Cold water cistern If there is a leak in your cold water cistern, you should call a plumber. In the meantime, to avoid damage from leaking water, turn off the water supply at the main stopcock, which is generally under the kitchen sink on the main feed pipe to the cistern. Then drain the cistern by turning on all cold taps. If you can't find the main stopcock, you can stop water from flowing into the tank by tying the lever of the ball valve to a piece of wood laid across the top of the tank, so that the valve is closed even when the water level has fallen.

> **WARNING**
>
> If your hot water is heated directly by the boiler, rather than by a heat-exchange coil, you must put out the boiler before draining the cistern.

Once the water has stopped running from the cistern it will be almost empty, but you may have to bale out some water.

After the leak has been mended and the cistern is refilled, the taps should be turned on until the water is coming through satisfactorily, and then turned off.

Lavatory cistern If the leak is in a lavatory cistern, which is not usually supplied from the mains, it is possible to cut off the water supply by a stopcock near the lavatory cistern. Otherwise, tie up the lever as described above. Flush to empty the cistern.

Overflowing cisterns

If your cistern develops a constant drip from the overflow pipe, certain faults can easily be put right.

Faulty ball float If the float is submerged below the water level, partially or wholly, you may have a leak in your ball float. Stop the water flowing in as previously described. Unscrew the ball float from the end of its lever. If you cannot see a hole, shake it to see if any water has got in. If it has, you will need to replace the float with a new one.

If the cistern still overflows, you probably have a faulty valve. In this case it is advisable to call in a plumber.

As a temporary measure, until you have a new float, drain the water out of the old float, screw it back on to the lever, and cover it with a polythene bag, tied tightly round the lever.

High water level Take the cover off the cistern and look at the float inside. If it is floating, but the water level is so high that it comes up to the overflow pipe, you can prevent the overflow by bending down the arm supporting the ball float. This lowers the level at which the valve shuts off the flow.

Drains

Building regulations which concern drainage are designed to protect health and are very strict. In no circumstances may you alter your existing system or install a new one without first consulting your local authority.

Always check the regulations carefully before you embark on any drainage work – they may vary slightly between each area authority.

Maintenance responsibility Once a drainage system is installed you, the householder, are obliged to maintain it. The local authority can insist that you repair a faulty system, or they may even carry out the work and then send you the bill.

For cleaning and minor repairs – see CLEANING THE HOUSE – Drains.

Dry and wet rot

Rot is one of the most destructive attackers of timber in the house. Both dry and wet rot are fungi which require moisture in order to thrive, so wherever there is damp timber, there is a high risk of rot.

Prevention

Make sure that you trace and eliminate all sources of damp in your house and that there is good ventilation throughout – including loft, cupboards and under stairs and floorboards.

As an added precaution, treat all

timber with a wood preservative, obtainable from most timber merchants. Both clear and coloured preservatives should be applied liberally to all surfaces of the wood, really soaking the timber and paying particular attention to ends and undersides and to joints. Give three coats, allowing each to dry thoroughly. Small wooden items can be immersed in preservative for at least 10 minutes.

Dry rot

The less common of the two, dry rot is by far the more dangerous.

Signs The first signs of an attack are small, whitish, rubbery growths producing rust-coloured spores which settle like dust on wood and furniture.

It is important to locate the source before it spreads further, even if you have to lift floors or remove panels. If the fungus growth is already advanced, there will be a white, fluffy growth over the affected timber and adjoining damp masonry. Dry rot also has a strong and unpleasant smell.

Treatment Unless you are very experienced in do-it-yourself work, and confident of your abilities, it is best to call in professional help for an accurate diagnosis and expert treatment. This may well entail stripping the walls of plaster, and treating them with injections of fungicide as well as treating the timber. Rotten timber should be burned.

Dry rot specialists generally give a 20-year guarantee against recurrence.

Wet rot

This is easier to deal with. It develops slowly in hardwoods, but rapidly gains a hold on softwoods.

Signs Often there is no outward sign until the damage is extensive. When it is visible, it may be as a yellow-brown skin, a network of dark strands or a blackening of the wood.

Treatment All dampness must be eliminated and ventilation improved. If the rot has not weakened the timber and dry conditions are maintained, there should be no further trouble. Unsound wood will have to be replaced.

★ **HANDY HINT** ★
You can make certain there will be no recurrence of wet rot by treating all wood, new and existing, with preservative.

Electrical repairs

There are many small electrical jobs around the house which can be carried out safely and easily, provided that sensible precautions are taken.

 WARNING
Never touch any electric appliance, even a light switch, with wet hands.

You can save time and expense by doing some simple jobs yourself, but call in a professional if you want new sockets or wiring, or if any of your electrical equipment goes wrong.

One job which can be done at home is connecting or replacing flex. The flex of an appliance is often ignored because it seems so straightforward, but it does wear out and become dangerous.

Cores and sizes

Flex comes in two- or three-core form and various sizes:

Two-core flex Used only for unearthed appliances. Ideally, all the appliances in your house should be earthed unless they are marked with the international double-insulated box symbol.

Three-core flex Contains a live wire (brown insulation sleeving), a neutral wire (blue) and an earth wire (green and yellow stripes). Older flexes with different colours (red for live, black for neutral and green for earth) should be changed.

Size The thickness of a flex, known as its size, determines the amount of current it can carry. There are three basic sizes:

● 2-amp (ampères) lighting flex, *only* for a single ordinary lamp or a clock.

● 5-amp flex for small appliances such as hair dryers and televisions.

● 15-amp flex for larger power users such as heaters.

When buying flex, go to a proper electrical shop and tell the assistant what you need it for. You will then be sure of getting the correct size.

Connecting flex

To connect a flex to any appliance or plug, a certain amount of the core, insulation and outer sheath must be stripped off. Remove as little as possible, so that the screw-down clamp in the plug or appliance presses on to a piece of sheath rather than on to the cores which, if pinched too closely, could fray and break. Enough bare wire should be exposed to go right around the screw of a 'nut and bolt' terminal and hook around itself to make a secure fixing (see Plugs and sockets).

Connectors

Electrical appliances which have flexes too short to enable them to be used satisfactorily can have the flex extended by using a flex connector or by replacing the flex completely.

Fitting a connector Insulated flex connectors consist of a box with a screw-down plastic cover and screw terminals inside. Buy one to suit the flex and appliance. Make sure the new flex is the same as the old one in size, measured in amps.

1 Remove just enough of the outer insulating sheath to allow the cores to enter the hole in the connector.

2 Strip a short piece off the end of the sleeving of each core.

3 On *heavy* flex twist the strands of wire to stop them splaying out; on *light* flex, twist and bend the exposed wire in half so that it can be fixed securely to the terminal screws.

4 Poke the wire ends into the terminal holes as far as the insulation, making sure that the wiring colours match across each link. Do up the screws tightly and re-assemble the box.

Fitting new flex

It can be easier and cheaper to buy a new piece of flex of the right length and have it fitted permanently to an appliance rather than use a connector.

1 Buy the same thickness of flex in the length you require.

2 Unplug the appliance from the mains and dismantle the casing until you find the place where the mains leads are connected.

3 Undo the terminals and attach the new flex wires. Make sure you connect the new wires to appropriate terminals.

 HANDY HINT

As a guide, when removing old flex, mark the terminals with tags stuck on with adhesive tape, giving the colour of each wire.

---

4 Do not forget to thread any grommets (rubber sleeves to prevent chafing) on to the new wire before attaching the wires to the terminals and screwing them in.

Electrical repairs – fuses

Overloading an electric wire makes it become hot. To avoid excessive overheating, which might lead to a fire, part of the electric circuit is closed by a fuse, or short piece of wire made of metal with a low melting point. If a fault causes an overload, the fuse melts, or 'blows', and stops the flow of current. Before current can be restored, the fault must be located and 'dealt with' and a new fuse fitted.

Types of fuse

Many fuse-box systems are rewirable, a short replacement piece of fuse wire being strung across a heatproof, insulated porcelain or bakelite fuse carrier in the fuse box.

Protected fuses are also made of porcelain. It is more difficult to see if the wire has blown, however, because the wire is poked through a hole and secured at each end with an exposed screw.

Modern systems have the wire enclosed in a ceramic or glass tube and the whole cartridge has to be replaced.

The most modern type is a miniature circuit breaker, a switch that automatically turns itself off when overloaded and can be switched on again when the fault has been corrected.

Plug fuses come in different sizes to suit appliances according to the amount of current they use.

● 3-amp fuse for appliances such as hair dryers, food mixers, or televisions.

● 13-amp fuse for heaters and other heavy current users.

Always use the correct fuse rating. Too low a rating will result in constant blowing of fuses; too high a rating may lead to overheating and fire.

Mending fuses

In the fuse box If your circuit fuses are of the re-wireable type, they are quite easy to mend.

1 First turn off the mains supply of electricity to the fuse box.

2 Open the fuse box and, if the fuse carriers have not been labelled with the circuit they serve, remove each carrier in turn until you find the one that has the broken wire.

3 Replace the wire, being sure to use the

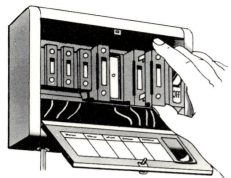

Above: conventional fuse box.

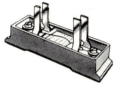

Left: In this type of fuse the wire runs across an asbestos mat.

Right: In a protected fuse the wire is covered.

Left: A modern cartridge fuse is easiest to repair.

Right: To mend a bridge fuse, wrap wire clockwise around screw, under washer.

Left: Finally tighten the screw using an insulated screwdriver.

right amperage replacement, and put back the carrier.

4 Switch on the power. If the fuse blows again immediately, look for the fault in the flex, plug or piece of equipment.

Cartridge-type fuses are simple to replace, the only snag being that it is generally impossible to pinpoint the blown fuse unless you test each fuse separately.

In a plug The most vital cause of failure in a piece of equipment is not the fuse in the fuse box, but the small cartridge fuse in the plug. This is very easy to replace.

Unscrew the base of the plug, lever the old fuse out and push in a new one of the correct amperage.

Always keep a supply of the relevant types of fuse and fuse wire handy. It is worth testing your fuse box in daylight by switching off, removing one fuse carrier, switching on again and going round the house to see what has stopped working. Do this with all the fuse carriers, one at a time, *switching off* before removing and replacing them. Make a list of which fuse controls which circuit, to keep near the fuse box or consumer unit.

Consumer units

These are modern, compact devices combining the function of fuse boxes for an entire dwelling, and the mains switch. When this is off, no electricity will reach the house, so repairs are made simpler.

The consumer unit acts as a distribution board for the different sub-circuits and provides overload protection in the form of wire fuses, cartridge fuses or circuit breakers.

Electrical repairs – plugs and sockets

The standard plug now in use in Britain is a three-pin 13-amp one with rectangular pins. It contains a cartridge fuse which 'blows' if there is an overload or short circuit in the appliance. You should not always use a 13-amp fuse, however; this is the maximum size for heavy current users such as electric heaters. Smaller appliances should have lower rated fuses (see Fuses).

Wall sockets may be single or multiple – the latter saves having to use an adaptor.

★ **HANDY HINT** ★

If you have children in the house, make certain your wall-sockets are of the modern type with shutters to cover the live and neutral holes. Unshuttered sockets can, however, be blocked off with special safety covers.

---

fused plug, is in contact with the cartridge holder.

● The neutral, blue-cased wire goes to the left-hand terminal.

● The green and yellow earth wire goes to the top, earth terminal.

Remember: BRown to Bottom Right, BLue to Bottom Left

Keep a small, insulated screwdriver in a handy space for dealing with the very small screws in terminals and cord grips.

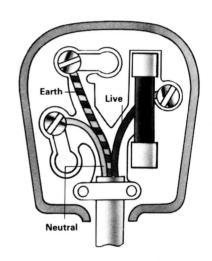

Connecting a plug

Two-pin plugs These cannot be connected to three-core flexes. A two-core flex must be used and it does not matter which wire goes to which terminal.

Three-pin plugs These can be connected to a two-core flex, ignoring the terminal.

When using a three-core flex with a three-pin plug, the same wires go to the same pins in all cases.

● The live, brown cased wire goes to the right-hand, live terminal which, in a

Extension leads

These may be necessary for portable appliances such as power drills and vacuum cleaners when they are being used a long way from a socket.

Extension leads can be bought ready made up with a plug at one end and a single or twin trailing socket at the other. The plug and socket should be made of rubber to stand up to hard use.

Always choose a lead with a 13-amp rating; one with a lower rating might inadvertently be used for a high wattage appliance, in which case it would overheat and might cause a fire.

Ordinary plugs and sockets are not suitable for outdoor use.

 WARNING

Never use a mains appliance out of doors when it is raining.

Furniture, damaged

Treatment of damage

Cracks in wood grain These are due to wood shrinking and can be disguised with coloured wood filler pressed into the crack. Allow the filler to harden and then rub smooth with glasspaper. You can disguise the repair with a touch of matching oil paint or shoe polish and, when dry, a touch of shellac for protection.

Dents in bare wood Protect the surrounding surface near the dent, particularly if it is veneered. Lay a damp rag, or damp blotting paper, over the dent and place a warm iron on top. Be very careful not to scorch the surface by letting the iron get too hot or leaving it there too long.

Loose joints First clean and remove old glue before re-setting and clamping the joint.

Scratches These can be dealt with by using a commercial scratch remover, or working some old paint into the scratch. Use wax polish for polished surfaces and commercial French polish for French polished surfaces.

Unwanted marks may be removed by gentle scraping with a very sharp blade or by wiping gently with a rag dampened with an appropriate solvent.

White heat marks On cellulose or French-polished finishes, rub these marks with a mixture of one part turpentine and one part linseed oil. Clean off with vinegar and repeat the process if necessary. A proprietary ring remover can also be used.

 HANDY HINT

Ease a sticking drawer by rubbing the runner with candle wax.

Woodworm

Furniture, structural timbers and all kinds of wood can be damaged by woodworm, the grubs of the furniture beetle, which hatch from eggs laid in cracks in the wood. The grubs live for about three years in the wood, where they tunnel inside, before coming to the surface again, hatching and laying a new batch of eggs.

 WARNING

Woodworm is not necessarily confined to old pieces. If you see a fine wood dust under new furniture, however, this is not necessarily worm.

Recognising woodworm The tunnelling grubs leave small, round holes in the wood. If the grubs are still active there will be little piles of wood dust round the holes, or clean wood dust will fall out if you tap or shake the wood. Holes that do not show wood dust, and where the inside of the hole looks dark rather than light, have probably either been treated, or the grubs have gone.

Treating woodworm A piece of furniture which is affected should have any bare wood painted all over with a proprietary woodworm killer. The liquid should also be injected into the holes—and legs can be immersed. Valuable antique furniture may have to be professionally fumigated.

Floorboards and structural timbers which are seriously affected should be treated professionally as it entails the use of pressure sprayers. In cases where the wood has become dangerously fragile, the infected parts will have to be cut out and replaced.

A professional firm will generally give a 20-year guarantee.

Furniture, renovating

The order in which the various processes should be carried out is as follows: cleaning, stripping, sanding, bleaching, staining, grain, hole and crack filling; final finishing if needed – oiling, waxing, varnishing, etc.

Cleaning wood furniture

The first essential in renovating old furniture is to clean it thoroughly. Never use vast amounts of soapy water over wooden furniture as it may become so waterlogged that it warps. If your piece is only lightly soiled, a well squeezed out washleather and mild detergent may be enough to clean it.

Painted, varnished or lacquered finishes These can be cleaned with a proprietary paint cleaner. After washing, the furniture should be thoroughly dried.

A build-up of thick, dark wax polish On a stained wood or French polished surface, this can be removed with turpentine or white spirit. Rub over the surface with fine wire wool dipped in turpentine, then wipe the surface with an absorbent rag or, for a gentle finish, wipe over with a mixture of turpentine substitute and vinegar on a soft cloth. On a French-polished surface, if you do not want to remove the French polish, use cotton wool rather than wire wool.

Removing French polish Use methylated spirit. Wipe it on generously and leave for a few minutes; this will soften the polish. Take the polish off with a cabinet scraper. To remove any remaining polish, rub the area with fine wire wool dampened with methylated spirit. When dry, rub it down with fine glasspaper.

Other finishes can be removed by chemical or mechanical stripping (see Stripping furniture).

Stripping furniture

Whether you are stripping or cleaning, you will not want to remove the old finish and attractive colouring entirely, so *don't* clean or sand off the old surface completely, but retain some of the 'old' look.

Types of stripper The two best methods of stripping furniture are with a proprietary paint and varnish stripper or with caustic soda (sodium hydroxide). While the proprietary strippers are easier and safer to use, caustic soda is much quicker and cheaper to use on heavily painted furniture – but don't use on good pieces.

 WARNING

If any stripper accidentally gets on your skin, wash it off at once with water (neutralise caustic soda with vinegar first.)

Using proprietary stripper You will need stripper, a stripping knife for flat surfaces, grade 1 wire wool for curved surfaces and plenty of old newspapers.

1 Before starting, read the manufacturer's instructions.

2 Place the piece of furniture on newspapers, preferably outside or in the garage.

3 Apply the stripper with a brush, according to the instructions.

4 When the paint bubbles and blisters, scrape it off with a stripping knife on flat surfaces and with wire wool on curved and carved areas.

5 Apply as many coats of stripper as needed to clean the surface, scraping between each application.

6 When the wood is clean, wash down according to the instructions and leave to dry.

Sanding and bleaching

After stripping a piece of furniture, decide whether it is the colour you want and only needs sanding. In some

furniture, different woods have been used in the same piece, and you may want to bleach it so that it is all one colour.

Sanding The best type of paper to use is cabinet or garnet paper. You will need four grades – medium, fine, very fine and extra fine. For flat surfaces you will need a sanding block and for carved surfaces and corners, you will need fine wire wool.

Wrap the paper round a conveniently sized rectangular block of wood and sand *with* the grain, never across it, starting with the coarsest paper and working up to the finest. An orbital sander (*not* a disc sander) will completely remove the surface, which should then be finished off by hand. But do take care: you can get a very uneven surface.

When the surface is completely smooth, wipe away the sanding dust with a lint-free cloth soaked in white spirit.

 WARNING

Getting rid of all the dust is most important as clinging dust will spoil the subsequent finish.

Bleaching If you just want to remove a stain that has been applied to wood, you can use ordinary household bleach. If you want to remove the natural colour of the wood and lighten it generally, you must use a special two-part solution, either proprietary or made up at home.

To remove stain from wood Having stripped and sanded the article, try out some household bleach, applying it with a sponge on a concealed part. Rinse with water and let it dry before deciding if the result is what you want. Try different strengths of bleach and vary the length of time you leave it before rinsing off. When you have found the right combination, bleach the whole piece. Rinse off with water and dry thoroughly with a clean cloth. Leave to dry for at least two days before finishing.

To bleach out natural colour Good results are obtained from using proprietary wood bleaches.

Finishing bleached wood Use a very light finish, or you will destroy some of the effect of bleach. A coating of white shellac and a light rub with glasspaper is quite sufficient to seal the finish.

If you prefer to wax or oil the wood, bleach it a little lighter to compensate for the darkening effect of the finish.

Staining and filling stripped wood

Staining If you find you don't like the colour of the wood when it has been stripped, there are several types of stain available.

Oil-based stains are probably the easiest for a beginner to apply evenly. Dye colours can be mixed to get the shade wanted. Oil-based dye can be diluted with white spirit to make it lighter or two coats can be applied to make it darker.

To help the stain go on more evenly, coat the wood first, either with a mixture of equal parts of boiled linseed oil and turpentine, or with a very thin layer of shellac. Linseed oil can, however, make light wood look very yellow. Allow to dry before applying the stain.

Oil-based stains may bleed through subsequent coats of varnish. The best finish to apply is a coat of shellac. (These processes have an effect on the colour, so try it out first.)

The stain can be wiped on with a sponge or brushed on. Oil stain dries fairly slowly and can be brushed and re-brushed to a smooth finish. If too dark it can be wiped off to make a lighter finish. Two light coats are better than one dark one, but allow at least 12 hours between coats.

Water-based stains are easy to use. Earth colours are effective and cheap. Aniline dyes are available in bright colours, in powder form to mix with water.

Water-based stains penetrate quite deeply and do not fade easily. They are applied by brush, pad or spray and take about 12 hours to dry. Water raises the grain of the wood, so you need to sand the piece down lightly between each application. Any type of varnish can be applied over a water-based stain.

Spirit-based stains are based on commercial alcohol or methylated spirit. They are penetrating and quick drying, but may fade on prolonged exposure to daylight. They do not raise the grain of the wood. An oil-based varnish is best over a spirit-based stain.

Filling

If the wood has a very coarse grain, it is best to fill it in. Buy grain filler of the colour nearest your wood, choose natural for very light woods.

1 Using white spirit, mix the filler to the consistency of thick cream.

2 Apply with a stiff brush, scrubbing it well into the wood and working against the grain.

3 When the filler is nearly dry – when it begins to look dull – rub it off, working with the grain and using a piece of hessian or other lint-free cloth. Do not rub before the filler begins to dry, or it will rub out of the grain.

Cracks and holes Fill with special wood filler or plastic wood. Plastic wood shrinks when it dries, so fill it a little full and sand it smooth when dry.

Glazing

The glass in both doors and windows is apt to crack or get broken. It is not difficult to replace small panes yourself, but large expanses should be professionally replaced.

Wood-framed windows

You will need a putty knife, a heavy woodworker's chisel, a hammer and a pair of pincers.

1 Remove all the old putty with the knife or chisel.

2 Wearing gloves, dislodge the glass and tap out the pane with a hammer.

3 Use pincers to remove the sprigs (headless nails) which have held the glass in place.

4 Remove the rest of the putty, scrape the rebate down to the bare wood and repaint with wood primer.

5 Measure the frame for the new pane which should be 1.5mm ($\frac{1}{16}$in) smaller than the rebate. Get the glass cut by a glazier.

6 Form a thin bed of putty in the rebate, for the glass to rest against. (Putty can be bought in do-it-yourself shops.)

7 Place the new pane in position, starting with the bottom edge. Press the glass firmly into the putty and remove surplus putty on the inside, leaving 1.5–3mm ($\frac{1}{16}$ to $\frac{1}{8}$in) between the glass and the rebate.

8 Tap new, 15mm ($\frac{5}{8}$in) sprigs into the rebate, using the side of a wide chisel as a hammer.

9 Apply the rest of the putty, covering the sprigs and working round the whole of the pane, using thumb and forefinger to press the putty into place. Smooth the putty off neatly at an angle of 45° to the glass, and finish off by running a finger along the join between glass and putty to seal it. Paint it after 14 days.

Locks

Check all locks regularly to make sure that no springs are broken and no parts badly worn. If they are, it is probably best to replace the entire lock as the cost of parts is high, and they are sometimes difficult to find, particularly if the lock is an old one.

Make sure that locks are clean and that the parts work smoothly. Simple locks may need a little oil applied to the bolt but take care with very high security locks; if you oil them they may seize up. Yale-type locks should be lubricated with graphite powder, or a soft lead pencil rubbed along both sides of the key. (See also HOME SAFETY – Locks.)

Metals

Aluminium

Rub off corrosion from anodised fittings with fine wire wool. Finish by rubbing lightly with paraffin, thin oil or furniture polish. Aluminium window frames should be washed every time the windows are cleaned and specks of white powder or dark spots removed by a bristle brush or nylon cleaning pad.

Brass

Mainly used for ornaments, candlesticks, door handles, bell-pulls and other door furniture.

Brass tarnishes fairly quickly especially out of doors, and must be cleaned regularly, though tarnishing does not cause it to deteriorate. Antique brass should not be lacquered.

Bronze

This alloy of copper and tin 'patinates' or corrodes, darkening to brown and turning green when out of doors. Antique pieces should have the patina left intact, but excessive patina or corrosion can be removed by scraping with a brass bristled brush or wire wool.

Wine goblets in bronze should have a different lining so that they cannot react with the acids in the wine. Bronze platters are designed to be put under plates rather than eaten off directly.

Chromium plating

This cannot be renovated if a lot of rust spots appear, other than by replating.

However, removing the rust with wire wool and a proprietary rust remover, followed by a special neutralising wash and a thin coat of polyurethane varnish, protects the metal and prevents rust building up again.

Copper

Pots and pans made of copper must be properly lined with tin and, when the lining becomes scratched, must be re-tinned before being used again to avoid contaminating the food. It is sensible to use wooden spoons and stirrers to reduce the risk of scratches.

Any blue-green oxidation (verdigris) should be washed off or treated with lemon juice and salt, or a paste of methylated spirit and powdered chalk. On antique pieces, verdigris spots can be dabbed with olive oil and gently scraped away with a bone or plastic implement.

Pewter

Old pewter is often rather pitted and spotty – this is normal and you should not attempt to treat the spots. If the metal is actually eaten away, consult a professional jeweller.

Renovation Unless the item is really old and valuable, when professional restoration is needed, badly neglected pewter, where the surface is filthy and crusted, can be treated in various ways.

● Degrease the surface with paraffin, acetone or dry cleaning fluid. Articles can be left to soak in paraffin; the other solvents should be rubbed on. Polish gently afterwards.

● Make up a mixture of whitening (powdered chalk) and oil (mild cooking oil) or paraffin or ammonia. Rub on the mixture and gently polish.

● A solution of 15g ($\frac{1}{2}$oz) soft soap in 150ml ($\frac{1}{4}$ pint) hot water, well mixed, left to cool and shaken in a bottle with 50g (1$\frac{3}{4}$oz) fine jeweller's rouge and 4 tablespoons turpentine. Rub on, leave for a day, wash off and polish.

Repairs Pewter is so soft that it is often dented. Serious dents on valuable articles should be hammered out by an expert, but this may spoil the patina.

You can flatten dents in less valuable items yourself – the main danger is stretching the metal. Use a domed, polished hammer, a wooden mallet or soft-faced rubber or plastic hammer. Tap out the dent very gently, where possible from the back. Rest the other side of the metal against a suitably shaped piece of wood or, for plates, a bag of sand.

Broken parts These can be soldered on, but must be done by a soldering expert. A safer method is to use an epoxy resin adhesive.

See also CLEANING THE HOUSE – Metal cleaners.

 WARNING

Work in a well ventilated place when renovating pewter with these materials as the fumes are toxic

---

Pipes, frozen and burst

When water freezes it expands and therefore can burst pipes. This damage can be prevented if all pipes, for both cold and hot water, are well lagged.

Frozen pipes

If, during an icy spell, one of your pipes is frozen up with no water coming through, try melting the blockage carefully. Open the tap to which the pipe runs and apply cloths wrung out in hot water, starting at the tap end of the pipe and working backwards until the blockage is located and the water begins to flow again.

 HANDY HINT

A hair dryer can be used to melt the ice in a frozen pipe.

When the ice has melted, lag the pipe (see HOME IMPROVEMENTS – Insulation) to prevent a further occurrence.

Burst pipes

If a pipe actually bursts, the main problem is to prevent flooding. Place a bucket or container under the leak, use plenty of old towels, etc. to mop up, and turn off the appropriate stopcock so that no more water will come through. Run off the water and put out the boiler if necessary. Send for a plumber immediately.

A temporary repair may be possible, using a short piece of garden hosepipe split along its length and held over the burst with wire twisted tight with pliers. A split in a lead pipe can sometimes be closed by hammering gently.

Rust and corrosion

Rust is a destructive form of corrosion affecting iron and steel. There are several methods of rust prevention.

Prevention

Ironwork Clean gutters, drainpipes and gates thoroughly with a wire brush and then paint either with a lead-based paint or a zinc chromate rust inhibitor. Finish with two undercoats and then a gloss coat.

Locks and window latches Smear regularly with petroleum jelly. When installing, smear screws and bolt threads with a graphite-free grease.

Screws and hinges Preferably use brass or bronze fittings. If these are too expensive, use steel hinges with screws that are either zinc-plated, galvanised or sherardised. The latter screws should not be used with brass hinges as they react on each other when damp.

Tools Keep in a dry atmosphere, covered with a thin film of oil. Keep cutting tools in a baize-lined drawer with a bag of silica gel to take up damp (this should be reactivated regularly by being dried in a warm oven). The correct wrapping for tools is silk soaked in machine oil.

Power tools Keep in a warm, dry place in the house, not in a damp shed.

Water tanks (galvanised) These will eventually corrode. In some areas the trouble can be partially avoided by hanging a 'sacrificial anode' in the tank. This is a piece of metal which will waste away instead of the protective galvanising. The local water authority should be able to advise on this. When replacing a tank, install a plastic or fibre glass one.

Treatment

General rust Remove with a wire brush and emery paper or hire a small industrial angle grinder. Treat with a rust-neutralising chemical and paint with a good metal primer before painting in the normal way. Use a rust-binding paint for inaccessible corners.

Bolts, nuts and screws Those which have rusted in can often be released by tightening them a quarter turn before undoing. If this fails, a rust-releasing fluid should be applied and after it has penetrated, the screw or nut will come loose. If this fails, cut off the head of the bolt or nut with a junior hacksaw.

Screws in wood will generally respond to a hot soldering iron or tip of a red-hot skewer or poker held to the screw head. The metal expands and breaks its hold as it cools.

Tools Remove rust with very fine wire wool and light machine oil.

Water tanks Inspect galvanised water tanks regularly. If corrosion is apparent, drain the tank, dry with a blow lamp and remove rust with a wire brush and abrasive emery cloth. A wire cup brush in an electric drill is ideal.

Treat the affected part with an aerosol rust-neutralising liquid, then paint the whole of the tank interior, including the inlet and outlet holes, with a specially made odourless bitumen paint. After about 24 hours, when the paint has dried, the tank can be refilled.

Sash windows

To control the sliding action of sashes, counterbalancing weights run in pockets are installed at each side of the frame. These are connected to the sashes by cords passing over pulleys near the top of each side. There are two weights and cords to each sash.

Replacing the cords

Cords generally break as a result of old age. Replacing a cord is not very difficult, but makes a mess of the paintwork as you have to prise off one of the nailed-on beadings and centre beading to remove the window. It is a good idea to make a thorough job of it and replace both cords at the same time.
1 Lever the side (staff) beads off with a broad chisel, taking care they do not break.
2 Take out the bottom sash window, cutting the sash cord if necessary.
3 Remove the centre beading. Take out the top sash window, cutting the cord if necessary.
4 Remove pocket pieces covering weight compartments. Take out the weights.
5 Remove the nails holding the remains of the sash cord in the grooves of the windows.
6 Tie a bent nail to one end of a piece of string and a new sash cord to the other.
7 Feed the nail and string over the pulley. The weight of the nail will pull the string through.
8 Feed the sash cord through. Pull the cord through the compartment opening. Thread the cord through the weight and knot the end.
9 Replace the upper window in the frame. Hold about 12cm (5in) above the sill. You will need another person to help you measure the cord.
10 Pull the cord until the weight is at the top of the pulley. Nail the cord to anchor it temporarily to the top of the frame. Measure the cord until it almost reaches the bottom of the groove in the window. Cut the cord and nail into the groove. Remove the temporary nail.

Repeat the process on the other side.
11 Replace the centre beading then repeat the whole process for the lower window. Replace the outside beading.
Chain-type sash windows These do not suffer from broken cords, but any problems with them should be dealt with by a professional joiner. The same applies to aluminium sash windows.

Tap rewashering

Washers are quite simple to replace, both in conventional taps (see illustration overleaf) and modern 'supataps'.

Conventional taps

1 Turn off the water supply to the tap. Turn the tap fully on.
2 Unscrew the cover over the headgear (use self-grip wrench and penetrating oil if stiff).
3 Raise the shield to expose the hexagonal nut. If it will not rise enough, remove the tap handle by taking out the grub screw which holds it and tapping

the handle gently upwards. Lift the shield right off.

4 Unscrew the headgear by undoing the large hexagonal nut and lift out the jumper which holds the washer.

5 Remove the worn washer and replace with the new one.

6 Reassemble the tap by reversing these instructions, preferably greasing the threads with petroleum jelly.

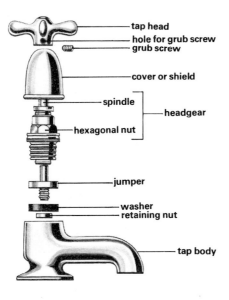

- tap head
- hole for grub screw
- grub screw
- cover or shield
- spindle
- headgear
- hexagonal nut
- jumper
- washer
- retaining nut
- tap body

Supataps

Supatap washers are not the same as washers for ordinary taps – they are a special type of combined washer and jumper. With these taps you do not have to turn the water supply off.

1 Loosen the large locking nut above the tap handle, between it and the top supply pipe. Loosening this anti-clockwise will cause water to flow, but carry on until the nozzle falls off, when the flow will stop.

2 Turn the nozzle upside down and tap on the table top to release the washer and anti-splash device.

3 Replace the anti-splash device making sure you put it back the right way.

4 Put on a new washer and reassemble.

Pull-off handles

Some modern taps have large handles which must be removed before you can get at the hexagonal nut. To get the handle off, prise up the little button in the centre of the top with a small screwdriver. Undo the screw underneath and pull off the handle.

Vacuum – belt replacement

Before buying a replacement drive belt, take details from the vacuum cleaner name plate to ensure the correct one is bought. The manufacturer's instructions will show where the drive belt is.

1 Disconnect the cleaner!

2 Remove the cover, held in place by spring clips or a metal catch.

3 Lift out the roller, and check the position of the drive belt before removing.

4 Slide the new belt over the roller and fit it back into the cleaner.

5 Stretch the belt until it fits over the drive pulley.

6 Check in the manufacturer's instructions that it is on the right way round, otherwise the belt will leap off as soon as you switch the cleaner on.

7 Replace the cover.

CHAPTER 4
CLEANING THE HOUSE

Brooms•Brushes•Carpets•Cleaners
Curtains•Drains•Furniture
Glass•Soft furnishings

CLEANERS AND EQUIPMENT

Basic cleaners

Floors
● Special carpet cleaning fluid.
● Dual purpose cleaner/polish for vinyl floorings.
● Wax polish for wood floors.

Furniture
● Aerosol polish for some plastic or cellulosed surfaces.
● Wax polish for French polished or waxed furniture.
● Colourless furniture cream for painted furniture.
● Hide food for leather-covered furniture.
● Teak oil or cream for teak.

Metals
● Brass and copper polish.
● Silver polish.
● Stainless steel cleaner/polish.
In addition you will need a selection of: soaps, detergents (powder and liquid), abrasive cleansers (powder and liquid), grease solvents (aerosol and liquid), an all-purpose cleaner/polish, upholstery shampoo and a window cleaner.

Basic equipment

● Brooms, soft and stiff
● Brushes, short-handled
● Carpet shampooer
● Cleaning materials (see Basic cleaners)
● Dustpans
● Dusters and soft cloth
● Dusting mop
● Sponge mop
● Steel wool in various grades
● Vacuum cleaner

Abrasive cleaners

Abrasive cleaners come in both powder and liquid form. They will remove dirt and stubborn grease from hard surfaces. Powders are not so gentle as liquids and if excessively used can sometimes damage the surface. Mildly abrasive cleaners are made especially for baths but a different type of cleaner is necessary if the bath is made of plastic or fibreglass.

Scouring pads
Those made from steel wool impregnated with soap are excellent for removing burnt-on dirt and grease from metal surfaces. The knitted or woven pads or cloths made from nylon or other types of plastics are gentler.

Bleach

Ordinary chlorine household bleach is useful for cleaning lavatory pans when they are badly stained. Flush to clear away chlorine before pan is used again.

> ▲ **WARNING** ▲
>
> It is dangerous to mix proprietary lavatory cleansing powders and chlorine bleach as the combination gives off dangerous fumes.

A mild solution of household bleach (1 part bleach to 10 parts water) will clean badly stained sinks made of enamelled metal, acrylic and glass fibre reinforced surfaces. Bleach solution will also clean stained flower vases.

Brooms and brushes

These are simple cleaning tools and invaluable for quick, quiet work and for jobs that the vacuum cleaner cannot do.

Brooms

Handles Sometimes sold separately from the heads, they can be made of wood or tubular aluminium. Make sure you buy the right size handle for your broom head as diameters can vary.

Heads Cheap, wooden heads have a hole cut for the handle. If it is not a tight fit, hold it firm with a thin screw. Other types of broom head may have plastic sockets or screw holes.

Soft brooms Use for sweeping dust and general household debris from smooth floorings such as vinyl, wood, tiles, cork, etc. Natural bristles are split naturally at the ends, which helps to hold dust. If you buy synthetic brooms check that the ends have been artificially split, making them equally efficient. Vegetable fibres are also used for some soft brooms.

Hard brooms Excellent for use on carpets or cord and matting; for this kind of abrasive work synthetics such as PVC, nylon or polypropylene have a longer life than vegetable fibre.

Special brooms for lifting the pile on long shag carpets are now available; they look more like rakes.

Yard brooms They are satisfactory for outdoor use if made using stiff vegetable bristles, but stiff synthetic bristles may last longer and can be washed.

Brushes

As with brooms, the fibres of a brush can be natural or man-made. Short-handled brushes come in many shapes and sizes for various purposes.

Hearth brush If you have an open fire you will need a brush with natural fibres and a metal dustpan. Heat will melt synthetic fibres and plastics.

Kitchen brushes Scrubbing brushes are usually made from vegetable fibres which hold water well. Washing-up brushes are best made from stiff synthetic fibres. Bottle brushes are handy for cleaning out vacuum flasks and storage jars.

Lavatory brushes These should be made of synthetic fibres, easily sterilised, with curved head and handle. Sterilise lavatory brushes by swishing in a weak bleach solution, then rinse and shake dry.

Small brushes and dustpans Essential for transferring dust collected after sweeping and for reaching into awkward corners. Soft brushes are excellent for general dusting or sweeping while those with stiff fibres are especially useful for carpets, particularly where limited space makes vacuum cleaning tricky.

Wall and cornice brushes These have long handles which can sometimes be extended for reaching high ceilings, etc.

Detergents

A detergent is a cleansing agent and can be made either from soap or a synthetic substitute.

Household detergents

There are many powders and liquids available for cleaning floors and paint-work. Most have to be diluted for normal dirt, but can be used neat for stubborn marks. Read all instructions carefully and make sure you have the type of detergent you need for the particular job.

Washing up

Washing-up liquids are generally synthetically produced. Always use a minimal quantity to avoid waste. Wear rubber gloves, use hot water and rinse your washing up in clean hot water before drying or leaving to drain. Buying washing-up liquid in bulk can save money.

Dishwashers These need a specially made, strong powder. A measured amount is placed in a special container and released into the hot water at the appropriate time.

Washing clothes

If you live in a hard water area, synthetic detergents will prevent soap scum and be more economical. Some detergents have an 'optical whitener' in addition to a certain amount of bleach. Enzymes are also added to some powders to help remove food-type stains. Front-loading washing machines need a 'low lather' soap or detergent. Soap-based powders, or soap flakes are better for wool, leaving it softer. (See also CLOTHES CARE – Laundering.)

Dusters and cloths

Every home needs a good assortment of cloths for different purposes. Old torn sheeting, towelling and interlock cotton or wool are all useful. Cut the fabrics into good sized pieces, removing any elastic, buttons, fasteners, etc. and hem round to prevent fraying.

Types of cloths

Chamois leather Ideal for cleaning windows. Wash in warm soapsuds, rinse in *soapy* water and hang to dry, rubbing to soften it as it dries.

Dusters These should not have a fluffy or raised surface. Wash after use.

Floor cloths Must be tough and absorbent, while *dishcloths* are softer.

Synthetic cloths Sold in boxes and in packets, these last for quite a time and can be cleaned in the washing machine.

Tea towels Linen, cotton or part cotton tea towels are essential. Wash them frequently in hot soapy water. (See also SOFT FURNISHINGS – Tea towels.)

Rinse and wring wet cloths after use and other cloths regularly. Boiling and bleaching may occasionally be necessary for very dirty cloths.

Metal cleaners

Clean metals regularly, using soft cloths and an old toothbrush for those difficult crannies.

Types of metal

Aluminium Keep clean by normal washing up, preceded by soaking if food is burnt on. Remove discoloration by boiling up a mild acid solution, such as water containing apple peelings, lemon juice or vinegar. Soap impregnated steel wool pads give a good finish.

Brass Use ordinary or long-term brass polish. Lemon juice and salt removes light stains and badly neglected brass can be restored by wiping with a solution of 1 part hydrochloric acid to 5 parts water. Hydrochloric acid is a dangerous poison (see HOME SAFETY – Poisons) and the utmost care is essential when using and storing.

Bronze Dust regularly and occasionally rub over with a few drops of cooking oil on a soft cloth to maintain the sheen. Rub with a clean cloth to remove.

Carbon steel While most knives are made from stainless steel, some high-quality kitchen knives are still manufactured from carbon steel, which can be sharpened to a very fine edge. Clean with a harsh nylon scourer and abrasive powder, or with steel wool pads. A specially treated emery paper can be obtained for the purpose. Keep knives in a dry place for everyday use, and cover with a very thin film of oil when storing for any length of time.

Chromium plate Wipe regularly. Chrome or silver polish will shine it up.

Copper Clean with ordinary or long-term brass polish, or a special copper polish. Copper tarnishes very quickly and you may wish to lacquer copper ornaments.

Pewter Clean with pewter polish, ordinary metal polish or a mixture of powdered whiting and oil. Old pewter should only be rubbed up with a soft cloth so as not to damage the patina.

Silver Clean regularly with a proprietary silver polish. Long-term polishes are available (but do not use them on table silver) and foam cleaner and liquid dip can also be used. It is useful to keep an impregnated silver polishing cloth on hand for a quick shine.

Stainless steel This normally remains clean if regularly washed in hot detergent suds and dried with a soft cloth. Marks can normally be removed with a stainless steel cleaner/polish.

Wrought iron Dust with a soft cloth or brush. If rust appears, rub it off and paint first with a metal primer, then paint.

See also REPAIRS AND MAINTENANCE – Metals.

Oven cleaners

Whether an oven is electric, gas or solid fuel, it is likely to be lined with enamel unless it has easy-clean linings. The best way to keep an enamel-lined oven clean is to wipe it with a damp cloth, and perhaps a little detergent, every time it has been used and while it is still warm.

Abrasives

The simplest and most economical way to clean burn marks off an oven is to use an ordinary household abrasive cleaner and apply it with a steel wool or nylon scourer. There is a chance that enthusiastic rubbing may scratch the enamel and make burn marks even harder to remove next time.

Aerosols

These are easy to use and do not usually need to be left on for long. However, they are relatively expensive and less effective than steel wool pads and paste cleaners. It is often necessary to use two applications. The oven must be heated before using an aerosol cleaner and if it becomes too hot, the cleaning foam will slide down the sides and it will be necessary to cool the oven and start again. Fumes from aerosols can also be unpleasant.

Polishes

Floor polishes

These can be divided into three types:
Pastes These are designed for use on wood, wood composition and cork floors which have not been sealed with a polyurethane finish. They may contain silicones as well as wax. They clean surface grime and fill in and renovate worn or rough patches. They do not shine the floor.
Self-shine finishes These are designed specifically for thermoplastic, vinyl and rubber flooring. They are simply applied, without rubbing, to a clean floor, using a cloth or sponge mop and as they dry, produce a shine that lasts for several weeks. Constant use sometimes produces a build-up of polish which has to be removed with a special stripping solution. However, some polishes contain a cleaning substance that removes the previous finish as the next is applied.
Tile polishes For use on unglazed quarry tiles, brickwork and stonework. These polishes can be paste or liquid with slip-retardant properties for rough surfaces or a self-shine type for doorsteps and tiled floors, which can be washed over between applications.

Wood polishes for furniture

There are four basic types of furniture polish – aerosols, creams, liquid waxes and wax pastes. Whichever you use, it is regular application and sparing use that gives the best results.
Aerosols Contain silicone cream polish and should be used only on modern hard finishes. Multi-purpose aerosol cleaner polishes can also be used on kitchen units, the outside of refrigerators, windows and mirrors.
Creams Traditionally containing hard wax in a water and oil emulsion, they are used on older furniture and antiques. They are good for cleaning off fingermarks. *Silicone creams* are intended for the hard, high gloss finish found on most modern furniture.
Liquid wax This contains natural and synthetic waxes, plus a cleaning solvent. It is easier to rub in than wax paste.
Wax pastes These need to be well rubbed in and polished hard to give a good shine. Some wax pastes contain

silicones to repel water and resist fingermarks. Do not use these on antique furniture where the absorption of wax into the wood is important. Beeswax-based polishes are best, if you can find them.

Other finishes Modern furniture with a matt finish, such as teak and afrormosia, should *never* be polished. Dust regularly and give a rub with teak oil or one of the aerosol liquid sprays specifically designed to protect this wood.

French polished furniture Best treated with cream polish, used very sparingly.

Oil polishing If you have a piece of stripped furniture, *linseed oil* will give a deep, rich gleam on woods like mahogany or cherry, but tends to darken or yellow lighter woods, for which it is best to use *olive oil*. Make sure the surface is well prepared, as the oil treatment shows up any imperfections.

The linseed oil must be mixed with turpentine and heated and applied once a week for up to 10 weeks, then monthly for a year, after which a yearly oiling is needed.

★ **HANDY HINT** ★

Polish or oil the underside of table tops now and then to prevent warping.

Vacuum cleaners

Vacuum cleaners may seem expensive, but they are worthwhile. Efficient cleaning makes a pleasant home and adds to the life-expectancy of carpets and rugs.

Types of cleaner

Decide first whether you want an upright or a cylinder type.

★ **HANDY HINT** ★

If you have fitted carpets throughout, then the upright is best, but for a mixture of carpeted and hard-surfaced floors a cylinder model would cope better.

Upright cleaners These cover carpeted areas quickly, and are easy to use. Many of them have adjustment for pile depth. Often they do not clean well right up to the skirting board. Choose a model with re-usable paper dust bags.

Attachments for upright cleaners Usually the weak point, first because they are an extra expense and secondly because they are not very convenient. An upright vacuum cleaner with a nozzle attached is less manoeuvrable than a cylinder model, especially on stairs, and less powerful.

Cylinder cleaners The most satisfactory for coping with nooks and crannies and cleaning hard floor surfaces. They are usually provided with a two-way attachment for all flooring and several other accessories for dusting, upholstery, crevices, etc.

One disadvantage is that, with one or two exceptions, the carpet attachments do not adjust for pile depth or have beaters. However, most models incorporate suction controls so that you can have a strong suction for lifting dirt from carpets and a weaker one for cleaning curtains.

Cylinder models are generally quite easy to empty and many have disposable or re-usable paper dust bags.

Wet and dry cleaners It is now possible to buy several different types of these cleaners. They can be used to sweep up dust, to wash floors or even unblock a sink. Some are available by mail order.

Maintenance Vacuum cleaners should be professionally repaired, though the rubber drive belt (see REPAIRS AND MAINTENANCE – Vacuum cleaners) is easily replaced. Check name plate to ensure that you buy the correct belt.

HOUSEHOLD CLEANING ROUTINE

Bathrooms and lavatories

The bathroom can be kept shining and clean in very little time, if you get into a regular cleaning routine.

Daily care
● Every time the bath is used, wipe it round with a clean, damp cloth and a little non-abrasive liquid cleaner. Polish up the taps with a clean, dry cloth.
● Clean the washbasin with non-abrasive liquid on a damp cloth, finishing the taps with the dry cloth.
● Polish up the mirror with a clean, dry cloth and wipe down any glass shelves.
● Pour a little bleach into the lavatory pan *or* sprinkle it with a proprietary powder. DO NOT use both together as the combination can be dangerous.
● Wipe round the lavatory seat with a weak disinfectant solution.
● If the floor is carpeted, sweep or vacuum.

Weekly care
● Follow the daily pattern, but in addition pay special attention to the bases of the taps and to the plug holes in the bath and basin, which can become encrusted in hard-water areas.
● Clean the lavatory with a brush, washing the brush in hot, soapy water after use.
● Use an aerosol silicone polish on plastic lavatory seats and bath panels.
● Clean the medicine cupboard.
● Wash down the floor with a weak disinfectant solution.

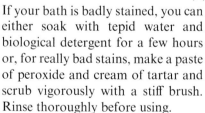

★ **HANDY HINT** ★
If your bath is badly stained, you can either soak with tepid water and biological detergent for a few hours or, for really bad stains, make a paste of peroxide and cream of tartar and scrub vigorously with a stiff brush. Rinse thoroughly before using.

Carpet cleaning

Basically there are three types of dirt. Surface litter and light dust, which include hair, threads, bits of paper,

Dealing with carpet stains

Stain	Treatment	Stain	Treatment
Beer	A squirt from the soda syphon; sponge, rinse and blot dry	**Milk**	A squirt from the soda syphon; sponge, rinse and blot dry. Follow with mild carpet shampoo solution; sponge, rinse and blot dry. Finish with dry cleaning fluid
Blood	A squirt from the soda syphon; sponge, rinse with cold water and blot dry		
Candle wax	Scrape off as much as possible. Melt and absorb the remainder by covering with blotting paper and applying the toe of a warm iron. Do not let the iron come into direct contact with the carpet or use this method with polypropylene or nylon carpets. Dab with methylated spirit to remove any remaining colour	**Soft drinks**	Sponge with mild carpet shampoo solution; rinse with warm water and blot dry
		Soot	Vacuum up as much as possible and treat with dry cleaning fluid
		Tar	Gently scrape up the deposit. Soften with a solution of 50 per cent glycerine and 50 per cent water Leave for up to an hour, gently wipe, rinse and blot dry. Obstinate marks can sometimes respond to treatment with dry cleaning fluid or eucalyptus oil
Chewing gum	Treat with Holloway Chewing Gum Remover or dry cleaning fluid		
Coffee	As for beer, but remove final traces with a dry cleaning solvent	**Tea**	A squirt from the soda syphon; sponge, rinse and blot dry. Finish with peroxide, 250ml to 250ml water
Egg	Remove with salt water and blotting paper		
Ice cream	Mild carpet shampoo solution; sponge, rinse with warm water and blot dry. Finish with a dry cleaning solvent	**Urine**	A squirt from the soda syphon; sponge and rinse. Sponge with mild carpet shampoo solution, rinse and blot. Then rinse several times using cold water with a few drops of antiseptic added. Blot dry
Ink	A squirt from the soda syphon; sponge, rinse with warm water and blot dry. Finish with dry cleaning fluid if mark persists		
		Wine	Squirt with soda water. Shampoo with 15ml white vinegar in carpet shampoo solution
Lipstick	Gently wipe away with paint remover, rinse with warm water and blot dry		

crumbs and so on, are comparatively easy to remove. Light dirt, such as fluff from clothes, ash and normal household dust, settles part of the way down the carpet pile and is not too difficult to remove. If this type of dirt is allowed to build up, however, it can dull and sometimes change carpet colours. For dealing with this type of dust and dirt, see Carpet sweepers. Vacuum cleaners (see Vacuum cleaners) are needed to remove gritty dirt such as sand and mud.

The third type of dirt is grease from spills, ground-in food particles and so on. Shampooing or dry cleaning are the best methods of dealing with this. All spills should be cleaned up at once. Mop the surface with a dry, clean, white cloth and then sponge several times with a clean white cloth wrung out in warm water. Many stains can be removed by this method.

If this method does not work, however, try a carpet detergent, following the manufacturer's instructions carefully. If the stain remains, then the recommended antidote (see chart) must be used.

Carpet shampooing

A badly soiled carpet can be shampooed, dry cleaned or steam cleaned. All of these can be carried out professionally – shampooing is the only method you can use yourself.

⚠ WARNING ⚠

Avoid an uneven use of shampoo solution on the carpet and over-wetting which can cause shrinkage.

Application by hand Make up the shampoo solution according to the directions and apply to small areas of carpet, using a sponge or small brush. Small hand applicators make even distribution easier.

Electric shampooers Quick and thorough as well as easy to use. An electric machine is best for medium pile carpets, but it is sometimes possible for shag piles to become entangled.

Manual carpet shampooers These are easy to use, distribute shampoo evenly and avoid over-wetting the carpet.

Hints on carpet shampooing Follow the manufacturer's instructions both on the appliance and the shampoo. Test for colour fastness by rubbing with a little shampoo solution. If the colour runs, seek professional advice.

Before shampooing Vacuum the carpet thoroughly and remove as much furniture as possible. Put foil under the feet of remaining furniture to prevent marking. Tackle any heavy stains by rubbing with shampoo solution first.

China, bone

Bone china looks and feels fragile, but is tough and strong, often withstanding generations of wear. However, it should be heated gradually and never subjected to extremes of hot and cold. Most breakages are caused by simple carelessness.

Washing

Some acids, such as fruit juices, can affect the decoration and therefore all food scraps should be gently scraped off immediately after a meal and the plates rinsed in cold water. Do not leave china soaking. Any plates with leftover egg on them should be rinsed first in cold water before being washed.

Use hand-hot water and mild liquid detergent for washing up. Wash each item separately and, after rinsing, place separately on a plate drainer to dry.

Stain removal
Tea and food stains can normally be removed fairly easily during normal washing up. For obstinate stains, dip a damp cloth in salt, bicarbonate of soda or borax and rub the marks with this. This method should also remove the black stains caused by contact with aluminium or silverware.

For old, obstinate stains, or dark tea or coffee stains inside a bone china tea pot, a special tea or coffee stain remover is the easiest way. Follow the manufacturer's instructions.

★ **HANDY HINT** ★

If you cannot obtain special stain remover to clean your china, try using denture cleaner.

Drains

Day-to-day maintenance of drains is important – they must be kept clean and free of germs. You should never be tempted to use drains as general waste disposal units.

Interior drains
Heavy paper, thick cotton wool, food, fat, soil, plaster filler and even tea-leaves can cause blockages which may be extremely difficult to clear.

By their very nature drains encourage germs, so keep them disinfected with regular use of bleach or a proprietary cleaner. Lavatories should be cleaned every day and sink and bath drains as regularly as possible.

★ **HANDY HINT** ★

A little washing soda and boiling water poured down sinks will prevent fat from collecting in the pipe.

Exterior gullies
If you live in an older house with an open gulley, this should be cleaned regularly. There should be a grille over it to stop leaves from blocking the pipe – keep this grille unblocked and clean. Wear rubber gloves and scrub it with hot water and washing soda.

Scrape and scrub the walls of the gully clean of any sludge and lift out any silt from the bottom. Finally, swill out with clean water and disinfectant before replacing the grille.

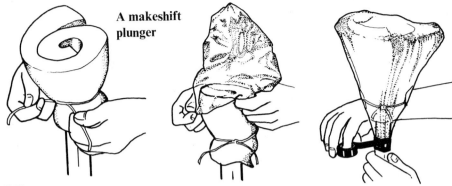

A makeshift plunger

Minor blockages

Using a plunger Buy a rubber plunger from any hardware store, or in an emergency, make your own. Block the sink overflow with an old rag and, if the water has seeped away, fill the basin or lavatory – the pipe must be filled with water. Place the plunger over the plug hole or the opening at the bottom of the lavatory pan, and work it up and down vigorously. The plunger causes a vacuum to form and the blockage should be forced through behind the airlock.

Caustic soda Grease and dirt blocking a sink can be dispersed by pouring a caustic soda solution down the plug hole. (Always use it carefully as it can burn the skin. Wear rubber gloves if possible.) Or use a proprietary drain cleaner with a base of caustic soda.

Unblocking the S bend If a plunger fails to unblock a *sink*, place a bowl under the S bend (or trap) and undo the screw plug at the bottom. If the water remains in the sink, the blockage is above the trap and it may be possible to shift it with a flexible wire poked through the plug hole. If the water pours out when you remove the trap, the problem lies

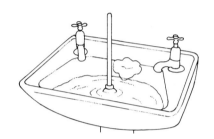

beyond the trap. Again, a flexible wire should shift it.

Stiff wire can be used to hook a blockage from behind the S bend of a *lavatory*. Twist it to and fro and then pull it and the blockage back into the pan. Badly blocked drains will need the services of a professional plumber or drain specialist.

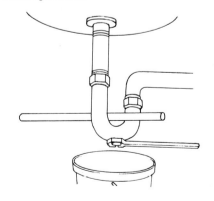

Furniture

Polishes for furniture may be wax, liquid or cream. Some contain silicones and some come in aerosol cans. Different woods and their finishes require different treatment and so does plastic, so unless all your furniture is made of the same material you will need to keep a variety of polishes in your home. (See also Polishes.)

Material of furniture

Cellulose lacquered wood Treat high-gloss like French polished furniture; matt and semi-matt do not need polishing but dust regularly and wipe over from time to time with a matt furniture cream.

French polished wood Dust regularly and polish occasionally with furniture cream.

Laminated furniture Use a non-abrasive kitchen or bathroom cleaner on marks; otherwise a damp cloth should keep it clean.

Leather furniture Dust regularly and give an occasional feed with hide food. Do not use furniture polish on it as a sticky residue will build up. Wash very dirty leather with glycerine soap and warm water.

Painted furniture Wash down from time to time and use a colourless furniture cream to maintain the sheen.

Plastic furniture Keep clean by wiping over with a damp cloth. Use soapy water if marks are bad, but do not over-wet.

Teak furniture Needs little care other than dusting. About two or three times a

year apply special teak oil or cream and rub it in well so that no stickiness is left.

Waxed furniture Treat in the same way as French polished furniture.

Glass

Modern methods of glassmaking have led to the production of many different kinds of household glassware, needing different care.

Washing

Wash glasses individually in a clean, warm (not hot) weak detergent solution, preferably in a plastic bowl. Use a soft brush to clean the facets of cut glass and a long-handled brush for the inside of long necked items.

Rinse in clean, warm water and dry on a soft, non-fluffy cloth, holding the bowl of stemmed glasses in the palm of your hand. Do not try to push your hand inside fragile items when drying. Buy linen glass cloths for the best finish.

Some everyday glassware may be strong enough to be washed in an automatic dishwasher, but better glass should be washed by hand. *Never* put lead crystal in a dishwasher.

Flat glass Clean with a chamois leather squeezed out in warm soapy water (not synthetic detergent). There are also many proprietary glass cleaning creams and liquids, including aerosols.

Stains and scratches A little paraffin or methylated spirit, mixed with whiting powder may be successful on stains, but scratches and chips must be professionally treated.

HANDY HINT

Clean stained decanters with a mixture of 1 tablespoon common salt to 150ml ($\frac{1}{4}$ pint) vinegar. Leave to stand for some time before rinsing well.

Kitchen cleaning

As the kitchen is the place where food is prepared and dishes washed, absolute cleanliness is essential for good health.

Daily care
● Wipe down working surfaces thoroughly after use.
● Wash the kitchen floor.

 HANDY HINT

If you have a vinyl or linoleum floor covering, a self-shining liquid polish can be applied. The shine lasts well and the floor is easily wiped clean.

● Sinks and draining boards can harbour germs. Always wipe over both with hot water and washing-up liquid after use. Clean stainless steel sinks with a special stainless steel cleanser to protect it from scratch marks.

△ WARNING △

Do not use steel wool pads or abrasives to clean stains in a stainless steel sink. Neat washing-up liquid on a damp cloth should do the trick.

Weekly care
● Clean all woodwork.
● Clean kitchen windows, Venetian blinds, air extractors and ventilators; they all acquire a greasy film from cooking steam.
● To clean the oven, see Oven cleaners.
● Clean items such as the cooker, refrigerator and washing machine with a solution of washing-up liquid and water, or with an all-purpose cleaning polish.

Living rooms and bedrooms

Daily care
● Empty out and clean ashtrays and waste paper baskets.
● Brush or vacuum the upholstery and shake up the cushions.
● Vacuum the floor; dust wood floors with a polishing mop.
● Dust the shelves, mantelpiece, windowsills, skirting.
● Dust furniture.

Weekly care
Follow the daily pattern, but also:
● Dust picture rails, tops of doors, light fittings, etc. using the vacuum cleaner attachments or a long-handled mop/duster.
● Apply polish to furniture, wood floors or surrounds.
● Clean the glass of display cabinets, mirrors and pictures.
● Clean televisions, stereo equipment and radios with an all purpose

cleaner/polish. Remember to wipe the television screen over with window cleaner.

Refuse

General rules

● Rinse out and flatten empty food cans before throwing them away, to save space and avoid smells.

● Wrap food scraps tightly in newspaper or an old polythene bag.

● Broken glass and crockery and other sharp, dangerous refuse should also be wrapped very carefully.

● Hot ashes or lighted cigarette ends will damage plastic containers and could start a fire. Allow any ashes to cool completely in a metal bucket before throwing them away.

● If your local authority does not collect paper separately for recycling, fold papers and flatten cardboard packs so they do not take up too much room.

Wastepaper baskets

Keep a wastepaper basket in every room, including the bathroom. Line the bottom of the baskets with kitchen paper or brown paper to prevent dust and dirt lodging in the corners. Watch out if there are smokers around and provide plenty of ashtrays; some baskets are fireproofed but you cannot be too careful when it comes to smouldering cigarette ends. Try to keep wastepaper baskets for paper only.

Empty baskets regularly into a large bucket or polythene bag and take straight to the dustbin. If you have metal or plastic baskets, give them a quick wipe round with a damp sponge.

Kitchen bins

Choose your kitchen bin carefully, bearing in mind how easy it will be to use, how strongly it is made and how big it is.

Pedal bins These allow you to use both hands, but the spring and hinges are not always very strong. Check the 'works' carefully when you buy one.

Swing-top bins Usually larger, but make sure that the top fits well, does not swing out of place too easily and is simple to remove for cleaning.

Plastic bin liners Convenient and do a good job of keeping the bins clean, but for large bins they are expensive. It is possible to line a bin with several thicknesses of newspaper, to catch any drips, but if you do this it is best to wrap any soggy rubbish separately.

Another type of bin consists of a circular or oval fitment attached to a door or wall, to which a disposal bag or special bin liner is fitted.

Washing bins

Regular washing of bins is important to prevent germs and smells building up. Use mild detergent and a little household bleach or disinfectant. Swilling round the solution may be sufficient, but for a bad build up you may have to scrub the sides of the bin – this is where a smaller one is more convenient.

Dustbins

These are made of metal or plastic; in some areas regulation bins or paper or plastic sacks attached to a metal framework are supplied by the local authority.

Metal dustbins are strong, but noisy, and tend to get bent so that the lids no longer fit. *Plastic* bins are not so strong, but quieter. It is possible to get *dustbin liners*, but these work out quite expensive. However, it is worth having a small supply for extra rubbish, especially over public holidays, when collections may be fewer. Some local authorities supply black polythene sacks which fit inside the dustbin.

Dustbin hygiene Keep your dustbin fresh with regular scrubbing out with disinfectant and water. Turn it upside down to drain and dry thoroughly. Dustbin powders, sprinkled inside, kill off flies and their eggs; sachets of time-release insecticides, attached to dustbin lids, have the same properties. Always keep the lid firmly in place to avoid unpleasant smells and to keep out flies and scavenging animals such as dogs, cats and foxes.

Soft furnishings

All soft furnishing fabrics should be cleaned thoroughly at least once a year.

Blinds

Do not wash as this will distort their shape. Provided they are vinyl or have been treated with a proofing spray (see HOME DECORATION – Blinds) you can sponge them with a mild detergent solution, taking care not to over-wet. If blinds are kept dusted regularly no drastic cleaning should be required.

Venetian blinds Dust with a special brush or with the dusting attachment of your vacuum cleaner. Alternatively, you can put an old clean sock over a small brush and clean the slats with that. Wash from time to time with a weak detergent solution. *Small* Venetian blinds can be put in the bath and washed in soapy water. *Large* ones will need to have their slats cleaned individually. Hang the blinds out with the slats open to prevent the tapes from shrinking.

Covers

Fitted covers Clean fitted covers on chairs and stools with upholstery shampoo kits which work on the same principle as carpet shampoos, and are suitable for most colourfast fabrics. Bad marks should first be removed with a proprietary spot cleaner.

Loose covers Remove from the furniture and wash or dry clean according to the type of fabric. If loose covers are washed, put back on the furniture while still slightly damp to prevent shrinkage.

Curtains

Wash or dry clean according to the type of fabric. If you are in doubt, have them dry cleaned. If the linings are a different fabric from the main curtain, it is sensible to choose dry cleaning as this is less likely to cause shrinkage.

 HANDY HINT
Do remove all metal and plastic hooks, and any delicate trim before having curtains dry cleaned.

Net curtains Wash frequently so that dirt does not collect in them and discolour them. If they are badly soiled, soak for 30–45 minutes in warm water before washing. Most can safely be washed in a washing machine at the correct setting. Hang while still damp.

Lampshades

Keep well dusted and clean according to the type of material.
Stitched shades Wash suitable fabrics in warm, soapy water and hang up out of doors to dry.
Glued shades Rub over with a proprietary dry cleaning fluid or carbon tetrachloride applied on a clean white cloth.
Plastic and glass shades Wash in warm soapy water and dry with a soft cloth.
Valuable or antique shades These should be cleaned professionally.

Unpleasant smells around the house

Everyone would like a fresh-smelling home.

You'll find that scrupulous cleanliness and good ventilation are your chief allies against bad smells.

Bathrooms and lavatories

Various types of commercial deodoriser are available from chemists, hardware shops and stores, and these will freshen the air either continuously or when required. Perfumed lavatory cleaners hook inside the cistern – one type releases detergent, disinfectant and a perfume. Small blocks of perfumed cleanser clip to the rim of the bowl and release perfume when the lavatory is flushed.

There are aerosol air fresheners which will mask unpleasant smells; they are available in a range of perfumes.

Some products absorb smells rather than disguising them. These include bottles with pull-up wicks, and plastic containers containing scented smell-absorbing substances.

Adding disinfectant to the washing water when cleaning bathrooms and lavatories also helps to keep them fresh.

Kitchen

Sometimes you cannot easily track down the cause of kitchen smells. Here is a list of possibilities to check when your nose cannot immediately lead you to the source of the trouble.

● A neglected, damp and dirty dishcloth. *Solution:* boil dishcloth, or soak it in a strong solution of household bleach at least once a week. Spread out to dry when not in use. Throw dishcloths away as soon as they begin to get worn and ragged. Synthetic, lighter household cloths can be machine washed.

● Forgotten neglected, rotting vegetables at the back of or hidden in your vegetable bin or rack. *Solution:* always sort through old vegetables before putting in fresh supplies. Discard any which show traces of going soft or bad. Keep vegetables dry and well ventilated, removing them from any polythene wrappings as these cause condensation, leading to rot.

● Small quantities of stale food on a shelf, working surface or in a cupboard – or trapped behind it.

Solution: remove the stale food and wash the area thoroughly if necessary with detergent and hot water.

● A sink drain that needs cleaning.

Solution: put half a cup of washing soda crystals over the plug hole and pour boiling water over them. This will not only clean grease from the drain, but can sometimes dislodge blockages as well. Wear household gloves as soda crystals can affect the skin.

● If dishwashers are run infrequently on full cycle and are stacked with dirty dishes, they often give off a smell, particularly in hot weather.

Solution: use the cold pre-wash rinse to remove food debris from plates each time you add another batch. Alternatively, rinse plates well under the cold tap before stacking them in the dishwasher.

● Sometimes food goes bad inside a refrigerator, often because of a breakdown in the appliance or a power cut.

Solution: remove all food and wash the refrigerator out thoroughly with a solution of 1 tablespoon bicarbonate of soda to 1 litre (1¾ pints) warm water, using a clean cloth.

Before going on holiday, etc., empty and defrost your refrigerator, turn off the electricity, and leave the door ajar, otherwise the interior will smell musty and unpleasant. Special smell-absorbing products can also be obtained for use in either empty, closed refrigerators or ones in use. (See also KITCHEN SENSE – Refrigerators.)

Living rooms

Adequate ventilation and regular cleaning should ensure that the general rooms in the house smell sweet. However, there are some smells which may need treatment.

Tobacco The smell of stale tobacco in a room can be lessened by emptying all the ashtrays every night and giving the room a few sprays with an aerosol air freshener. If you can, leave windows open to air the room thoroughly. Alternatively, a wick type deodoriser placed in the room should help to freshen it.

Vases The water from cut flowers can give off a very strong odour in a living room. You can prevent this by putting a few drops of household bleach in the vase when you arrange the flowers. It will not harm them.

Use a strong solution of household bleach to clean and freshen a slimy vase.

★ **HANDY HINT** ★

One quick way of neutralising an unpleasant smell is to strike a match and immediately blow it out.

Walls and ceilings

Paintwork

Wash paintwork on walls and ceilings using lots of warm soapy water and clean cloths. Care should be taken on emulsioned surfaces not to streak the paint or rub flakes off – non-washable wall paint should not be cleaned.

When washing walls work on a small area at a time and try to complete the whole wall in one go or difficult to remove lines may appear between washed and unwashed areas. Wash walls from the bottom upwards to prevent streaks.

Wallpaper

This is not washable unless it is specifically claimed to be.

Washable wallpaper Sponge vinyl and polyester wallcoverings with warm soapy water, again starting from the bottom and treating the whole wall in one go. Some vinyls can be scrubbed gently – follow manufacturer's instructions.

Non-washable wallpaper Brush down or dust thoroughly. Marks on non-washable wallpaper can sometimes be removed with an aerosol grease solvent or by gently rubbing a piece of bread over them.

Specialist wall coverings Clean hessian, grasscloth and silk carefully, using the brush attachment on a vacuum cleaner to remove dust from the surface. Do not apply any cleaning products unless the manufacturers recommend it.

Ceilings

Ceilings, on the whole, do not get as dirty as walls and so require cleaning less often. If you plan to clean both walls *and* ceiling, start with the ceiling, then go on to the walls. Clean by using a special ceiling brush or vacuum cleaner attachment, then go over with a weak washing-up liquid solution. Rinse and wipe off to remove the detergent.

Windows, glass and mirrors

These all tend to show every mark so should be kept free from smears and dirt. Regular use of a proprietary window cleaner will keep them shining. Clear spray-on types with ammonia are best – the type that dries to a white powder is much harder to polish. It's better to clean windows on an overcast day. If the sun shines on them they can dry too fast and show streaks.

Rubber squeegees are useful for cleaning large windows. Hold the squeegee and stroke downwards. Always wipe the blade after each stroke.

> **WARNING**
> Never use soap to clean a window. The panes will smear and these marks are hard to remove.

Mirrors can be cleaned with warm water and white vinegar. Be careful when washing mirrors to see that water doesn't seep between glass and frame. This will damage the mirror.

> ★ **HANDY HINT** ★
> Clean your windows by rubbing over with crumpled balls of newspaper (the printer's ink does the job).

Bad marks on any kind of glass can usually be removed with methylated spirit applied on a soft clean cloth.

CHAPTER 5

HOME SAFETY

Alarms•Child safety•Electricity
Fire•Gas•Locks and bolts
Poisons•Safes

Burglars

It has been proved that most burglaries take place during the afternoon and early evening. Such break-ins are far less likely if the defences of your house are such that a good deal of time would have to be spent overcoming them.

It is often easy to overlook ways in which a burglar can break in. In an older-type house there may be a skylight that could be reached. Anti-climb paint, which remains sticky and greasy, can be applied to the upper parts of louvred windows, drainpipes, etc. Cellar and attic doors which lead into the house need adequate strong bolts and locks, as do any other doors leading in from a garage, shed or sun lounge.

Precautions

Going out If you are leaving the house empty during the evening, it is sensible to leave a light on in a downstairs room and close the curtains. Time switches can be fitted to turn lights on and off.

Do not leave the door key under the mat or hanging from a string through the letterbox.

Do not leave ladders lying about. When you are out padlock them to a fence or (horizontally) to a drainpipe.

Going away If you intend to be away for more than a few days, inform your local police station how long you will be gone.

● Leave a set of spare keys with trusted neighbours and ask them to check your home from time to time (tell the police that you have done this).

● Cancel regular deliveries such as newspapers and milk.

● If you have any particularly valuable small possessions, consider renting a safe deposit box at your bank.

▲ **WARNING** ▲

Don't write your name and address on a key tag or key holder.

Burglar alarms

A large proportion of house break-ins could be prevented by the efficient use of locks and bolts. However, once someone as broken in, alarms can alert police, security firms, passers-by or yourself.

Trap devices

Doors These usually have a magnetic switch which activates the alarm when the door is opened.

Windows Protected in the same way as doors or by an inertia switch which is set off when the window vibrates.

Walls Protected in the same way by inertia switches.

Floors Pressure mats, fitted underneath the carpet in a doorway, under a window or in front of valuable items, set off alarms when someone stands on or walks across them.

Space detectors A picture or other valuable can be protected by microwave detectors or infra-red ray units which detect movement and set off the alarm.

Acoustic detectors These work by picking up sounds and triggering the alarm.

The control unit

This should be fitted into a cupboard within the protected area. It is connected to the mains supply but should have a battery which will take over if there is a power cut.

Some systems can be set to operate for different parts of the house while the family is at home. The different sections of the system can be turned on and off as required. Control units usually have two spare keys. It is sensible to give one set to trusted neighbours or to a security firm. The names and addresses of key-holders should be given to the police.

Alarm

A box outside the house can be a strong deterrent to burglars, although it can advertise the fact that the house may contain valuables. Any box installed should have an anti-tamper device.

Some alarms send a direct signal to the security company or police, with no audible bell. There is also an automatic telephone system connected with the security company, but this is expensive. Some security firms offer a group system for neighbouring houses.

Make every effort to see that the alarm is not set off accidentally. If false alarms are raised too often, the police will warn you that they cannot keep answering them. If the bell rings persistently you may be prosecuted by neighbours or the local council.

Choosing a system

Do not choose a more extensive system than you need. Too much complication can cause false alarms.

Choose a system that conforms to the British Standards specification 4737 and consult the National Supervisory Council for Intruder Alarms about both alarm and installer. All systems should be inspected quarterly.

Child safety

Toddlers and young children are particularly vulnerable to accidents in the home.

Electricity

● Make sure all sockets are shuttered. If they are not, fit safety covers over them.

Falls

● Fit safety catches or bars to upstairs windows.

● Do not put chairs under windows.

● Make sure cots are designed with bars no more than 7cm (2¾in) apart.

● Use a non-slip rubber mat in the bath.

> ▲ **WARNING** ▲
>
> Never leave a baby or child in the bath unattended.

● Fit gates to the top and bottom of the stairs – but teach toddlers to climb up and down safely as soon as they can.
● Make sure high chairs are firm and will not topple.
● Never leave a baby lying on a bed or high surface unattended.
● Top bunks should have a guard rail.

Fires
● Open fires must, by law, be guarded.
● Make sure the fire guard is firmly fixed to the wall.
● Portable oil and gas heaters should also be guarded and fixed firmly.
● Keep matches out of the way on a high shelf.
● Make sure clothing is flame-proof.
● Teach a child fire drill at home.

Gas
● Make sure that gas taps are secured, so that they cannot be turned on easily.

Outside
● Young children must be supervised when playing near ponds or rivers.
● Garden ponds should be covered or fenced off when there are young children about.
● Make sure garden gates close securely. Mend broken latches.

Poisoning
● Keep all drugs, medicines, household cleaners, etc. well out of reach.

● Never put poisonous substances in bottles or containers which have originally held food or drink.
● See also Poisons

Scalds and burns
● Never leave the handles of pans, kettles, etc. projecting over the edge of the cooker.
● Do not leave a pot of hot tea or coffee where it can be pulled off the table.
● Never leave a hot iron unattended.

Suffocation
● Do not leave a front loading automatic washing machine open.
● If dumping an old refrigerator, remove the door first.
● Do not leave polythene bags lying around for children to get hold of and put over their heads.
● Do not provide a pillow for a baby.
● Do not use plastic sheets on mattresses in cots.

Electricity

Don't
● Overload electrical circuits.
● Touch electrical gadgets with wet hands or use them in steamy rooms.
● Use frayed appliances or ones with frayed or twisted flex.
● Run flexes under carpets or let them trail about.
● Join two lengths of flex except with an approved connector. (See also RE-PAIRS AND MAINTENANCE – Electricity – Flex.)

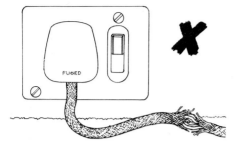

● Switch off electrical equipment when answering door or telephone.
● Switch off electric underblankets before getting into bed.
● Make sure electric blankets lie flat.
● Have electric blankets inspected and cleaned every two years and if they get wet.

Falls

Don't
● Take any portable electric gadgets into the bathroom.
● Leave hot irons unattended.
● Use an electric underblanket as an overblanket or vice versa.
● Attempt to repair electrical equipment until you have unplugged it.

Do
● Remove relevant fuses when drilling holes in walls which might contain wires.
● Switch off and unplug equipment for filling (e.g. kettles), for cleaning and when not in use, particularly televisions at night.
● Wire plugs correctly (see REPAIRS AND MAINTENANCE – Electricity – Plugs).
● Make sure equipment is properly earthed.
● Use the right fuse for the job.
● Have faulty wiring or equipment professionally repaired.
● Have shuttered sockets when there are young children in the house.
● Have any electric bathroom heater wall mounted with a pull switch and the plug or spur fuse box outside the bathroom.

Don't
● Have polished floors at the foot of stairs.
● Polish floors under rugs.
● Keep movable objects (which children could climb on to) under window sills.
● Polish treads of uncarpeted stairs.
● Allow stair carpets to work loose.
● Allow more than about 7cm (2$\frac{3}{4}$in) between baluster uprights.
● Have stairs with open risers if you have a choice.
● Leave items lying about on the stairs or piles of things at top or bottom to be carried.
● Keep bicycles, prams, toys, etc. where they can be tripped over.

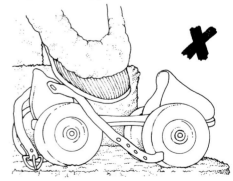

Do

● Use non-slip polish.
● Anchor loose rugs and mats and anchor carpet and lino edges securely in doorways.
● Highlight small steps with a contrasting painted edge on the step.
● Keep all areas well lighted.
● Reinforce or bar windows that go down to the floor.
● Use shatter-proof acrylic or protective mesh in glazed doors and use push-pull catches that give on impact.
● Use a firm stepladder when decorating or to reach high cupboards.
● Fit removable bars or safety catches to upstairs windows in children's rooms and bathrooms.
● Have correctly positioned hand-rails in the bathroom for the old or infirm.
● Have a non-slip bathmat next to the bath and a non-slip rubber mat in the bath or shower.

Fire

Don't

● Carry oil heaters when they are alight.
● Draw a fire with newspaper or use petrol or paraffin.
● Cut clothes over or around exposed heat or near cookers.
● Use gloss paint on polystyrene tiles.
● Leave lighted cigarettes unattended.
● Use inflammable materials while smoking or near a naked flame.
● Drape Christmas or party decorations round light fittings.

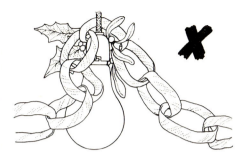

● Leave candles burning unattended.
● Leave magnifying glasses in the sun.
● Puncture, incinerate or expose aerosols to heat.

Do

● Keep an up-to-date fire extinguisher in a handy place.
● Use spark guards for open fires and guards round heaters.
● Fix oil heaters to floor or wall, away from draughts.
● Sweep chimneys regularly.
● Make sure nothing is still alight before emptying ashtrays into bins.
● Close downstairs windows and doors at night to prevent spread of fire.
● Buy children's clothing in flame-proof materials
● Keep all matches, lighters, etc. away from children.

 ▲ WARNING ▲

Don't open door if you think there is fire on the other side.

In the event of fire

● Get everybody out of the house, shutting windows and doors.

● Call the fire brigade.
● Try putting out the fire *only if there is no risk*.
Trapped by fire *If you are trapped upstairs:*
● Go into a room facing on to the street side of the house.
● Close the door and block the gap underneath with rugs or blankets.
● Open the window and shout. Do not jump unless it is absolutely unavoidable.
Fire drill Have an occasional fire drill, so that everybody knows what to do in an emergency. Teach the children how to telephone for help. Teach them not to hide but to go to a window and shout.

Various types of fire

Chimney Pour water on the fire. Close the doors and windows. Call the fire brigade. Move furniture, etc. away.
Chip pans Turn off the heat and smother the flames with a blanket or lid.

 WARNING

Never pour water over a chip pan which has caught alight or carry the pan outside.

Clothes Push the casualty down on to the floor. Roll or wrap in a rug, curtain or heavy coat to quench the flames.
If you are the victim, lie down on the floor and roll over to extinguish the flames. Get medical attention quickly.
Electric fires DO NOT USE WATER before plugging or switching off at the mains. Use a fire extinguisher if you have one.

Foam-upholstered furniture Get out at once. The fumes can be lethal.
Oil heaters Do not move or try to carry outside. Throw buckets of water over the heater from a few feet away.
See also FIRST AID – Burns and scalds.

Gas

Don't
● Search for gas leaks with a naked flame.

Do
● Put out cigarettes and extinguish naked flames.
● Ventilate rooms containing gas appliances.
● Switch off all gas appliances before putting money in the meter.
● Switch off gas taps as well as the appliances when not in use.
● Check connecting tubing regularly for signs of wear.
● Have flues and ventilators checked regularly for signs of wear or blockages.
See also FIRST AID – Artificial respiration.

Locks

Protecting your home from unwelcome intruders is becoming increasingly important as the incidence of burglary grows. However, most break-ins are the work of opportunists rather than professional, and so there is no real need to turn your home into the suburban equivalent of Fort Knox. You need a sensible selection of security devices, and a common-sense approach.

Mortise deadlocks

Surprisingly, the most vulnerable part of the house is often the least-expected one – the front door, or the door everyone uses to enter and leave the house. What you need to secure it when you are out is a *mortise deadlock*, which is set into a slot or mortise cut into the edge of the door, and which shoots a thick-square-edged bolt into a recess cut in the door frame. With the deadlock in operation it cannot be forced back; only the correct key will open it.

The mortise deadlock's one disadvantage is that when fitted to a door of less than standard thickness, or to a glazed door with comparatively narrow stiles, the mortise itself may weaken the door structure unacceptably. If this sounds like your door, the best alternative is to choose a cylinder deadlock that is screwed to the inside face of the door instead of being let into its edge. The most satisfactory types can be locked on the inside with a key instead of with a catch, so that even if a burglar breaks the glass in the door he cannot open it. Also the door cannot be used to make a quick getaway if entry to the house has been gained elsewhere.

Bolts

Bolts, added to mortise deadlocks, can give peace of mind as far as night-time security is concerned. Both barrel bolts (screwed to the top and bottom of the door), or mortise bolts (set into its edge and turned with a special key – although obviously these cannot be used when you leave the house) are suitable.

★ **HANDY HINT** ★

It is worth considering fitting a spy-hole and/or a door chain to the front door, especially if you live alone.

Mortise lock and latch

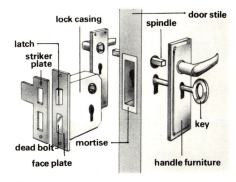

lock casing door stile spindle latch striker plate dead bolt mortise face plate key handle furniture

For other doors, the best security measure is to fit bolts at the top and bottom, and to make sure that they are shot across at night and whenever the house is left empty. The locks on outward-opening french doors should be backed up with bolts at top and bottom, engaging in holes in the door frame. In addition, you should fit hinge bolts to the hinged edges of these doors; as their hinges are accessible from the outside, a burglar could knock out the hinge pins and force the door.

Patio doors may already incorporate cylinder locks; however, these can be forced because of the softness of the aluminium frames used on many patio doors. You can buy special door bolts for patio doors (and for sliding windows too); these screw to the frame, and shoot a bolt into the sliding door at right angles to the direction of sliding.

Other devices

Garage and shed doors and ladders should be secured with a good padlock, attached to fittings that are either bolted to the door or else fixed with clutch-head screws that cannot be undone. Metal, wood and glass fibre up-and-over doors can usually be fitted with extra locks, available from the manufacturers.

For windows, the best security devices are variations on the mortise bolts mentioned for doors. Alternatively, surface-mounted key-operated locks can be fitted, but these are comparatively expensive. Wooden-framed opening windows you never actually open can be secured most effectively with a couple of woodscrews. On metal-framed windows, lockable stays or handles can be fitted. These are suitable for wooden-framed windows too, and have the advantage of allowing the window to be locked in a slightly open position for ventilation.

See also REPAIRS AND MAINTENANCE – Locks.

Poisons

Don't

● Keep old medicines. Flush them down the lavatory.
● Leave alcohol about for children to get hold of and drink.

● Leave keys in cupboards containing drugs or chemicals.
● Use toxic paint on toys or children's furniture.
● Store garden chemicals in unlabelled bottles or bottles that have been used for fruit drinks, alcohol, etc.
● Grow poisonous plants and berries where children can reach them.

Do

● Keep all poisons in their own or other carefully labelled containers.
● Lock away all medicines and household cleaners.
● Keep cosmetics away from children.
● Lock away all garden chemicals, weed killer, insecticides, rodent poison, etc.

See also FIRST AID – Poisoning.

Safes

If you have to keep large sums of money in the house, or if you have any valuable jewellery, it is wise to install a safe.

Types of safe

Floor safe This can either be of the type which is hidden under the floor boards, and securely embedded in concrete, or locked on to a base plate which itself is bolted to the floor. Such a safe presents no point of entry, as the only way to open it is by unlocking it from the base plate.

Wall safe This is roughly the size of a brick and will hold a fair number of small items. It is easily installed and can be hidden by a picture or mirror. Larger wall safes are also available.

CHAPTER 6

FAMILY HEALTH

Allergies•Antiseptics and disinfectants
Exercise•Home nursing•Illnesses
Insects•Quarantine

GENERAL HEALTH CARE

Antiseptics and disinfectants

Antiseptics are usually applied on the outside of the body to prevent the spread of germs and infection. Disinfectants are stronger and kill germs, but undiluted disinfectants should not be used on the skin. Some brands, however, can act as an antiseptic when diluted.

A useful antiseptic to have in the home is a paste or solution made from magnesium sulphate (Epsom salts) for skin abrasions, cuts, bites, etc. A proprietary antiseptic for cleaning wounds and gargling will also be useful. When there is a baby in the house, an antibacterial powder for soaking nappies and a sterilising agent for feeding bottles will be needed.

Ants

If ants invade the house, the only sure way of getting rid of them is to find the nest by following the ant trail. Make a hole in it and pour down a kettle full of boiling water. Finish by dusting the surrounding ground with a special insecticide, obtainable from garden shops.

If the nest cannot be found, or is under a path or wall, lay down a proprietary poison bait near the ant runs. This method may take about a week to eradicate the ants.

 WARNING

Keep the ant bait away from children and animals, and protect it from rain.

Entry points

Paint a diluted solution of one part chlordane to one hundred parts water or paraffin, on to grass and soil surrounding the house and around the base of the walls in a continuous 30cm (1ft) band.

Inside the house a solution of one part 20 per cent solution to ten parts water or paraffin can be painted with a brush around doors, window frames and other possible points of entry. Fill gaps in walls, skirting boards and floors with cement or wood filler.

Insecticides indoors

Some insecticides are safe for use on painted areas such as table legs and shelves. Whichever brand you decide to use, follow the instructions carefully. Before treatment, remove plants, animals or fish. Move or cover food. Wash off splashes on the skin at once and wash your hands after using. Store chemicals under lock and key. (See also HOME SAFETY – Poisons.)

Prevention

Keep all sweet foodstuffs covered and in inaccessible places such as cupboards and refrigerators. Cover refuse bins and keep surfaces free of crumbs, spilt sugar, etc. by wiping frequently.

Cockroaches

The most common species are the *Common cockroach*, which is almost black and 20–24mm (¾–1in) in length, and the smaller *German cockroach*, which is light brown. Cockroaches have long, whip-like antennae, flat, oval bodies and rapid, jerky movements. They have a hard outer casing.

Cockroaches thrive in warm, humid areas such as centrally heated buildings, bakeries, kitchens and laundries.

The German cockroach is often found under sinks, cookers and refrigerators. It will scuttle up walls, tiles, etc., whereas the Common cockroach forms colonies below ground level. They have nocturnal habits and are seldom seen by day.

Health threat
Scavengers by nature, cockroaches are fond of drains, sewers and rubbish. They foul more food than they eat, leaving a trail of excreta and regurgitated material and can carry many diseases, including food poisoning. They have an unpleasant smell.

Eradication
Recently developed formulations for use by specialist pest control companies have proved successful in most cases. Alternatively, use baits containing special insecticide or boric acid powder.

If you have an infestation, consult your local authority or a specialist pest control company. If the infestation is slight and you want to tackle it yourself, long-lasting insecticidal puffer packs or aerosols can be effective so long as you can ensure the insecticide has penetrated the haunt of the insects.

 ▲ WARNING ▲
Remove all foodstuffs from the area to be treated.

Keeping cockroaches out Practise scrupulous cleanliness and hygiene in the kitchen and avoid leaving food residues or dregs from drinks which will lure the insects out. Search areas where you suspect their presence and block up every possible crack through which they might squeeze. Regularly use a torch, pull out the refrigerator, look behind disposal bins, etc.

Exercise

A sensible amount of exercise helps to keep you fit, to tone-up sagging muscles, will increase your sense of well-being and energy and help to combat overweight problems. People who eat properly and exercise regularly are also less prone to heart disease. Exercise can mean anything from specially constructed exercises, to be done daily or weekly (see overleaf), a regular jog or walk (a good, brisk 20-minute minimum per day) to regularly playing games such as squash, tennis, badminton, football.

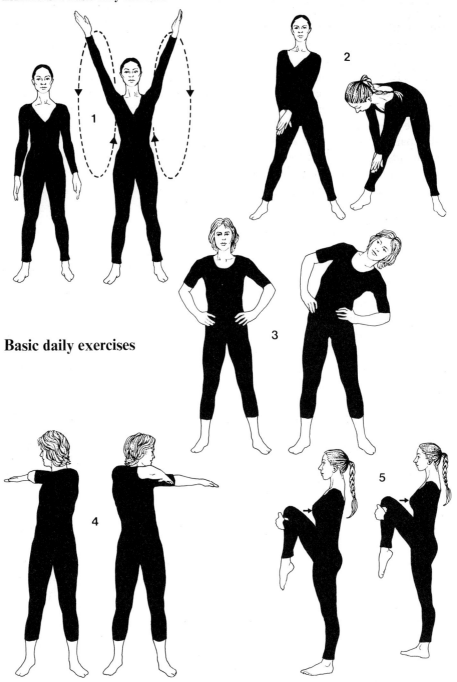

Basic daily exercises

Basic daily exercises

There are innumerable exercises which you can do, which will exercise your total body and/or various parts of it. Some basic warm-up exercises to increase mobility are given below.

Exercise 1 Arm circling. Stand with feet wide apart, hands by your sides. Raise your hands up in front of you, circling above your head, stretching back as you bring them down. Repeat at your own pace, breathing freely, for 30 seconds.

Exercise 2 Ankle reaching. Stand feet wide apart, palms of both hands on one thigh. Bend forwards and sideways, sliding hands down the leg as far as you can comfortably go. Do not strain: let the spine bend naturally and hang your head with neck muscles relaxed. Breathe out when bending forward, and in when straightening up. Repeat with alternate legs for 30 seconds.

Exercise 3 Side bending. Standing with feet wide apart, hands on hips, bend first to the left, gently pressing down, then to the right. Tilt your head and neck with your shoulders each time. Repeat for 30 seconds, breathing freely.

Exercise 4 Trunk rotating. Stand feet wide apart, arms raised in front at shoulder level. Keeping hips and legs straight, turn head, shoulders and arms first to the left and then to the right. Again, continue for 30 seconds.

Exercise 5 Knee bending. Stand upright, feet together, hands at sides. Raise one knee as high as possible, grasp the shin with both hands and pull towards the body. Repeat with the other leg, keeping the back straight throughout. Continue for 30 seconds.

Flies and mosquitoes

The feeding habits of flies make many species carriers of a wide variety of diseases from food poisoning and dysentery to cholera and polio. As they move from filfth to food, they carry bacteria on their feet, legs, bodies and in the gut. Flies with piercing mouthparts like mosquitoes get their food from human or animal blood.

Eradicating flies

Breeding sites To deny flies their breeding sites, all empty cans, bottles and other containers must be disposed of quickly, especially in hot weather. Where possible, burn refuse. All peelings, dregs of food, etc. should be wrapped before being thrown into bins and not left lying around.

Dustbins should be sited well away from windows and have sound, close-fitting lids. Bins should be regularly hosed out and dusted with insect powder or a dual purpose insecticide. These are usually based on chemicals called lindane, carbaryl or diazinon, and have a residual effect which helps to kill eggs and maggots as well as mature flies.

Left-over food Never leave left-over food exposed, especially meat, fish or dairy products. Keep them in a refrigerator where possible and cover foods in a larder, or left out, with cloths, gauze covers, glass or plastic covers.

Killing flies

A fly swat is cheap and handy, but its use

requires good co-ordination of hand and eye.

Aerosol insecticides Those containing pyrethrins will wipe out flies. When spraying, remove all food and make sure there are no pets in the room.

Barriers and fly-papers Flexible fly screens which can be attached to window frames with Velcro are available. Old-fashioned sticky fly papers are not ideal, but will eliminate many flies.

Vapour releasers These are impregnated resin strips which are hung from the ceiling. They continuously give off a vapour which is poisonous to flies.

Eradicating mosquitoes

Place a little paraffin on the surface of water in guttering, water butts and stagnant pools. Clean bird baths out regularly. If you live near a large area of stagnant water, the local authority may be able to help eradicate mosquito pests.

Inside the home Aerosol fly sprays containing pyrethrin will kill individual mosquitoes. Follow the manufacturers' instructions and spray carefully, avoiding food and pets.

See also FIRST AID – Bites and stings.

Hygiene

Hygiene is almost entirely a matter of cleanliness. A house that is regularly cleaned (see CLEANING THE HOUSE), clothes that are washed properly, care in personal cleanliness and in the preparation and storage of food, will all help to prevent the growth of bacteria.

Some rules for hygiene

● Fresh air and good ventilation in the house.

● Regular cleaning of the house.

● Regular washing or dry cleaning of clothes.

● Protection of food from flies and other types of contamination.

● Storage of perishable food in the refrigerator or cold larder.

● Scrupulously clean dishcloths and tea towels – these should preferably be boiled or washed on the hottest cycle in the washing machine.

● Clean hands. Wash every time after visiting the lavatory and teach children to do so. Always wash hands before handling food.

● If a member of the family has a heavy cold, cough or other infectious illness, keep special towels and face cloths, cups and cutlery, for their use alone.

Inoculation and immunisation

Immunisation by an inoculation or series of inoculations saves countless lives by preventing serious illnesses such as polio, diphtheria and smallpox. Inoculations have also proved successful against tetanus, whooping cough, typhoid, measles and tuberculosis as well as some of the virulent tropical diseases.

Children are inoculated against different diseases at different ages. The *triple vaccine* shown in the chart is a combination of diphtheria, tetanus and whooping cough. Smallpox has now been declared eradicated as a disease.

Immunisation programme

3 months	**Triple vaccine** **Polio** ⎫ 1st dose
4–5 months	**Triple vaccine** **Polio** ⎫ 2nd dose
10–12 months	**Triple vaccine** **Polio** ⎫ 3rd dose
1–2 years	**Measles**
5 years (school entry)	**Diphtheria booster** **Tetanus booster** **Polio booster**
10–13 years	**B.C.G. (tuberculosis)** **Rubella (German measles)** **for girls**
15–18 years (school leaving)	**Tetanus booster** **Polio booster**

Contra-indications

There are some people for whom immunisation by certain vaccines may prove dangerous. It is important to inform the doctor involved in the immunisation about any condition that you or your children are suffering from, or any previous reaction you may have had to a different vaccination. If you are suffering from any form of infection, immunisation should not take place.

Whooping cough Seek your family doctor's advice on the subject. Children who have had convulsions, recent chest infections or who have a history of fits or asthma in the family should probably not have the vaccine.

Mice and rats

Both mice and rats have a compulsive need to gnaw in order to keep their constantly growing incisor teeth worn down. They will strip insulation from electric cables, chew up polystyrene insulation and damage woodwork and even plastic and lead pipes. Both rodents contaminate far more food than they consume and are capable of carrying many diseases.

Mice

Mice shed about seventy droppings every 24 hours and food is contaminated by their urine as well as their dirty feet.

Getting rid of mice Mouse holes and any other holes should be blocked with wire wool embedded in cement. Pipes and cable ducts should fit closely to holes they run through, without leaving gaps.

Metal strips can be fitted to the bottoms of damaged doors. Store away all foods.

'Break-back' traps can be useful for dealing with a few mice, but must be correctly placed, running across the path of the mouse with the bait against the wall. This traditional mousetrap has about a 50 per cent success rate and should be baited with nuts, chocolate and bread rather than cheese!

> ★ **HANDY HINT** ★
> The best cure for mice is – get a cat!
> The very smell of a feline in the house
> prevents vermin from staying there.

A *galvanised steel mousetrap* is now available, which does not need baiting and has overcome the problem of the mouse springing the trap without being caught.

If you do not want to kill the mice, put the bait into the bottom of a smooth sided plastic bucket or bin and place it near a table or chair. The mice will be able to leap into the bucket but not climb out, and you can carry them outside and let them out – preferably a long way away.

Rodenticides are available, in particular 'Warfarin', but many mice are now becoming immune to this. Other substances include mouse killers based on the drug alphachloralose and calciferol. If you are using mouse killers, dispose of the bodies carefully in a sealed polythene bag in the dustbin.

Most local authorities offer free *rodent control* services to householders and if mice persist you should contact the local health department.

Rats

Rats live in filthy surroundings, such as refuse tips and sewers. They can harbour or transmit more than twenty diseases, including Weil's disease (leptospiral jaundice) which is often fatal to people and dogs, and they can transmit food poisoning. They are potential carriers of foot and mouth disease on farms and their urine can pollute stagnant water.

Rats can destroy poultry, game, crops, stored grain and eggs.

Getting rid of rats Block up holes and seal gaps as for mice. Chemical rodenticides, of the same type as those recommended for mouse control can be used. *Acute rodenticides* are quick-acting and efficient, but for professional use.

In any case of rat infestation call your local public health department because a cornered rat is dangerous to humans.

TREATMENT OF ILLNESS

When illnesses occur, there are usually medicines to be taken. They should be used with the greatest respect as almost all of them can have harmful effects if they are misused.

Medicines on prescription

When your doctor prescribes a medicine, make sure you understand the dosage before taking it. If in any doubt, telephone the doctor or pharmacist.

Storage

● Keep medicines clearly labelled and dated and store in a locked cupboard out of the reach of children.

● When medicines are no longer needed, flush them down the lavatory or return them to the chemist.

● Many medicines, especially liquids, do not keep well once they are opened. Find out how long they will keep when you get them.

Side effects

Many medicines have side effects, so ask about them when they are prescribed.

Long-term drug taking Some common drugs can be dangerous, even at normal dosage, if they are taken for prolonged spells. Tell your doctor what you are taking if you buy any medicines without a prescription.

Interaction with other drugs, etc. Some tranquillisers have dangerous reactions with other drugs and foods; other drugs can react with aspirin or alcohol.

Allergies

About one person in every ten of the general population develops a special sensitivity, or allergic reaction, to everyday substances.

These allergy-provoking substances can cover a wide range from house dust and pollen to strawberries, penicillin, cosmetics and washing powders. Some babies are allergic to cow's milk.

The body's reaction uses the release of a chemical, histamine, which can react on the skin, producing weals and rashes, on the lung tubes, producing asthma, and on the inner lining of the nose, producing hay fever. These symptoms occur soon after exposure. In acute cases (like shellfish allergy) people sometimes swell up, and the respiratory tract can be affected.

Delayed reactions can appear some seven to ten days after exposure to the allergen.

Treatment Doctors can offer a wide range of therapies and advice for relief and control of the problems provoked by an allergy. Among these are *antihistamines* for hay fever – these have the disadvantage of causing drowsiness and the drug is not compatible with alcohol. A long-acting injection of *cortisone* can be given just before the hay fever season. *Sodium cromoglycate* in the form of a nasal spray has none of the side effects of antihistamines or cortisone.

Skin tests can be carried out to discover which substances are causing the allergic reactions. Some people are allergic to more than one substance.

Long-term precautions

In the case of immediate or delayed allergy to drugs, this information should always be given when seeking any form of medical treatment. A suitable reminder card can be carried in the purse or wallet in case of an accident.

Avoid contact with substances that are known to be allergenic. This might require applying skin barrier creams, even self-adhesive plasters or wearing rubber gloves or overalls.

Desensitisation Tolerance can, in 70 per cent of cases, be improved by a series of injections under the skin, but this process cannot be used on young children.

Boils

Painful boils often occur in anyone who is particularly run down, who has not been maintaining a balanced diet; or, occasionally, a crop of boils can be a symptom of diabetes.

Carbuncle

This is a many-headed boil which needs prompt medical treatment to prevent it from spreading.

Both boils and carbuncles will usually leave scars.

Treatment NEVER touch or squeeze a boil or carbuncle, or touch the pus. This can spread the infection both under and on the surface of the skin.

Sometimes a boil can be hastened to its end or relieved by applications of warm poultices. Antiseptics added to these are useful for discouraging secondary infections. Applications of magnesium sulphate paste also help draw out the boil.

Occasionally the boil will not burst on its own and will require lancing to allow the pus to escape and relieve the sufferer. This should be performed by a doctor.

 HANDY HINT

If a member of the family has boils, make sure they only use their own towels, to prevent the boils from spreading to other parts of the body.

Bronchitis

Bronchitis is inflammation of the lung tubes (bronchi) and appears either as acute bronchitis, which comes quickly over a period of days, or chronic bronchitis, which develops slowly.

Acute bronchitis

The initial virus infections that often start acute bronchitis include the common cold, influenza and children's fevers such as measles and German measles (rubella).

Acute bronchitis is more common in cold, damp, foggy or smoggy conditions and can be brought on by a sharp drop in body temperature, inadequate nutrition, severe stress or as the aftermath of illness. Heavy smokers (twenty or more cigarettes a day) and people who work in dusty environments also run a greater risk of bronchitis.

Signs and symptoms The first signs are cold, influenza or other virus conditions. This is followed by a dry, irritating cough causing pain behind the breastbone. There is loss of appetite, feverishness and wheezing. Coughing produces sticky yellow (infected) phlegm.

Treatment It is essential to call the doctor who will prescribe antibiotics and other remedies. The patient should be kept in bed in a warm room until the fever abates. Steam from a kettle or bowl of hot water may make breathing easier in the early stages.

Give hot, non-milky drinks. A teaspoonful of bicarbonate of soda in a glass of warm water helps to bring up phlegm. Smoking is forbidden and the doctor will say when work may be resumed.

Chronic bronchitis

If unchecked, chronic bronchitis takes between ten and twenty years to develop into a crippling disease, producing permanent disablement with problems of breathing and heart weakness.

Heavy smoking is one of the main causes and must be stopped at once.

Overweight people, especially men over forty are more at risk.

Dusty jobs give rise to bronchitis. Occupational safeguards such as masks or dust extractors should always be used. Cold and foggy conditions worsen the condition.

Signs and symptoms A 'smoker's cough' during the winter months, with large amounts of white or grey (uninfected) phlegm especially early in the day. After several years the cough becomes chronic. Shortness of breath worsens over the years and eventually the heart becomes strained.

Treatment The doctor can prescribe medicine which relaxes the lung tubes and allows them to be cleared easily.

Physiotherapy departments of hospitals generally have special classes to teach breathing exercises.

Central heating can help by providing an even temperature, but a humidifier may be needed if the air is dry.

Antibiotics may be prescribed to help ward off colds and influenza.

Bugs and body parasites

Animal parasites may arrive in the home via many different routes. Children may pick them up at school; adults may come into contact with carriers in sports or social clubs. Domestic animals and pets can be carriers and second-hand furniture, particularly when it is upholstered and in a poor state of repair, can be infested.

 ★ HANDY HINT ★
Once animal parasites are discovered, do inform other contacts who can then take precautions.

Bed bugs

These have a sweet, offensive odour. They can be detected by black stains left on bedding and walls, as in fact they live in cracks in the wall and only come out at night. They are about 5mm ($\frac{1}{4}$in) long.

Bites Some people have no reaction at all, others react quite severely, sometimes needing medical treatment. A mild antiseptic will soothe a bite.

Eradication requires help. Consult your local environmental health officer.

Bed Bug

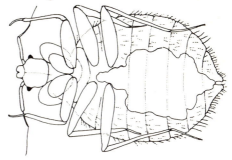

Fleas

Comparatively few fleas trouble humans. Most infestations are due to cat fleas, which are also found on dogs. These fleas lurk in the animals' bedding or in furniture and their eggs usually hatch out on the floor.

Bites Many people show no reaction at all on being bitten by a flea. Others may have painful bites which can be treated with calamine lotion or insect bite creams. They become infected if scratched and need medical attention.

Flea

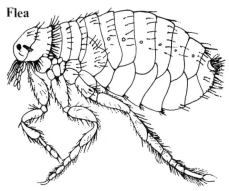

Eradication Scrupulous cleaning of carpets and floors can help to keep adult fleas from developing. Consult a vet if your pet is infested and carry out scrupulously the treatment he prescribes. Regular grooming will help reveal flea infestations so that they can be dealt with promptly.

Lice

Body lice These live in the seams of underclothing which is worn continuously in a dirty condition. They are associated with conditions of poverty, disaster and war and are the sole distributors of epidemic typhus.

Head louse

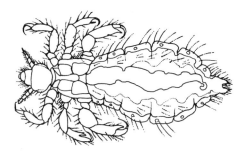

Head lice These tend to affect children more than adults. This louse, about the size of a match head, spends its whole life in the hair, sucking blood from the scalp. The eggs are glued to the hair shafts by the female. They are whitish, oval objects about the size of a pinhead and are difficult to remove.

Signs of infestation Persistent scratching of the head often indicates that there are head lice present. Head-to-head contact is the major method of transmission. Some lice can lurk in hat bands, hairbrushes and combs, and it is very important that such articles should not be used by other people (as frequently happens in schools).

Treatment These can live happily on the cleanest of heads with the shortest of hair. Washing the hair with ordinary shampoos will not remove them. School health services or a chemist can supply the necessary lotions for killing lice and special fine combs for removing the eggs from the hair.

Regular grooming and weekly inspection, especially of children's heads, can help to prevent lice from becoming a serious problem.

Crab lice Most frequently found in

Crab louse

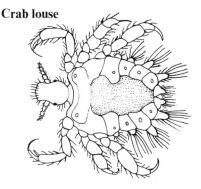

pubic hair, they are transmitted by sexual contact.

A special lotion is available for *crab lice* from chemists. Use according to the manufacturer's instructions. Do not have sexual contact until the condition clears up.

Scabies

These are small parasites which burrow into the outermost layers of the skin. An allergic reaction causes an itchy rash on shoulders, waist, legs and ankles.

Treatment Once diagnosis has been made, a special lotion will clear up the problem. Consult your chemist for specific details.

Colds

There is no 'cure' for the common cold, though there are many remedies to relieve some of the symptoms.

Infectious colds are caused by viruses which cannot be killed by antibiotics. Because there are so many different types of virus, vaccination is not practical.

Avoidance of infection

A cold-sufferer is most infectious in the acute 'streaming nose' stage, when the virus is spread into the air by coughing and sneezing.

To reduce the chances of catching a cold, try to avoid crowded, stuffy places as much as possible. Pay particular attention to washing your hands thoroughly and avoid touching eyes or nostrils with unwashed fingers.

It is sensible for people who suffer from bronchitis to avoid cold victims, even at the risk of seeming antisocial.

Treatment Many people believe that large doses of Vitamin C are good for relieving cold symptoms, and certainly a balanced diet which includes all the essential vitamins builds up resistance to all kinds of illnesses (see FOOD – Nutrition).

Hot drinks and aspirin or paracetamol will help a sore throat. Decongestants, which make breathing easier, may be temporarily useful, but whatever you take to alleviate the discomfort, the cold will run its course.

Colds and small babies Keep the baby warm and consult your doctor as to what treatment you can carry out safely to relieve some of the symptoms. This might include junior aspirin, an inhalant and plenty of warm drinks.

Contagious diseases

When a child first goes to school, he is likely to pick up any infection that is going around, but he will gradually build up immunities over the years.

However, the various immunisation and inoculation procedures are important to maintain control over possible epidemics. By the time a child goes to school, he should have had a full course of immunisation against measles, poliomyelitis, diphtheria and whooping cough. The World Health Organisation has reported that smallpox has now been eradicated, so it is no longer deemed an essential inoculation.

Chickenpox

The illness starts 10 to 20 days after contact and the patient is infectious for two days before and about 14 days after the rash.

Symptoms The patient may have a vague headache, generally feel unwell and occasionally have a blotchy red rash which quickly fades. Within a day, the first spots appear in crops, spreading rapidly on the back, abdomen and chest, then usually to the face, scalp and limbs. The blister-like spots eventually dry out and scabs form. Once this has happened the patient is no longer infectious.

Treatment The patient should stay in bed if he has a temperature but otherwise do not insist on bed rest. Give mild painkillers to ease sore throats and headaches, cut down on food when the temperature is raised but give plenty of liquids to drink. Calamine lotion applied to the spots will soothe irritation and help to prevent scratching. This is important as the secondary infection caused by scratching may leave scars that last for life. If the itching becomes intense, a soothing bath containing potassium permanganate (available from chemists) will help. After the bath, pat the patient dry (don't rub because of body scabs) and use talc to soothe.

Complications from chickenpox are rare, but it is highly infectious and the infection can sometimes be passed to adults as shingles. Children with chickenpox should, therefore, be isolated.

German measles

German measles is a fairly mild illness. Epidemics occur every three or four years in the winter and spring months.

Symptoms These appear 17 or 18 days after contact and the patient is infectious for a week before and after the appearance of the rash. This rash starts on the face and behind the ears, spreading downwards to trunk, arms and legs. The rash fades after four days.

Treatment Treatment is virtually unnecessary and there is no real need for isolation.

WARNING

A patient with German measles should never be allowed to come into contact with a pregnant woman, as contact with German measles during the first four months of pregnancy can result in damage to the foetus.

Girls should be brought into contact with the disease before puberty to provide immunisation in the child-bearing years. Alternatively, a vaccine can be given at the age of thirteen.

Measles

This is a highly infectious virus disease, which is passed by droplets from the nose and mouth.

Symptoms The patient will be unwell for three or four days before the rash appears. There will be a temperature, symptoms of a bad cold with a harsh cough, red eyes and a runny nose. These may be combined with earache, irritability and drowsiness.

Small white spots like grains of salt can be seen on the inside of the cheek, called Koplik's spots. The rash starts behind the ears and spreads rapidly, fading after two or three days.

Treatment The patient should stay in bed during the acute stage of the illness. Give him plenty of liquid. Eyes become very sensitive to light during measles and should be protected by keeping the curtains drawn. If the eyes are not protected, corneal ulceration can result.

 WARNING

Earache, with a persistent temperature, after the measles rash fades, may be a sign of secondary infection and the doctor should be consulted.

Mumps

This is caused by a virus and though mainly a childhood disease, can occur in infants and adults.

Symptoms The patient may feel unwell for a time before the characteristic swelling of the glands behind the ears occurs. Sometimes only one gland swells, but most commonly the other swells within a few days, or both swell at once. They are very tender to touch; it is painful to open the mouth, laughing is agony and there is sometimes earache.

Treatment The patient should stay in bed for the first few days. Give plenty of liquid, using a straw to drink through to avoid pain. The application of heat to the swollen areas, by wringing out pieces of linen in fairly hot water, may ease the pain. If the patient develops a headache or vomits, call the doctor again.

Mumps orchitis

This is a rare complication in children, but occurs in about 20 per cent of adult males. There is swelling or tenderness in one or both testicles, sometimes followed by a reduction in size of the testes; but sterility is thought to occur only rarely.

Scarlet fever

This fairly uncommon illness starts two to four days after contact with an infected person, but can also be transmitted by infected clothes.

Symptoms Onset of symptoms is rapid, with a high temperature and a very sore throat. The patient may vomit, complain of a headache, will look flushed with a characteristic pallor round the mouth. The rash, which appears within 24 to 72 hours on the face and spreads rapidly downwards, consists of an overall flush which may be superimposed with tiny red pin-point spots. The rash lasts for a few days and is followed immediately by a fine peeling of the skin where the rash was.

Examination of the throat and mouth shows bright red swollen tonsils which may be covered with a white coating.

At the beginning of the illness, the tongue appears to be covered by a thick white coating through which red points can be seen, the size of pinheads. After two or three days, this will disappear leaving a red shiny surface, again with the prominent red spots. The lymph nodes in the neck are usually enlarged and tender.

Treatment General care of the patient is similar to that of measles, keeping him in bed with plenty to drink and aspirin to relieve pain in the throat. As scarlet fever is a bacterial infection, it is one of the few contagious diseases for which antibiotics are indicated. The antibiotic may have to be given by injection to begin with. Within 24 to 48 hours the patient will begin to feel better. However, watch out for signs of complications after a few days, such as earache or a rise in temperature.

The patient should be isolated until the infection has cleared – usually about three weeks. The doctor will advise you about quarantine for contacts.

Whooping cough

This disease is highly infectious and is caused by a bacterial germ which cannot be treated by antibiotics.

Quarantine table

Disease	Incubation	QUARANTINE	
		Patients	Contacts
Chicken pox	10–20 days	Until scabs fall off	14 days
German measles	5–21 days	7 days from rash appearing	21 days
Measles	7–14 days	10 days from rash appearing	14 days
Mumps	14–28 days	7 days after swelling gone	28 days
Scarlet fever	7 days	Consult doctor	Consult doctor
Whooping cough	6–18 days	28 days from start of illness	21 days

Note Quarantine for contacts of chicken pox, German measles and mumps is often not required nowadays, as it is considered sensible for children to have these diseases early. They can be much more serious if caught later in life, particularly mumps in the case of males and German measles in the case of females. If a woman catches German measles during pregnancy, the foetus can be affected.

Formerly dangerous diseases, such as poliomyelitis and whooping cough, are normally avoided by early immunisation and inoculation, as is tuberculosis.

Symptoms The disease develops seven to ten days after contact, with a temperature, a general feeling of illness and a cold. During the second week coughing spasms develop and the sufferer may cough up to thirty times without stopping, possibly vomiting after coughing. The disease usually settles within four to six weeks.

 WARNING

If a child under one year contracts whooping cough, hospital treatment will be necessary, as there may sometimes be difficulty in breathing after a coughing spell.

Treatment Keep the patient in a warm, draught-free room, though well ventilated – the slightest stimulus will set off a bout of coughing. The doctor will prescribe cough medicine.

Coughs

The cough reflex depends on sensitive nerve endings in the linings of the windpipe and the lung tubes. When these are irritated by any foreign substance, coughing follows.

Treatment If a cough is not painful, is bringing up colourless phlegm easily and is not keeping you awake, there is little point in taking anything for it. There are, however, many proprietary brands of cough medicine sold over the counter, usually expectorant mixtures designed to 'loosen the phlegm' and soothe the discomfort caused by persistent coughing. Mild versions are available for children.

When a cough is due to an infection, medically prescribed antibiotics are the real curing agents.

 WARNING

If a cough persists, do not attempt to suppress it in the hope that it will go away. It is a signal that something is wrong and should be referred to a doctor.

Home treatment The use of a vaporizer, steam or balsam inhalations and rubbing the chest with a proprietary vapour rub can all be soothing and provide relief, especially if the chest feels tight. Hot drinks of lemon, which acts as a mild expectorant, and honey, can help to soothe an irritated throat.

Cramp

Cramp most commonly affects the feet, calves and hands. Old people, diabetics and those with a low blood calcium level are often prone to cramp, for which medical help should be sought.

Cramp from cold

A cold atmosphere and contact with cold material can both provoke muscle cramp. Contact with cold bedclothes and a cold bedroom can combine to produce a rapid cooling of the feet, the feet and legs move restlessly and then the muscles, especially those leading to the toes, go into cramp.

Treatment This type of night cramp is

treated by applying vigorous massage to the cold feet and by stretching the toes, feet and calves. A warm bed and bedroom reduce the risk.

Cramp from heat

An excessively hot working environment, strenuous exercise and very hot weather may also cause cramp, the spasm being thought to come from a loss of fluid and salts through excessive sweating. The sufferer may become dizzy and unsteady, with a flushed face and body, dilated pupils and laboured breathing.

Treatment Get medical attention and give the patient salt water drinks.

Avoiding heat cramp In very hot conditions, drinking water should contain salt added in the proportion of about $\frac{1}{4}$ teaspoon to one glass. This replaces salt lost by sweating. Alternatively, salt tablets can be taken with water.

Cramp from food and drink

Food 'Stitch' or diaphragm muscle cramp and cramp in the leg muscles may occur during vigorous exercise immediately after a heavy meal. For this reason people are usually advised to rest for a while after eating, before taking exercise. The cramp usually passes soon if the sufferer rests.

Alcohol Cramp may be a symptom of excessive drinking. Massage and warmth applied to the affected area will ease the discomfort.

Cramp from menstruation

Many women suffer from menstrual cramps at least some time during their menstruating lives. For those with severe pain, a doctor can usually help. Otherwise hot-water bottles and painkillers are the most effective cures. Some authorities also suggest gentle exercise, particularly yoga, as a means of lessening the strain.

Ear disorders

Catarrh with deafness

This may follow colds or influenza. If it persists for more than three days, consult a doctor.

Discharge from the ear

Whatever the type, a discharge from the ear needs urgent medical attention. Never put anything into the ear unless prescribed by the doctor.

Earache

If a child wakes at night with earache, check if there is fever, sweating and sickness. If so, call the doctor at once. Otherwise give a dose of junior aspirin and put a warmed blanket or warmed cotton wool on the outside of the ear.

Persistent earache, particularly in children, always needs proper medical diagnosis.

Giddiness

This may be caused by inflammation or infection of the inner ear balance mechanism. A doctor can prescribe a drug to relieve this.

Persistent giddiness may be caused by otitis media, or occur after a blow on the head. This always needs medical investigation.

Inflammation

If the ear flap or outer ear canal becomes inflamed it can be caused by water from swimming or by accidental roughening. If the ear flap and ear canal become sore and red and little blisters or boils occur, consult a doctor.

Middle ear infection (otitis media)

This is a common cause of earache in adults and children. It is usually accompanied by fever and sweating, and sometimes by vomiting and loose bowel motions. A doctor should be called.

Wax

Hard or excess wax can be cleared by softening drops prescribed by the doctor, or he may clear the wax by syringing with warm water.

Fever

The normal temperature for most people is 37°C (98·6°F) but temperatures slightly above or below this may be normal. Provided that the temperature does not go over 40°C (104°F) there is no need to resort to extreme measures to try and lower it. Lightheadedness sometimes occurs where the patient appears to have hallucinations.

Convulsions

Children under the age of six who have temperatures over 40°C (104°F) may suffer from fits and loss of consciousness. Cool the child immediately by removing clothing, sponging with cool water and using a fan. Get medical attention. Let the skin dry naturally.

Taking the temperature

In adults and children over six, the temperature should be taken by mouth. The thermometer is placed under the tongue and kept there for two minutes.

In younger children take the temperature under the armpit with the arm pressed firmly against the side of the chest, or in the groin with the legs kept together. The skin temperature is always 0.5°C (1°F) lower than the oral temperature.

Care of thermometers

Clean with cold water and antiseptic after use, do not put under a hot tap.

Shake the mercury level down by holding the stem firmly, with the bulb away from you, and giving several good shakes.

Breaking a thermometer If a thermometer breaks when not in use, clear up the mercury, wrap it and put into an outside dustbin.

If one breaks in use, check that the bulb and glass are present and rinse the mouth with water. If glass or mercury has been swallowed, take the patient to the nearest hospital immediately.

Food poisoning

Food poisoning is caused by eating food which contains either too many dangerous germs or too high a concentration of a poisonous substance. The contamination may be by chemical poisons, by the toxins of certain germs or by the germs themselves.

Symptoms The three main symptoms are diarrhoea, vomiting and abdominal pain.

Symptoms may appear anything from 20 minutes to two days after eating contaminated food. Generally the earlier cases are associated with vomiting and tend to last only five or six hours, whereas the later cases are associated more with diarrhoea and abdominal pain and tend to last one or two days.

If more than one person develops symptoms of this type at the same time, food poisoning should be suspected

Treatment In general there is no specific treatment for food poisoning. The main hazard to the sufferer, apart from acute shock and collapse, which is rare, is that he may lose too much body fluid and become dehydrated.

Treatment therefore consists of rest and replacement of fluids. If frequent vomiting goes on after four to six hours call a doctor. A doctor should also be called if diarrhoea persists.

▲ WARNING ▲

The danger signs to look for are those of shock – cold, pale, sweaty skin and fast, faint pulse. If these signs occur in any person with severe diarrhoea or vomiting, call a doctor immediately.

Gastric disorders

Disorders of the stomach can cause loss of appetite, some degree of pain, diarrhoea or vomiting – or even a combination of all these symptoms.

▲ WARNING ▲

Diarrhoea in a baby under the age of one year should be reported to your doctor, in case the infant has become dehydrated.

Acute gastritis

This can result from infection, excessive eating or drinking or taking of drugs in excess.

Symptoms They are nausea and discomfort in the abdomen, accompanied by diarrhoea in cases of *gastro-enteritis*. Most forms of acute gastritis settle down in a few hours. If symptoms persist after 24 hours, consult your doctor.

Treatment Keep the patient warm and in bed. Do not give solid food, only small sips or spoonfuls of water.

Half a teaspoon of bicarbonate of soda dissolved in a tumbler of warm water will give some relief if there is acute acidity with sourness in the mouth.

Provide only light food, avoiding fatty or spiced dishes until recovery is complete.

If blood or blood-stained stomach contents are vomited up, this is an emergency needing immediate hospital treatment.

Chronic gastritis

Is usually found in heavy drinkers or people with a history of acute gastritis, but can also occur as part of an emotional upset or anxiety state.

Symptoms These are the same as for acute gastritis but include poor appetite, particularly early in the day.

Treatment This includes avoidance of too much fatty food. Meals should be small and frequent rather than bulky and occasional. Milk is useful in relieving symptoms.

Simple dyspepsia

Indigestion is usually relieved by milk, milky drinks or by antacid preparations which can include ingredients for relieving flatulence.

Home nursing

Nursing minor ailments at home is largely a matter of common sense. Serious illnesses are generally treated in hospital. However, you may find yourself with a child suffering from one of the common childhood illnesses (see Contagious diseases) or perhaps someone having to face a long convalescence.

Nursing a convalescent

Choose a well-ventilated, sunny room or even a room downstairs where the patient can feel more involved with the family and can get some interest from looking out at the garden or seeing passers-by in the street.

The sickroom should be simply furnished without a lot of heavy drapes or thick rugs that need constant brushing and cleaning. This may mean removing some of the furnishings temporarily. Make sure that there is a table of convenient height next to the bed so that the invalid can reach books, papers, spectacles and so on. Place a small hand bell so that the patient can call for help whenever necessary. See that the bed is not in a draught – a screen can help here. Make sure there are plenty of pillows for anyone who has to be in bed for any length of time.

 ★   **HANDY HINT**   ★

Triangular-shaped foam pillow supports which are easily available, are often more satisfactory than a pile of pillows which are apt to slip about.

A fleecy, mock-sheepskin underblanket is both warm and soft, and completely washable.

When necessary ask your visiting nurse to show you the best way of making the bed and giving a 'blanket bath'.

Travel sickness

A common form of nausea suffered by people of all ages is travel sickness (whether by air, sea or land) and motion sickness, experienced in lifts, on fairground machinery and cable cars.

Travel sickness, with or without vomiting, is generally more common in children, many of whom may soon grow out of it. However, it can persist into adulthood or even appear then for the first time.

Treatment The most effective way of dealing with this distressing complaint is by use of the modern anti-nausea drugs available from chemists or by prescription. Treatment generally involves taking a tablet half an hour before setting off and another about halfway through the journey, if it is a fairly long one.

These proprietary drugs are safe for children, provided the instructions on the packet are followed or the doctor's instructions adhered to. They are not always safe for pregnant women, so check with your doctor before taking any if you are pregnant.

Safeguards Whether or not the sufferer has taken an anti-nausea drug, it is sensible to take with you on a journey a supply of small, strong bags in case of sickness – such as those provided on aircraft – or polythene bags, together with a damp face cloth.

Worms

In humans, worms are manifested by a parasitic infestation of the bowel.

Pork worm
This can result from eating under-cooked pork. It causes nausea and vomiting for about 24 hours, followed a week later by a high temperature, aches and pains and puffy eyes.

A doctor will prescribe tablets to clear the condition.

Tapeworm
These are white, flat and ribbon-like in form, made up of many segments.

Signs The tiny head of the tapeworm sticks firmly to the small bowel. Segments of the tapeworm break off from time to time and pass out recognisably in the motions.

Treatment The sufferer should take a stool sample with segments for medical tests. Most tapeworms can be removed by a two-day therapy which kills the worm. However, the doctor will want to see the actual head of the worm in the motion, for if this is not dislodged the tapeworm will simply grow again.

Threadworms
These roundworms are most common in children and are visible in the stools, looking like tiny wriggling white threads.

Symptoms Itching of the anal region, particularly at night, is the main symptom.

Treatment The worms may be treated by several forms of medication prescribed by the doctor.

Strict cleanliness – regular bathing and washing – is important. A doctor may prescribe a local anti-itch cream as well. Other members of the family may be harbouring threadworms and should go for examination if the worms return.

It is important that the sufferer or the parent of the child should not feel embarrassed to come forward for early and effective treatment. Worm infestation can be troublesome, uncomfortable and prolonged if not recognised and treated.

CHAPTER 7

FIRST AID

Artificial respiration•Bandages
Bleeding•Broken bones•Burns•Fits
Hypothermia•Poisoning

Artificial respiration

If confronted with a person who has stopped breathing, from whatever cause, start forcing air into the unconscious person's lungs immediately. Seconds count as the brain cells cannot survive more than three to five minutes without oxygen; the victim may die or sustain permanent brain damage.

The most effective way to do this is by mouth-to-mouth or 'kiss of life' artificial respiration.

Check for breathing

These signs will help tell you if someone has stopped breathing:

● Lack of chest movement.
● Blue or grey colour in cheeks, lips, ears or fingernails.
● Frothy breathing attempts.

Listen closely against the mouth and nose or check if a mirror held in front of the mouth or nose mists over.

Start artificial respiration immediately you are sure there is no breathing.

▲ WARNING ▲

Victims of carbon monoxide poisoning are not blue but a bright, unnatural cherry red.

Clearing the airway

Lay the patient on his back and tilt the head back as far as possible so that the tongue falls against the palate and the airway is clear. Victims of collapse or accident often have vomit blocking the mouth, or the tongue has fallen back to block the back of the throat.

If there is debris, for example from drowning, or vomit in the mouth, turn the patient on his side and quickly clear out the mouth with your fingers. Leave false teeth in place unless broken.

If breathing does not restart IMMEDIATELY, turn the patient on his back and start artificial respiration.

Mouth-to-mouth artificial respiration

1 With the casualty on his back, support the back of the neck with one hand and press the top of the head so that it is tilted backwards, pulling the chin upwards. This may be enough to restart breathing. If consciousness does not return, but you can see that his breathing continues, turn the casualty into the recovery position.

1

2 If breathing does not restart by itself, take a deep breath, pinch the patient's nose so that it is closed, and blow steadily but gently into the mouth, making a good air seal with your lips. This should make the chest rise.

3 Turn your head away and take another breath. Watch for the chest to fall again.

2

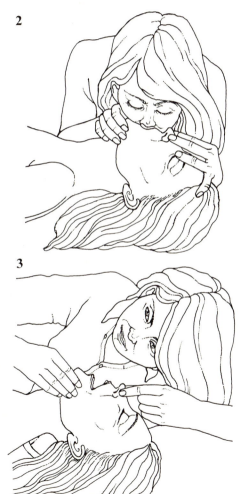

3

4 Start with fairly quick breaths to inflate the lungs, then continue with one breath every five seconds or so.

5 Once the airway is clear and you are getting air into the lungs, the casualty's colour should soon improve.

If the stomach inflates, turn the patient on to his side and firmly push the stomach down to expel the air before resuming resuscitation.

6 You may have to continue artificial respiration for some time before breathing restarts naturally. Once it has restarted, place the casualty in the recovery position, lying on his side with his uppermost arm and leg both bent, extended on the ground in front. Tilt the chin well upwards.

7 Cover the casualty with a blanket or coat and send for medical help.

Alternative methods

Nose Sometimes due to injuries or other reasons, it may not be possible to blow into the casualty's mouth. In this case hold the mouth closed and blow steadily but gently into the casualty's nose every five seconds, as previously described.

Babies If the casualty is a baby, make a seal with your mouth over the *mouth and nose together*. Breathe gently, never violently, into its lungs with a puff of your cheeks. This should be done at approximately double the adult rate – that is about *20–25 times a minute*.

Bandages and slings

To apply a bandage or sling correctly is most important and yet not very easy.

149

Here are a few points to remember:

● Make sure the bandage or sling is large enough to cover the injured area and secure a dressing.

● Always support the limb to be bandaged at an angle comfortable for the patient.

● Never apply a damp bandage, as it will tighten as it dries and become uncomfortable.

● Make sure the bandage is not too tight as it may impede circulation.

● Fingers or toenails should not be covered by a bandage as the colour of the skin beneath the nail indicates excessive pressure. If it is white or bluish and the fingers are cold, loosen the bandage.

● A bandage covering a sprain or bleeding must be secure and firm, but again not too tight.

● Make knots and fix pins where they cannot chafe or catch.

● Fasten triangular bandages and slings with a flat reef knot. Pad underneath with cotton wool if the patient is uncomfortable, or re-tie the knot.

Using triangular bandages
Arm sling

1 Place the whole cloth under the injured arm, with the top point beyond the elbow and one end over the good shoulder.

2 Carry the other end up over arm and shoulder on the injured side.

3 Adjust so that the arm is fully supported and fasten with a knot just above the collar bone.

4 Finish by bringing the point forward over the elbow like an envelope flap and fastening with a safety pin.

Triangular sling This is an alternative way of applying an arm sling.

1 Lay the open bandage over the forearm and hand with the point facing outward and going well beyond the elbow, and the upper ends on the sound shoulder.

2 Ease the base of the bandage under the forearm and elbow (the hand should

1

2

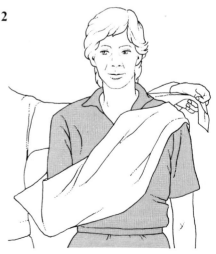

be resting on the sound shoulder) and bring the lower end up around the back and over the sound shoulder.

3 Gently adjust the tension of the sling to give maximum support; tie the ends in a flat reef knot in front of the hollow under the collar bone on the same side.

4 Tuck the point round the elbow and fasten with a safety pin.

3

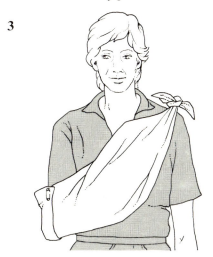

Folded triangular bandage Folded into a broad or narrow strip, the triangular bandage can be very versatile and binds wounds of the thigh, knee, elbow, lower leg and arm.

Hand and foot bandages Fold the triangular bandage to make a smaller triangle when bandaging a smaller area.

Head bandages Place the base around the forehead, cross the ends at the back and tie in front, pull down the point at the back and pin on top of the head.

Roller bandages

These bandages really do need practise as they are fairly difficult to apply well.

1 Bandage the limb in the position in which it is to remain.

2 Hold the bandage with the rolled-up part uppermost and the outer surface against the skin area to be dressed.

3 Unroll only a few inches at a time so that you can always keep a proper hold on the tension as you proceed.

4 With each successive turn of the bandage, cover two-thirds of the preceding turn and make sure that the free edges are lying parallel.

5 Start bandaging from the inside of a limb and work outwards, and from below an area, upwards.

Reversing When bandaging a gradually broadening area such as the forearm, you will find after several turns that the bandage will not lie evenly, but makes a 'cuff' of slack bandage. When this happens, make a reverse.

1 Place your finger across the turn being made and, using it as a bar, fold the bandage diagonally inwards and downwards the way you have come.

2 Take it round the limb and, when you come to the area of the previous fold, repeat the fold.

3 Continue until all the slack has been taken up and the bandage lies evenly.

Fastening If you have no safety pin, cut the end of the bandage in half for about 15cm (6in), wind the two ends round the limb and tie with a reef knot.

Bites and stings

Insect Bites

Prevention People who are susceptible to reactions from the bites of midges, flies and mosquitoes should wear a proprietary fly repellent cream or lotion on the face, ankles and wrists.

Treatment In most cases calamine lotion can bring relief to reactions from insect bites. For less severe reactions, a mild antiseptic lotion, or soluble aspirin rubbed on the bitten area, will reduce swelling and discomfort. Warm salt water will also soothe bites and act as a mild antiseptic.

Any severe reaction to an insect bite should be referred to a doctor.

Horseflies, midges, mosquitoes, sandflies The bites of these flies do not vary much – after the bite there is an acute itch, followed by a red itchy spot which persists for a day or two and can form a blister. These bites rarely cause trouble, but can become infected if scratched. In some parts of the world mosquitoes and sandflies carry diseases. Consult your doctor about vaccination if you are travelling to a tropical country. Treatment is as for insect bites above.

Bee and wasp stings

The normal reaction is a painful red area surrounded by blanched skin. The blackish sting is embedded in the centre of the reddened area.

Treatment If possible, scrape away the sting immediately with your finger nails, or ease out with tweezers, taking care not to squeeze the poison sac. If this is difficult, do not persist as it will just spread the venom. Clean the area, then treat with a bicarbonate of soda paste or surgical spirit for bee stings; dab with vinegar or lemon juice for wasps. If the swelling is severe add a cold compress.

 WARNING

Bee and wasp stings are dangerous if the victim is stung in the mouth or throat. Give a mouthwash of 1 teaspoon bicarbonate of soda to a tumbler of water, and then ice to suck. Get medical attention.

If there is difficulty in breathing, pains in the abdomen, vomiting or shock, the victim should be taken to hospital or a doctor called immediately. People known to have severe reactions should always have a treatment kit at hand.

Nettle stings

Nettle sting is acid so a paste made from bicarbonate of soda and water or weak ammonia will ease the pain. In emergencies, use cool leaves or water.

Snake bites

There is only one poisonous snake in the British Isles – the adder. This may be grey, yellow or reddish-brown with a dark zig-zag or diamond shape down its back. It has a wide head with a V-shaped mark on it. The bite is rarely fatal.

The bitten part swells up and appears inflamed or bruised. If you do get bitten, keep calm and try to rest. Take a painkiller such as aspirin, wash the bitten area with soap and water and remove any venom you can see.

Cover the wound with a clean dressing. Occasionally symptoms such as sweating, vomiting, diarrhoea and abdominal pain ensue, but if nothing has happened in two hours it can be assumed that nothing will happen.

If symptoms do develop the victim should be taken to hospital or a doctor called.

Animal and bird bites

All wounds inflicted by animals and birds, however minor, should be treated with respect.

Treatment Bites should be washed immediately with plenty of water, then antiseptic. Take the victim to hospital or a doctor for an anti-tetanus injection, and to have the wound stitched and dressed if necessary.

Prevention It is a wise precaution to ensure that all your family receive anti-tetanus injections every five years.

Cats Scratches occasionally become infected, in which case the doctor will probably prescribe antibiotics.

Dogs Bites should be treated as those from other animals. If there is any suspicion that the animal is rabid, anti-rabies injections are essential.

Bleeding

However and wherever bleeding occurs, the first priority is to stop it.

External bleeding

Bleeding from skin wounds, punctures, cuts, grazes, etc. is quickly visible.

Arterial bleeding Bleeding involving a cut artery can be recognised because it is bright red and flows in jets or spurts, pulsing with the heart beat. *Urgent medical attention is needed.*

Blood from a vein This is dark red and tends to flow steadily in a brisk stream.

Medical attention is needed.

Capillary bleeding Bleeding, as in the case of a cut finger, is recognised by its slow oozing and welling of blood. It is generally much less serious.

Internal bleeding

Internal bleeding may not be noticed until the victim becomes pale and shows symptoms of shock with rapid pulse beat and breathing. Other signs are bruising and swelling round the joints, blood in urine or bowel movements, or when a person coughs or vomits blood.

 ▲ WARNING ▲
Urgent medical attention is required if internal bleeding is suspected. Keep the victim lying down and resting.

Blood loss

Although a healthy adult can lose 0.5 litres (about 1 pint) of blood without serious harm (*the amount is much less for children*), any bleeding should be stopped as soon as possible. If a person loses more than this amount of blood, he or she will be seriously weakened.

What to do

Arterial bleeding Urgent medical attention is needed.

Blood from a vein Apply pressure and elevate injured area, if possible. Apply ice or cold compresses. If the bleeding is serious, urgent medical attention is needed.

Capillary bleeding Remove any dirt, etc. with cold, running water. Clean the surrounding area. Apply a sterile dressing large enough to cover the area generously. Use a dry gauze or vaseline soaked dressing depending on the injury. Apply further dressings on top if the blood seeps through.

Nose bleeds The casualty should sit up, lean slightly forward and pinch the nose just below the bony area where it is soft for 10 minutes while breathing through the mouth. In some cases an ice pack applied to the nose will stop the flow. After bleeding stops, breathing should be through the mouth; the nose should not be blown for several hours.

If the bleed was caused by a blow, a doctor should check to make sure there are no other injuries to the nose.

Bleeding from the gums (usually following a tooth extraction). Place a thick pad of cotton wool over the source of bleeding. The casualty should bite on the pad while supporting the chin with the hand. Bleeding should stop within 10 to 20 minutes.

▲ WARNING ▲

Do not fill the bleeding socket with a plug of cotton wool as this will disturb the blood clot when the plug is removed.

Bleeding from the tongue, lip or cheek The casualty should sit up. Firm pressure on the wound, compressing the area between finger and thumb, using a clean cloth or handkerchief, should stop the bleeding. If possible, give very cold water mouthwashes.

Tongue bleeding can be stopped by putting out the tongue as far as is comfortably possible and holding it out for about 10 minutes. This causes pressure on blood vessels at the root of the tongue. If the bleeding persists, get medical help.

Palm of the hand The arm should be raised and the fist clenched around a thick pad covering the wound. A bandage can be applied to the whole fist, helping to keep the pad in place.

Bleeding from the ear This can be a sign of possible skull fracture. Medical help should be obtained quickly.

Internal bleeding The casualty needs urgent medical attention.

Spontaneous bleeding Bleeding with no known injury as the cause. The bleeding should first be stopped then medical advice obtained.

Bones, broken

Types of fracture

Closed (or simple) fracture The bone is broken but there is no wound or break in the overlying skin.

Open (or compound) fracture There is a break or wound in the skin and the broken ends either stick out from the wound or create an opening from the outside down to the broken bones inside. Fractures such as these require *urgent medical attention* to stop the wound and the broken area from becoming infected.

Greenstick fracture This is only seen in a child. The bone bends on impact with a force and breaks on one side of the bone only, without cracking right across.

What to do
● Reassure the patient.
● Watch for shock in a major fracture.
● Keep the casualty warm and, *as long as spine fracture is not suspected*, prop up a small pillow under the head and turn the head slightly to the side. This will prevent the tongue falling back should the casualty fall unconscious.
● Don't move a major fracture casualty unless in danger.
● Don't try to put bones back into a normal position.
● Don't try to give casualty anything to eat or drink – in case an anaesthetic is needed.
● Stop any severe bleeding and cover with a light sterile dressing.
● Tie bandages firmly but not tightly.
● Be ready to loosen them if swelling continues.
● Tie bandages with reef knots or bows. Tie on the side away from the break.

Emergency treatment of fractures
Elbow This can be a serious fracture because the artery to the arm may be involved. Support the head with a pillow. Place loose padding between injured arm and body. Secure the arm to the body with three broad bandages.

Arm Place a roll of padding in the armpit and then support the arm with a sling.

Shoulder and collar bone As for arm.

Hip and thigh Pad the natural hollows of the body (under neck, small of back, behind knees and ankles) with soft packing. Place packing between thighs, knees and ankles. Bring the good leg towards the injured one *slowly and*

gently. Tie the feet and ankles together with a bandage in a figure of eight. Keep the shoes on. Bandage around the knees and above and below the break.

Pelvis Lie the casualty comfortably (usually on the back) and pad and bandage as for a hip fracture. The casualty should not try to pass urine.

> **▲ WARNING ▲**
> Unless you have medical training, don't try to move a casualty with suspected spine fracture unless absolutely necessary.

Knee to foot Pad between the thighs, knees and ankles and bandage as for thigh. A temporary splint can be helpful for these fractures; umbrellas or folded newspapers are suitable.

Feet and toes Leave the shoe on but remove fastenings. Don't let the casualty put weight on the injured foot.

Jaw Place a broad bandage or scarf under the chin and tie on top of head.

Skull Any casualty unconscious for even a short time should have medical attention. Watch the patient for any change in his conscious state or for sleepiness. Look for bleeding or a watery flow from around the eyes, nose and ears. If there is an open wound, cover it with a light sterile dressing.

Burns and scalds

Burns are caused by dry heat, such as flames and electricity; scalds by wet heat such as boiling water or steam; and by corrosive chemicals.

Dry burns and scalds

1 Flood the burned area with cold water. Use the running cold tap, basin, bath or shower. Areas like the face or chest that cannot be immersed should be covered by a thick cloth soaked in cold water.

2 Continue this for 10 minutes. Don't remove burned clothing.

3 Cover the burned area and surrounding skin with a sterile dressing or clean non-fluffy piece of material. Secure loosely with a bandage.

4 If badly burned, replace fluid loss by giving small drinks of water every 10 minutes. Never try to give water by mouth to an unconscious person.

5 Get medical attention immediately.

To the eye Cool by holding the head under gently running cool water, or put the face into a basin of cool water and make the casualty blink continually. Or lie or sit the person down with his head tilted back and turned towards the affected side. Flush the eye with tepid or cool water, holding the lids apart with your fingers. Put on a dry, light dressing and get medical attention.

To the mouth Arrange for removal to hospital. Lie the casualty in the recovery position (see Artificial respiration). Watch for breathing difficulties and be prepared to give artificial respiration. Give sips of cold water, if conscious, and put cold wet cloths on the throat.

Burning clothing If clothing is burning, wrap the casualty in a rug or blanket or similar heavy material, or roll him across the floor. This will put out the flames. Do not touch the clothing. Get the casualty to hospital as quickly as possible.

Chemical burns

1 Remove the chemical immediately by flushing with copious quantities of running cold water. Remove contaminated clothing while doing this.

2 Continue washing for 10 minutes.

3 Continue as for Burns and scalds.

To the eye As for burns to the eye, but milk can be used to flush the eye at first. Make sure no chemical is held under the eyelids. Rinse under the lids. Protect the uninjured eye.

To the mouth Flush with water. Treat as for burns and scalds to the mouth.

Electrical burns

1 Make sure the current is switched off before going near the casualty.

2 Listen for breathing. If none, apply artificial respiration. (See Artificial respiration.)

3 Get medical attention immediately.

See also HOME SAFETY – Fire.

Choking

This can often result from spasm due to panic. Attempts should be made to calm the patient. Adults can sometimes be helped by giving them three or four sharp slaps between the shoulder blades.

Choking children

Children should be placed either over an adult's shoulder in a position with the head forward and hanging downwards, or across an adult's knee with the head and chest pointing downwards. Give the child three or four sharp slaps between the shoulders.

Small children Hold by the feet upside down. Slap between the shoulders three or four times.

Bones in the throat

Any bone stuck in the throat may give rise to reflex actions such as coughing or vomiting, either of which may help to shift the obstruction.

Other measures are swallowing a chunk of dry bread or pieces of raw apple – the bone may be swallowed with it. Large gulps of water, smaller sips of oily liquids such as olive oil or medicinal liquid paraffin, or sucking an ice cube, all lubricate the lining and may free the bone as well as soothing the scratched throat.

Concussion

Concussion is a temporary disturbance of brain function, caused by a blow to the head or a heavy fall which jars the spine.

Symptoms

Usually the victim of concussion is dazed or knocked unconscious for a few seconds or minutes and is pale, cold and clammy. When he comes round he will almost certainly have a bad headache and feel sick and giddy.

Very often, concussed people cannot remember the actual blow or fall or the minutes (in extreme cases, hours) leading up to it. With severe concussion, this state can last for weeks.

Delayed reaction Sometimes a head injury causes serious damage to the brain, which is not immediately apparent.

Signs of more severe damage Although the casualty may apparently recover from the initial knock-out he may later on become steadily more confused, slipping back into a coma. As his consciousness fades, the pupils of his eyes may become unequal in size.

Anyone who deteriorates in this way and becomes more and more difficult to rouse, must be admitted to hospital as an emergency.

What to do

● Place the casualty in the recovery position (see Artificial respiration), so that the tongue does not obstruct breathing.

● Loosen tight clothing and remove false teeth, spectacles, etc.

● If the casualty cannot be roused within five minutes, after shouting his name or pinching him hard, call a doctor or an ambulance immediately.

● DO NOT move or shake him.

● Inform the doctor of any special treatment you know the casualty is undergoing.

 ▲ WARNING ▲

Contact lenses and false teeth should be removed from a person who is unconscious for any length of time.

● When the casualty comes round, give aspirin or paracetamol tablets with water and make him lie down quietly for an hour or two.

● Ask him how he is feeling now and

then, to check his level of consciousness.

In most cases the casualty will be perfectly all right within a few days. Any unusual signs or behaviour should prompt immediate medical attention.

Dislocations

A dislocation occurs when ligaments and muscles that keep bone ends in position become stretched or torn, so that the bones are displaced from their normal position.

Symptoms

There is swelling round the joint and some bruising. The joint may be quite obviously deformed and can be moved only very slightly, or not at all. The amount of pain varies, but is increased by attempts to move the joint.

Compression of nerves may lead to weakness and numbness in the organs served by the nerves.

Blood vessels may similarly be compressed or torn by the dislocation. Any change in feeling, or marked difference in local skin colour or an unusual sensation should be taken seriously, and medical help obtained.

What to do

If you are in any doubt, treat a joint injury as if it were a fracture (see Bones, broken).

● Comfort the injured person and get medical help quickly.

● Do not try to move the bones back – this may lead to further damage.

● *Do not* give anything to eat or drink in case an anaesthetic is needed later.

● Move a casualty with an *upper joint* dislocation to hospital in a sitting position, one with *lower joint* injuries lying down. If possible support the injured joint with padding for comfort (see Bones, broken).

Jaw Carefully remove any dentures and support the lower jaw with a length of fabric or bandage tied under the jaw and over the head.

Elbow Do not use a sling, but secure elbow gently to the side of the body with a wide bandage.

Ear – foreign bodies

If a child has an object lodged in his ear, unless you can remove it easily with your fingers, do not try to remove it by poking about in the ear canal.

Removing an insect

If an insect has crawled into the ear, you can try to float it out by pouring a little tepid water into the ear. Place the good ear on a firm surface, hold the other ear firmly forward and pour the tepid water in from a small jug. If there is any pain in the ear get medical attention.

Electric shock

Shocks from mains electricity may range from a mild jolt to a very serious incident. Quick action is essential.

What to do

1 Ensure that the casualty is away from

the power source.

2 If still in contact, turn off the power.

3 If the power cannot be turned off, prise the victim away with a dry, non-conductive object: wood, plastic or rolled up paper, never metal.

⚠ WARNING ⚠

Do not touch the victim at this stage or you will also receive a shock.

4 Check that the victim is breathing.

5 If not breathing, check that the heart is beating. You must be *absolutely certain* about this.

6 If heart has stopped (and *only* if) start heart massage and mouth-to-mouth respiration, doing them alternately if alone (see Heart failure).

7 If the heart is beating but there is no breathing, start artificial respiration.

8 When the casualty is breathing, place in the recovery position (see Artificial respiration) until consciousness is regained. Keep warm.

9 When the victim is conscious, treat first for physical shock. Give hot, sweet tea with glucose rather than sugar if possible, but only if no internal injury or serious burns have been sustained.

10 In any incident except a minor one, get immediate medical attention.

Electrocution
See Artificial respiration.

Eye – foreign bodies

Never try to remove a foreign body from the iris and pupil (the dark part of the

eye) or any object embedded anywhere. Cover the eye, or both eyes, with a gauze pad, bandage it lightly and take the patient to hospital.

⚠ WARNING ⚠

Bandage both eyes if the injury is severe, as the injured one moves whenever the other one does, causing more pain.

What to do

● If the foreign body can be seen, is on the white part of the eye and can move around, moisten a piece of cotton wool or the corner of a handkerchief with cold water. Tilt the casualty's head back, and get him to move the eye in all directions until you locate the object. If you cannot remove it with a gentle wipe, it is probably stuck to the eyeball. Get medical attention.

● If the foreign body appears to be under the top lid, get the casualty to look downwards and then gently pinch the upper lid downwards and outwards over the lower lid.

● A water bath is another alternative. Place the casualty's head over a wash basin with the injured eye downwards. Pour warm water in from the inner corner of the eye.

Fainting

The most common causes of fainting are emotional upset, severe pain, fear, loss of blood, standing still for a long time in a hot atmosphere and standing rapidly from a seated position.

Symptoms

These sometimes give the sufferer time to ward off the faint or to call for help. The casualty may feel dizzy, giddy, weak or limp or everything may start to go black. Nausea, a tendency to yawn and a cold, clammy sweat are other possible symptoms. A person who is about to faint looks tense, pale and unsteady.

What to do

To yourself If the warning signs give you time, you should put your head down between your knees to allow blood to flow back into the brain.

To someone else If someone faints, here are several ways to help.

1 Loosen any tight clothing, particularly round neck, chest or waist.

2 Open a window or door or turn on a fan if possible.

3 Old-fashioned smelling salts can bring the person back to consciousness.

4 If the sufferer falls down flat as the result of a faint, this will allow the blood to flow to the head again. If not, place the casualty on his back on the floor and raise the feet on to a chair.

5 Give a hot drink on return to consciousness.

 ▲ WARNING ▲

Frequent faints within a short period, or faints during which the victim jerks or writhes, indicate that a medical check-up is needed.

Do not try to put head down between the knees once the casualty has lost consciousness.

First aid box

A family first aid box is absolutely essential in every home. Ready-prepared boxes can be bought, but it is cheaper to make up your own kit, using a biscuit tin or box with a well fitting lid to keep everything inside dust-free.

Contents

Adhesive strapping This should be 2.5cm (1in) wide. (Have a roll of non-allergic strapping, too.)

One tin of assorted adhesive dressings (or one tin of dressing strip).

Antiseptic A bottle of ready diluted antiseptic for cleaning wounds. One per cent centrimide works as a detergent and antiseptic.

Tube of antiseptic cream

Tube of antihistamine cream (or calamine lotion) For insect bites.

Soluble aspirin or paracetamol tablets Buy junior ones, too, if necessary.

Bandages One 5cm (2in) plain bandage, one 7.5cm (3in) plain bandage, one cotton crêpe bandage 5cm (2in) or 7.5cm (3in) wide and one triangular bandage.

Cotton wool and paper tissues Keep a roll of cotton wool for padding under bandages. Use paper tissues for some types of wound cleaning.

Cough medicines An expectorant to relieve 'wet' cough and a linctus to help 'dry' cough.

Gauze dressings Two packets of dry gauze dressings, 5cm (2in) square and 7.5cm (3in) square, and two packets of non-adherent perforated film or vaseline net dressings, 5cm (2in) and 10cm (4in) square should be adequate.

Small tubular gauze bandages For fingers and toes (with dispener).

Scissors, tweezers, safety pins (assorted sizes) and a packet of needles.

Thermometer

Fits

Epileptic fits are frightening to the onlooker, but cause little discomfort or danger to those who have them.

Grand mal or major fits

A typical epileptic fit starts suddenly. Sometimes the person has an advance warning. Sometimes he cries out. Then he falls to the ground. All the muscles go rigid for a few moments, the casualty does not breathe and his face goes blue. This is followed by a period of jerking which occurs in all the muscles, regularly and rhythmically. After this the casualty comes round, often feels sleepy and, having moved to a comfortable place, goes to sleep.

Minor fits

These rarely need any emergency aid.

Convulsions

These are common in childhood and are often due to a high temperature. Never leave a child who is having a convulsion. See FAMILY HEALTH – Fever.

What to do

1 Do not try to move the person having a fit unless he is in danger, but move any objects he may hurt himself against.

2 Put something soft under the casualty's head, or cradle his head in your hands, turning the face to the side so that any food or vomit will not impair breathing; this will also prevent the tongue from falling back. Make sure the throat airway is clear.

3 Place something soft, like a folded handkerchief, between the teeth, but do not use force or try to prise the casualty's mouth open.

4 Do not try to stop the limbs jerking.

5 When the fit is over, let the person lie quietly until conscious and stay with him until recovery, as he may be very confused and not know what has happened.

6 If one fit is followed by another, without a return to consciousness in between, get medical help.

Heart failure

The most acute type of heart failure is when a heart stops beating completely.

 WARNING

There is a maximum of four minutes to restart the heart and get blood circulating. After this short time, irreversible damage may be done to the brain cells.

Symptoms

● No pulse at the wrists or in the neck (feel with your fingers, not thumbs, on each side of the windpipe).

● No heartbeat, felt or heard, under the left breast.
● No breathing.
● Dilating (widening) pupils in the eyes.

What to do

1 Give the casualty one thump with your closed fist over the lower third of the breastbone, slightly to the left, or alternatively, three sharp slaps (as hard as you would do in anger).

Do not be afraid of breaking a rib, as restarting the heart is far more important. *Moderate the blow for children.*

2 Commence mouth-to-mouth artificial respiration (see Artificial respiration).

3 If, and only if, the blow has not restarted the heart, you will also need to apply external heart massage, while continuing the artificial respiration.

Method of external heart massage

1 Place the casualty on a hard surface on his back, face upwards.

2 Kneel to one side of the casualty and put one hand over the heel of the other, which has been placed over the lower third of the breastbone.

3 Apply full pressure straight downwards by raising yourself over the sufferer once per second. Keep your arms straight.

4 After each pressure, lift the hands to permit full chest expansion.

If you find yourself alone and have to do both mouth-to-mouth artificial respiration and applying pressure, for *adults* depress the chest about five times (once a second) to each blow down the mouth.

For *small children* use only one hand and give 80 pressures per minute instead of 60, with one breath every five seconds.

For *babies* use only two fingers on the middle of the breastbone and give 100 pressures a minute, again with one breath every five seconds.

5 Carry on the two processes until the vital signs return – pulses felt at neck and wrist, breathing established and pupils narrowing in size.

6 Where possible an ambulance should be called at once, but if you are single-handed your primary effort should be to restart the heart straight away.

7 Once breathing is established you can prop a pillow under the casualty's head until medical help arrives; but leave him lying on his back.

Heat exhaustion

Heat exhaustion

A person suffering from heat exhaustion has a normal temperature, fast and feeble pulse and pale, moist skin and sometimes shivers uncontrollably. Put the casualty in a cool atmosphere with plenty of fluids to drink, adding half a teaspoon of salt to each glass of liquid. Consult a doctor.

Heat stroke

A person suffering from heat stroke has a very high temperature, fast and strong pulse, hot dry skin and a headache. Get medical attention urgently. Sponge the casualty all over with cool or cold water or put into a tepid bath. Fan the casualty with anything suitable available. Take his or her temperature frequently, but do not let it drop below 39°C (102°F) as this might cause collapse.

Hypothermia

Hypothermia is a dangerous cooling down of the body as a result of persistent exposure to low temperatures.

Infants and elderly people are less able to maintain the normal body temperature of 36–37°C (96–98.6°F) in low temperatures.

 WARNING

Babies cannot communicate their coldness and many old people cannot feel it because of the diminished sensitivity of old age.

Preventing hypothermia

In babies Room temperatures should be at least 18°C (65°F), preferably warmer. A cold cot should be warmed with a hot water bottle before the baby is put into it, but do not leave the hot water bottle in the cot. Make sure the baby's clothing is warm, loose and covers the feet and limbs.

In old people Old people may not feel the temperature falling, or may be anxious to cut down on heating costs.

● Keep hands and feet warm with gloves, socks and stockings. Scarves and hats should be worn outside and inside, too, if necessary. Several layers of clothing are warmer than one thick layer. Wool is best for trapping heat. Warm nightwear should be worn in bed.

● Hot food and drinks help to maintain the body temperature. Eat regular meals – preferably in the room in which the food was cooked, to make the most of the cooker warmth.

● Keep bedrooms warm and heat the bed with a hot water bottle or extra low voltage electric blanket. Wear slippers and dressing gown if it is necessary to get up in the night. A nightcap or woolly scarf worn in bed can also help since heat can be lost quickly from the head.

● Old people should avoid sitting still too long and should keep as active as possible.

● Elderly people should be encouraged to make the most of any social service and financial assistance available to them for heating and insulation. In winter it can be helpful to live in one room and so conserve heat and fuel costs.

Symptoms

The sufferer will be drowsy, physically sluggish and may become unconscious. The skin feels cold and stiff and looks deathly pale. Breathing is shallow, the pulse slow and the pupils grow smaller.

A person suffering from hypothermia has a temperature between 28–32°C (82–90°F) and a special low-reading thermometer is required to assess the exact degree.

What to do

Anyone discovered in a state of hypothermia should be wrapped up with coats and blankets and taken to hospital as an emergency patient.

Poison and antidote chart

Poison	Antidote and first aid
Acids, e.g. acetic acid (vinegar).	No emetic; cupful milk; hospital quickly.
Alcohol-based liquids (perfume, aftershave lotion, white spirit, methylated spirit).	Cupfuls water or milk; hospital quickly.
Alkalis (ammonia, caustic soda).	No emetic; sips of lemon juice or vinegar; hospital quickly.
Ammonia and ammonia cleansers.	No emetic; sips of lemon juice or vinegar; hospital quickly.
Aspirin and aspirin-containing tablets or powders.	Give emetic* (these poisons often cause vomiting anyway); hospital quickly.
Berries, toadstools and all poisonous plants (yew, holly, laburnum).	No emetic; hospital quickly.
Bleach and bleaching agents.	No emetic; hospital quickly.
Caustic soda.	No emetic; hospital quickly.
Household cleansing powders.	No emetic; hospital quickly.
Curry powder and spices.	Cupfuls cold water or ice cream.
Disinfectants, antiseptics, deodorisers.	If not corrosive give emetic* (these poisons often cause vomiting anyway); hospital quickly.
Drain and oven cleaners.	No emetic; hospital quickly.
Dry cleaning agents, e.g. acetone.	No emetic; hospital quickly.

Poison	Antidote and first aid
Benzine, carbon tetrachloride. hydrogen peroxide.	No emetic; hospital quickly.
Ink.	No emetic; call doctor.
Insecticides.	No emetic; hospital quickly.
Medicines, e.g. cough mixture.	Give emetic*; hospital quickly.
Paints.	No emetic; hospital quickly.
Petrol, paraffin, petroleum products.	No emetic; vegetable or olive oil; hospital quickly.
Pills and tablets, e.g. sleeping tablets, vitamins in large doses.	Give emetic*; hospital quickly.
Polishes.	No emetic (often sick anyway); hospital quickly.
Rat poison.	Give emetic*; hospital quickly.
Soaps, detergents.	No emetic (invariably sick); plenty of water to drink; call doctor.
Tobacco.	No emetic; hospital quickly.
Turpentine.	No emetic; hospital quickly.
Washing soda.	No emetic; sips of lemon juice or vinegar; hospital quickly.
Weedkillers, horticultural chemicals.	No emetic; hospital quickly.
Whisky and alcoholic spirits.	Cupfuls water or milk; hospital quickly.
*Emetic = vomiting agent.	Do not use salt water or mustard water. Use ipecac syrup or place two fingers in back of throat.

Poisoning

Poisons are either corrosive or non-corrosive. If someone has swallowed a corrosive poison, such as caustic soda or bleach, he should not be made to vomit. If someone has taken a non-corrosive poison, such as medicines and pills, he should be made to vomit.

The cause of poisoning is usually obvious: either the victim has been seen to take the poison or there is evidence to be found.

Prevention
● Keep all medicines in a locked cupboard.
● Store all household cleaning materials out of the reach of children.
● Keep all dangerous substances in their original containers. Never put them in other bottles or containers, particularly bottles which have contained anything a child likes, such as lemonade.
● Throw away all leftover medicine, either by pouring it down the sink or flushing it down the lavatory.
● See also HOME SAFETY – Poisons.

Signs and symptoms
Poisoning should be suspected in any small child who becomes suddenly and unaccountably ill, particularly if the child is drowsy, uncommunicative, nauseous and shocked. The symptoms of shock are cold, pallor, sweating and a rapid, faint pulse.

Corrosive poisons
These burn the skin on contact and the most important sign of such poisoning is burning in or around the mouth.

What to do
Do not make the casualty vomit. If you do there will be further burning of the gullet. Give water to dilute the poison, or milk to neutralise the effect of the acid, or lemon juice or vinegar to neutralise the effect of an alkali. Egg white and vegetable or olive oil may also be helpful and have a soothing effect. Get medical attention.

Non-corrosive poisons
If the casualty is unconscious, do not make him vomit. Assess the pulse and respiration. If these are adequate, place him in the recovery position (see Artificial respiration).

If the casualty is not breathing, start mouth-to-mouth artificial respiration (see Artificial respiration).

If the casualty is conscious, make him vomit either by inserting two fingers far back into the mouth to cause gagging or, if it is available, by giving ipecac syrup (ipecacuanha). Keep a sample of vomit for medical testing.

It is no longer considered safe to use salt water or mustard water as emetics.

In all cases of poisoning, get medical help as quickly as possible.

★ **HANDY HINT** ★

Take the container with the suspected poison and a sample of any vomit with you, if possible.

Skin – foreign bodies

Fish hooks

If the fish hook has passed right through the flesh and emerged, cut the barb off with wire-cutters and pull the rest of the hook back and out.

If the hook is embedded in tissue, it must be pushed onwards and out, and dealt with as above. This is best done by a doctor or at hospital. A tetanus injection is advisable.

Once the hook is removed, the wound can be cleaned and dressed with an adhesive dressing.

Needles

These can become embedded in flesh and disappear. If they can be felt by the finger, they can be removed easily with an anaesthetic in the hospital. Otherwise it is best to leave them alone as they will eventually move nearer the surface. If any discomfort is felt, consult a doctor.

Splinters or thorns

If the end sticks out, remove with tweezers. Wash the area with antiseptic solution and apply antiseptic cream. If a splinter lodges under the nail and cannot be removed it may be necessary to get medical attention if it is causing discomfort.

Splinters under the skin should be removed with a sterilised needle. If it is too small to remove, cover with adhesive strapping and in a few days it will come out naturally.

For large visible embedded objects, like large splinters of wood or metal, get medical attention.

Sprains and strains

Sprains

Sharp twisting or over-stretching movements, or sudden pulling actions involving the ligaments and supporting tissue attached to joints, can cause sprains. The knee, ankle, shoulder and wrist are the most common joints to be sprained.

What to do

1 Place the affected joint in the most comfortable position.
2 Apply a series of cold compresses.
3 Rest the joint and, if possible, raise it, fully supported, a little above the natural position. A badly sprained ankle should be rested slightly raised, by giving support to the whole leg from heel to thigh.
4 A cold compress (a bandage soaked in cold water) can be bound firmly in place with a supporting bandage. A crêpe bandage is preferable, but any material, a scarf of a strip of cloth, can be used.

If a sprain occurs during walking or sport, support the joint by some kind of bandage until it can be properly treated. In the case of an ankle or foot, do not take off any footwear, but bandage over it, using a scarf, large handkerchief or other binding until you can reach home or get medical attention.

Sprains with fractures can occur (see Bones, broken), so medical attention should be sought if you suspect one.

Ruptured ligaments or tendons produced

marked changes in the joint and the appearance of the limb. Medical attention is usually needed.

Strains

These can cause swelling and pain and even some bruising. If the over-stretched or torn muscle is used the pain is increased.

Treatment Apply cold compresses to bring down any swelling and rest the affected part. Aspirin or paracetamol can be taken if necessary.

A supporting bandage is needed if the strain is a severe one. During the healing process, gentle exercise of the affected muscle helps to reduce stiffness.

Sunburn

It is essential, to prevent sunburn, to expose the skin only for short periods at a time and to apply a suitable screening agent. Always keep the head and back of the neck covered in strong sun, particularly those of children and elderly people.

Milder forms of sunburn can be soothed by the use of cold cream or, even better, calamine lotion.

In the case of severe sunburn or heat stroke, urgent medical attention is needed.

Some drugs cause an increased sensitivity to sunlight, so check with your doctor if you are on drugs and intend to do much sunbathing.

Heat rashes A sun-screening agent will help to prevent these. Calamine lotion can be used if a rash appears.

Swallowed objects

Small swallowed objects can pass through the gut quite normally, so do not panic.

The object should probably pass through the system within four or five days. An X-ray will be needed if it has not passed through by this time.

Sharp objects which have been swallowed need immediate medical attention.

Teeth

Knocked out tooth

If a child knocks out one of his permanent front teeth, place the tooth in a clean, wetted handkerchief. Take it and the child immediately to the nearest dentist.

If no dentist is available If there is no way of getting to a dentist, thoroughly clean the tooth, using only salt water and a toothbrush. Clean any cuts and abrasions in the mouth and then wash the mouth out with an antiseptic mouthwash. Re-insert the tooth into the socket.

After the insertion of the tooth, get the child to bite the teeth together on a handkerchief and try again to get dental help. Antibiotics and an anti-tetanus injection may also be necessary. (See also Bleeding.)

The same treatment can be tried when an adult knocks a tooth out, but it is usually not very successful.

CHAPTER 8

CLOTHES CARE

Dry cleaning•Dyeing•Furs•Ironing
Laundering•Mending•Shoes
Stains•Zips

No clothes can retain their smart, new look for ever, but regular care can help them to last and stay in good shape for longer, and cut down on cleaning costs.

Buttons

Sewing on buttons

On thick fabric, a flat button should be sewn on with a *shank* (a small stalk between the button and fabric) so that the button does not distort the button-hole or tear the fabric.

Take a couple of back stitches through the fabric where the button is to go. Slide a matchstick underneath the button and sew over it, *crossing* the thread between the button and the fabric to give a stronger shank. When the button is firmly fixed, bring the needle down through one of the holes in the button, slip the matchstick out and wind the thread round and round the shank, from top to bottom. Take the thread through to the back and fasten.

Strengthening A *thin material*, or one with a loose weave, can be strengthened with a small square of fabric placed on the inside of the garment and sewn on with the button.

For a *heavy coat*, button strain is avoided by placing a small keeper button on the inside of the coat and stitching through both buttons. Lay the top button over two matchsticks to allow room for the shank and sew on the button, at the same time sewing through matching holes on keeper button.

Remove the matchsticks and make a shank as before.

Darns

With garments where you want a real restoration job, there is nothing to beat darning by hand.

Fine drawing

This mends tears in thickish clothes with a nap.

1 Lay the edges of the tear exactly together and tack them lightly in place across the tear.

2 With a very fine needle and transparent thread (human hair is equally good) run diagonally to and fro across the tear, keeping the needle within the thickness of the cloth and bringing the needle out about 5mm ($\frac{1}{4}$in) above and below the tear. Keep the rows of stitching close together, working in any broken threads near the tear.

3 When the darn is finished, remove the tacking carefully and brush the nap of the material over the join. Press with an iron on the *wrong* side, over a damp cloth.

 ★ HANDY HINT ★

The colour range of darning wool sold on cards is limited. If you cannot get the colour you want, buy fine, crewel-type tapestry wool.

Making linen and hedge-tear darns

Examine the hole and check how far the thinning signs of wear extend by holding the fabric up to the light. Where the fabric is very threadbare, it is best to enlarge the hole by cutting away the thinnest parts round it. Extremely worn fabric does not give a sound foundation for darning.

Linen darns These are worked on the wrong side of the material, the lengthways threads being done first.

Run the threads through the material above and below the hole evenly, starting about 15mm ($\frac{5}{8}$in) from the worn area. Use small running stitches and keep in line with the existing threads (**a**). Carry the thread straight across the hole and into the material on the other side. Do not draw the loops too tight or the material may pucker.

When the hole is filled with lengthways threads, follow the same method crossways (**b**), weaving through the warp threads and keeping the threads close together so that the darned web is as close as the original fabric.

★ **HANDY HINT** ★

When darning materials that need to have some stretch, such as socks, work your second threads *diagonally* to ensure a little 'give'.

Hedge-tear darns Usually L-shaped tears, which can be darned with matching cotton or wool or with threads unravelled from the seams of the garment.

Darn with the usual running stitch, starting at one end of the L and working to the corner. Turn the work to complete the other half of the L, running

the rows at right angles to those of the first half, thus reinforcing the tear (**c**). Start work about 15mm ($\frac{5}{8}$in) outside the end of the tear and make the rows of stitching about 20mm ($\frac{3}{4}$in) long.

a
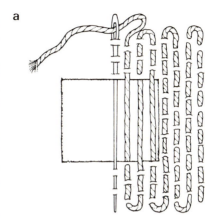

b
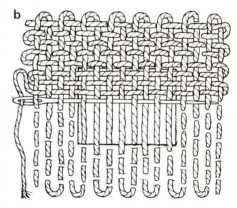

c
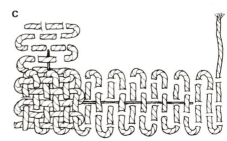

Darning knitwear (Swiss darning)

Use crewel wool, or a wool thinner than the knitting wool for strengthening.

Strengthening *Either* bring the needle out between horizontal threads, work upwards over a vertical thread, put in and bring out again between the next horizontals above.

Or bring the needle up through the base of a knitted stitch, round behind the head of the loop of the knitted stitch and back down through the back again, then up through the base of the next knitted stitch.

Mending holes Use wool of the same weight as that of the knitting.

1 First pick up any runs or ladders with a crochet hook so that the hole shape is as regular as possible.

2 Cut away any torn threads and free the loops round the hole. The threads must be cut so that a *square* hole is formed, with two or three extra stitches unravelled at each corner to allow the sides of the hole to be turned under and stitched in place.

3 Use a darning egg or mushroom as the threads must not be pulled tight. Run horizontal threads into the material, lining them up accurately with the rows of knitting needing to be replaced.

4 Make the stocking-web stitches by whipping over each 'rung' of horizontal threads in turn, moving up and down the darn.

Discoloured fabrics

White fabrics can become dull and discoloured for various reasons.

Restoring whiteness

Chlorine bleach This will whiten pure cotton or linen – do not use it on mixed fabrics. Follow the instructions and bleach at a low temperature.

Chloride of lime (powder) Also used for pure linen or cotton. Dissolve 25g (1 oz) powder in 4.5 litres (1 gallon) water. Let the articles soak for a little while and rinse thoroughly.

Fabric whiteners These can be bought for different types of fabric and can be added to the washing or rinsing water to remove discolouration. Be sure to choose the right type for the fabric you are treating.

Natural bleaching If you have a garden, sunshine is an excellent bleach for cotton and linen.

Dry cleaning

As its name suggests, 'dry' cleaning is a process of cleaning which uses special solvents rather than immersion in water. The fabric is usually steam ironed after the treatment. If you know that a garment needs special treatment, always tell the assistant.

Dry cleaning service

Re-texturing Many cleaners use a process of re-impregnation with resin for clothes which have been given a special finish during manufacture. This normally restores a cloth's crispness.

Stain removal Most dry cleaners will undertake to remove stains. If you know what caused the stain, tell the assistant or attach a label to the garment.

Special services These can include minor repairs, such as replacing zips, mending frayed cuffs and making invisible mends, as well as reproofing raincoats and cleaning suede and sheepskin clothing.

Coin-operated machines

These will remove dirt and some stains from clothes, but do not do a professional job. Remove spots and stains before putting clothes into the machine (see Stain removal).

▲ WARNING ▲
Never dry clean pillows, eider-downs or sleeping bags in these machines as fumes left in these articles can prove fatal.

Dry cleaning symbols

 Normal goods dry cleanable in all solvents.

 Normal goods dry cleanable in perchloroethylene, white spirit, solvents 113 and 11.

 Normal goods dry cleanable in white spirit or solvent 113.

 Do not dry clean.

 The article may be treated with chlorine bleach.

 Chlorine bleach must not be used.

Dyeing

Clothes can be given a new lease of life with a change of colour. Most fabrics – including many synthetics – can be dyed at home. Check manufacturers' labels for fibre content and washability. Generally speaking, if a fabric is washable it can be dyed, too, but not acrylics (Acrilan, Courtelle, Dralon, Orlon) and fabrics with drip-dry, showerproof or non-iron finishes.

Fabric dyes

Cold-water dye This dye comes in powder form only and is used in conjunction with a fixing agent. Mainly for use on natural fabrics, it can be used on viscose rayon and on fabric mixtures containing a high proportion of cotton although, as only the cotton will take the dye, the colour will be paler than shown on the dye pack.

Hot-water dyes Available in powder or liquid form, these may be used on all natural fabrics as well as a wide range of synthetics and fabric mixtures.

★ HANDY HINT ★
When washing a dyed fabric, use a mild detergent. Strong detergents tend to dull colours.

Both types of dye may be used for either hand or machine dyeing. There is also a special washing machine pack available which combines a hot-water dye with a low-lather detergent that washes and dyes in one go.

Choosing a new colour

Dyeing white or cream fabrics presents no problems, but when dyeing a coloured fabric you will have to take the new effect into consideration. The guide below tells you what effect you will obtain.

Base colour	Dye colour	Result
Brown + Red	=	Rust
Blue + Yellow	=	Green
Green + Red	=	Brown
Green + Yellow	=	Lime
Pink + Light blue	=	Lilac
Red + Yellow	=	Orange
Red + Blue	=	Purple
Yellow + Pink	=	Coral
Yellow + Purple	=	Brown

What to dye it in

Make sure that your dye container is large enough to allow the fabric to move freely, and that the fabric is *opened-out* when it goes into the dye. Too small a bowl prevents the dye from penetrating and gives patchy results. Use a flame-proof container for deep-dyeing small articles with hot water dyes. The bath, sink or a plastic bowl can be used for cold water dyeing.

The washing machine is particularly good for dyeing large articles or for colour-matching several smaller items.

Suede, leather and plastics

Suede, leather, plastic and PVC can also be revitalised with dyes. Suede and leather dyes, like fabric dyes, blend with the existing shade, but there are also obliterating paints for leather, plastic and PVC. Both dyes and paints can be used on clothes, shoes and bags.

Use a suede cleaner on suede, or special conditioner on leather, PVC and other plastic to remove surface dirt and grease. Pack out shoes, boots and bags with paper. Apply the dye or paint with a brush, working it well into any creases. When dry, brush suede to restore the nap, and bring up the shine on leather, plastic and PVC with a soft cloth.

Furs

Good furs are expensive to buy but, with minimal care, they will last for years.

Routine care

Try not to wear your fur every day – it will last better if 'rested' from time to time and stored correctly between use. When sitting in a fur coat, always undo the fastening – the leather beneath the fur could tear if stretched too much.

If your fur becomes damp, shake out then hang it up in a cool, dry place with freely circulating air – *never* dry close to a fire or radiator. If the coat becomes really wet, it will need remedial treatment to restore it.

★ **HANDY HINT** ★
Never brush a fur to clean it – just shake it out briskly after use.

To store during the wearing season, cover loosely with silk or cotton sheeting and hang on a suitable hanger – preferably padded – in an airy cupboard. Do not cover with plastic, since this may produce condensation.

Furs do become dirtier than you might think, so always plan an annual professional clean, especially of long fur coats which can become matted.

Summer storage

In summer, either store your fur coat with a professional cleaner, or put it into cold storage with a professional furrier. If you cannot do either, then wrap the fur loosely (to allow the air to circulate) and store in an uncrowded cupboard.

Home valeting

Everyday clothes care must be supplemented by more thorough treatment from time to time.

Suits and overcoats

Baggy knees and elbows These can be treated by ironing lightly over a very damp cloth to shrink the fabric back. Iron the area with the point of the iron, using small, light, circular movements, and then press the garment normally.

Brushing Every few weeks give a meticulous brushing out of doors, removing all traces of fluff and dust from pockets, turn-ups and trouser creases.

★ HANDY HINT ★

In an emergency, remove fluff, hairs, etc. from clothing by dabbing with the sticky side of adhesive tape.

Creases From time to time, apply ordinary washing soap or spray starch to the inside of creases, then arrange very carefully and press with a hot iron for a fraction longer than usual (see Ironing and pressing).

Dinner jackets and trousers They need similar treatment to ordinary suits, plus extra storage care. Remove hairs and fluff by dipping a clothes brush in methylated or surgical spirit and brushing quickly.

Pressing Suits and trousers should be pressed after every two or three wears to keep creases crisp. Use a hot iron and press over a silicone pressing cloth or damp muslin. When pressing a wool garment, place a fine woollen cloth, such as nun's veiling, under the pressing cloth. Hang suits and overcoats on wooden hangers.

Sponging On dark fabrics, sponge with an ammonia solution [1 tablespoon ammonia to 500ml (scant 1 pint) warm water], using a pad or cloth. Vinegar and water can be used on very dark fabrics.

Spot removal A spot-cleaning fluid or spray will deal with grease, shoe-polish, gravy and chocolate. Pay particular attention to collars, cuffs and trouser turn-ups. Wear-marks in these areas can sometimes be removed with a spot-cleaning fluid.

For further information on how to remove different types of stain, see Stain removal chart.

Raincoats

Hang up raincoats immediately after wearing and leave to dry before brushing. Mud should brush off easily once it is dry and any slight remaining stain can be sponged with warm suds and wiped off with a clean damp cloth.

Spot-cleaning fluid can be used to remove grease marks from a proofed raincoat, but a rubberised, foam-backed, plastic, PVC or impregnated fabric mackintosh should not be treated with any grease solvents. Instead, spread a paste made with French chalk and water on to the affected area, or try dry French chalk.

Some proofed raincoats can be washed safely, others must be dry cleaned only, so always follow the cleaning instructions sewn into the garment. Rubberised and plastic mackintoshes can be sponged or lightly scrubbed with warm suds, which are then wiped off with a damp cloth. Nylon raincoats can be washed and drip-dried.

Women's skirts and dresses

Garments made from heavy materials which cannot be washed, should be cared for in the same way as suits and overcoats – brushing well after use, removing spots and stains immediately, and pressing as instructed.

Ironing equipment

Dry irons

When choosing a dry iron, there are some general points to look for.
● It should be comfortable to hold.
● The weight should suit you.
● It should have a good pointed shape for ironing into gathers and round buttons. (Look for irons that have button slots built into the sole plate.)
● It should be well balanced when it is up-ended.

● It should have clear thermostatic controls and settings, and an on/off indicator.

Steam irons

These have a built-in container for water which evaporates as steam through holes in the sole plate. Most models can also be used as dry irons.

Basic points to look for in a dry iron also apply to a steam iron, but there are some additional factors to check.
● It should be easy both to fill and empty the water reservoir.
● A water level indicator is an advantage.
● Find out if the water must be distilled or whether the iron has a changeable filter to use with ordinary water.

Steam and spray irons These have a device which sprays water directly on to the fabric. The points to check are the same as for steam and dry irons, but also check the position and use of the spray control. Some irons have a control allowing extra steam to be pumped out of the sole plate. These are useful for heavy fabrics, such as denim.

Care of irons

Keep the sole plate clean. Most of the dirt which accumulates is the result of ironing a man-made fibre at too high a temperature.

Dissolve the deposit with methylated spirit when the iron is cold, or use a special iron cleaner. You can also use a *dry* soap-filled pad. Never scrape dirt off with anything which might scratch the sole plate.

A steam iron should not fur up if you

Ironing guide

Fabric	Damp or dry	Heat	Side
Acetate	Slightly damp	Cool	Wrong
Acrylic	Dry	Cool	Wrong
Cotton	Slightly damp	Hot	Right unless dark colour
Corduroy	Nearly dry	Fairly hot	Wrong
Linen	Damp	Hot	Right (shiny) Wrong (dull)
Nylon	Nearly dry	Cool	Either
Polyester	Slightly damp	Cool	Either
Silk*	Slightly damp	Warm	Wrong
Triacetate	Nearly dry	Cool	Either
Tussore/ Shantung	Dry	Fairly hot	Wrong
Velvet	Dry	Warm to fairly hot (depending on fabric)	Wrong
Viscose*	Slightly damp	Warm	Wrong
Wool**	Nearly dry	Warm	Wrong

*Do not sprinkle as fabric shows water marks
**Do not press ribbing or welts of knitwear

use distilled or demineralised water. If you have used tap water and suspect furring, use a special steam iron cleaner.

Keep the flex in good condition and renew when necessary. A flex holder helps to avoid kinking and rubbing.

Ironing aids

Cover A top cover of silver milium over the padded ironing board cover reflects the heat and helps retain damp, making ironing more effective.

Flex-holder This lengthens the life of the flex by keeping it away from the heat or the sole plate.

Needle board Covered with a mass of tiny metal spikes or pins which prevent velvet pile being crushed when it is ironed.

Pressing mitt (a large, well-padded mitten) This enables you to press curved or moulded seams neatly.

Seam roll (a very firmly packed, sausage-shaped roll) Useful for pressing seams on trousers.

Sleeve board Helps to iron sleeves and awkward corners more easily.

 HANDY HINT

If you have a dry iron, damp down fabrics with a small spray of the type used for indoor plants.

Ironing and pressing

Dampness and dryness

● If garments are too wet when they are ironed, they will have a poor finish and probably need re-ironing later.

● If fabrics are too dry, it is often impossible to achieve a smooth, crisp finish.

● Iron shantung, tussore, chiffon, georgette, crêpe and acrylic fibres when they are completely dry.

● Garments needing to be ironed when damp should be sprayed lightly, folded or rolled and put into a large polythene bag until you are ready to iron.

Temperature

Check the care label in the garment to ensure you have the right setting (see ironing symbols chart). It is most economical to start with a hot iron and deal first with cottons and linens, allowing the iron to cool gradually and working down to rayons and synthetics, but the reverse process may be safer if you are inexperienced. Some irons give a fabric guide on the temperature setting.

Ironing symbols

Hot iron (210°C)

Warm iron (160°C)

Cool iron (120°C)

Do not iron

Ironing technique

1 Damp down if necessary and set the iron at the required temperature.

2 Iron hems and seams first, then collars, sleeves and pockets.

3 Iron the rest of the garment.

4 Iron in the direction of the grain of the fabric, using long, smooth strokes over as large an area as possible except:

● Iron fine wool with a light circular movement.

● Iron knitted rayon and net curtains diagonally.

● Iron embroidery on the wrong side over a thick blanket or pad.

● Iron tucks and gathers with the point of the iron.

● Iron woollens or heavy materials over a damp, lint-free cloth. This is the only way to get crisp pleats or trouser seams. When the cloth is removed, the garment will be steaming slightly – it should be allowed to become completely cold before hanging up.

 HANDY HINT

Iron handkerchiefs round the hems first, so that they are set square before ironing the centre.

Laundering

Regular laundering helps things to last longer. Most clothes are now marked with clear instructions on the best method of laundering, but there are general guidelines to follow when an article does not have a care label.

Hand washing

Hand washing is essential for delicate fabrics such as silk and woollens. Soap or detergent should be thoroughly dissolved before the article is immersed in the water. Do not put too many articles in at once and change the water if the lather disappears. Rinse very thoroughly to remove soap deposits and keep the fabric soft. Do not twist or wring silk or woollens. (To dry woollens etc., see Laundering of different fabrics.)

Machine washing

Reliable washing machines, dryers and clothes lines are essential (see KIT-CHEN SENSE – Washing machines, dryers). Follow the manufacturers' instructions when sorting the wash and loading the machine. Many woollens

---

★ **HANDY HINT** ★

Deep-dyed materials should be tested for colourfastness. Wet a corner of the fabric and then iron between two scrap pieces of white cloth. If any colour comes out, the fabric should be washed on its own.

---

are now machine washable and these are clearly marked.

Most automatic machines have programmes for different fabrics and the code symbols indicate which wash cycle to use – see below.

 This programme is used for white cotton and linen articles without special finishes and provides the most vigorous washing conditions. Wash temperature can be up to boiling (100°C/212°F) and agitation and spinning times are maximum. This ensures good whiteness and stain removal.

 Programme 2 is for cotton, linen or viscose (rayon) articles without special finishes where colours are fast at 60°C (140°F). It provides vigorous wash conditions but maintains fast colours.

 Used for white nylon or white polyester/cotton mixtures, this programme is less vigorous than either 1 or 2. The wash temperature (60°C/140°F) is high enough to prolong whiteness, and cold rinsing followed by short spinning minimises creases.

 This process is for coloured nylon, polyester, cotton and viscose articles with special finishes, acrylic/cotton mixtures, coloured polyester/cotton mixtures. In all respects except for washing temperature, it is the same as programme 3. The lower temperature is hand hot (50°C/122°F) and safeguards the colour and finish.

Suitable for cotton, linen or viscose articles where colours are fast at 40°C (104°F) but not at 60°C (140°F), this programme has warm wash (40°C/104°F), medium agitation, normal spinning or wringing. The low wash temperature is essential to safeguard colourfastness.

This programme is for acrylics, acetate and triacetate including mixtures with wool, polyester/wool blends, which require low temperature washing (40°C/104°F), minimum agitation, a cold rinse and a short spin.

Similar to programme 6, this programme is for wool, including blankets, wool mixtures with cotton or rayon and silk, which needs low temperature washing (40°C/104°F) and minimum agitation but requires normal spinning. Washing in this way preserves colour, size and feel. These fabrics should not be subjected to hand wringing or rubbing.

This programme is for silk and printed acetate fabrics with colours which are not fast at 40°C (104°F), and need to be washed at a very low temperature (30°C/86°F), with minimum agitation.

This programme is for cotton articles with special finishes which benefit from a high temperature (95°C/203°F) wash but require drip-drying.

Laundering of different fabrics

Acrylics Wash frequently with soap or detergent in water not hotter than 40°C (104°F).

Acetate and Triacetate Wash as for acrylics.

Cotton Wash whites by hand at 48°C (118°F) or in the machine at a temperature up to 77°C (170°F). Coloureds should be washed at 60°C (140°F). Use a strong washing powder.

Drip-dries Wash in plenty of soapy water at the same temperature as for coloured cottons. Rinse thoroughly and hang to dry without wringing or squeezing. Do not bleach or boil.

Do not leave damp drip-dries crumpled up, or they will have to be ironed.

Knits and jersey fabrics Wash as for acrylics and rinse thoroughly. Knitted garments can be rolled in a towel to remove some of the moisture, or given a quick spin for not more than a couple of minutes. Dry flat. Jersey fabrics should be dripped dry, or dried off in a tumble dryer when partly dry; they may then need some ironing.

Mixtures Wash blended fabrics in the same way as the component fibre which needs the gentlest treatment.

Nylon, Dacron and Terylene Wash frequently. White nylon needs a temperature of 60°C (140°F) while coloured nylon, Dacron and Terylene need a lower temperature. Discoloured white fabrics can be improved by a specially made whitening powder (see Discoloured fabrics).

Linen Treat as for cotton.

Pleated fabrics Wash according to the fabric and hang to drip dry. Do not spin or rub too vigorously.

Silk Use a neutral soap or detergent in warm water 40°C (104°F). Swish through the suds, but do not rub. Rinse very thoroughly, finishing with cold water. Silk can be spun dry or wrapped in a towel to absorb moisture. Heavy silks should be dry cleaned.

Indian muslin Natural dyes are used on this material; they are seldom colourfast. Wash in cold, salty water and a mild soapless detergent. Rinse and spread flat on a piece of clean white cloth, placing white cloth between layers of material.

Stretch weaves These and bulked or crimped yarns, must be treated according to the fibre from which they are made – see the care label on the garment.

Wool Wash knitted garments by hand as for silk. Rinse in warm water. Support the weight of the garment while washing, to avoid stretching. Knitted wool can be given a short spin and dried flat, away from heat. Woollens which are not colourfast should be washed in cool water with liquid soapless detergent, thoroughly rinsed and dried with a cloth between the layers.

Drying

In addition to the washing symbols given on garment labels, you may also find drying symbols as shown in the table below.

Drying symbols

◯	Tumble dry recommended but not essential
▽	Line dry
‖‖	Drip dry; hang while wet
⊟	Dry flat; do not hang

Patches

Patching

Unless they are intended to be decorative, patches should match the worn fabric exactly. If only new fabric is available for patching, it should be washed several times before use, to match texture and colour and to pre-shrink it.

A patch must be oblong or square, cut straight along the thread, and should be placed so that the straight threads of the patch follow those of the garment.

Cloth or flannel patch Mark out the size of hole and cut the patch to this size, adding 16mm ($\frac{5}{8}$in) all round. Then fray the edges to a depth of 5mm ($\frac{3}{16}$in) all round and tack into position on the wrong side. (Do not turn the edges under.)

Use herringbone stitch to secure the patch to the garment, beginning in the middle of one side and covering the frayed edges.

Turn to the right side, cut away the worn material to within 10mm ($\frac{3}{8}$in) of the stitching, tack down and herringbone stitch the raw edge in place.

Patching printed fabric Find a straight grain of fabric and cut the patch so that the pattern matches that of the garment around the area to be patched. Allow 20mm ($\frac{3}{4}$in) extra all round. Fold edges under for 10mm ($\frac{3}{8}$in) along straight of grain and press.

Pin and tack the patch to the right side matching pattern exactly. Hem the patch to the fabric with tiny, even stitches. Cut away worn fabric on the wrong side to within 10mm ($\frac{3}{8}$in) of the stitches. Buttonhole over both raw edges together without carrying the stitches through to right side. Take out the tacking and press.

Leather patches Generally used for a worn elbow on a tweed or other casual jacket. They have no turnings, are cut large enough to cover the worn area plus about 8mm ($\frac{5}{16}$in) and are placed on the right side of the garment. Leather patches can generally be purchased in haberdashery departments.

 HANDY HINT

Sewing a leather patch is made easier if you first machine round it with large stitches but no thread on the machine, working about 5mm ($\frac{3}{16}$in) from the edge. Position the patch and hem in place, using machine holes.

Shoe care

Good shoe care need not take more than a few minutes a day and will amply repay the time and money spent.

General care

Try not to wear the same pair of shoes two days running. Leather shoes particularly benefit from resting and drying out completely. Shoes and boots should always be kept on shoe trees; put the trees in while the shoes are still warm, even if they cannot be cleaned until later. Clean shoes after every wearing.

Store Shoes should be stored in a dry, dark cupboard away from heat, sunlight, fumes or damp.

Repairs Always have shoes repaired just before they need it. Run-down heels distort the shoe and make repairs more difficult. Replace shoe-laces and insoles when necessary.

Shoe trees Well-fitting shoe trees are a must. Adjustable shoe trees fit the shoes like feet and hold uppers smooth and in good shape. They are expensive but, carefully treated, should last a long time. Use padded trees for the toes of soft leather shoes.

★ HANDY HINT ★

If you don't have shoe trees, stuff the toes and heels of shoes with wadded newspaper held in place with a piece of flexible cane.

Cleaning and polishing

Aniline calf, reptile skin, buckskin Special finishes for these leathers can be bought at the same time as the shoes.

Leather Remove caked-on mud and dirt as soon as possible. Stuff wet shoes with crumpled newspaper and dry in an airy place away from heat.

Clean stubborn dirt with a damp sponge and saddle soap.

When dry, wipe with a dry cloth, spread polish evenly on the shoes with a brush or cloth and polish vigorously with a brush, cloth or velvet rubber.

Man-made uppers Clean with warm, soapy water and wipe dry. Scuff marks should be polished with ordinary polish or cream.

Patent leather Dust off dirt and polish with special polish. As an alternative, wipe over with a cloth dipped in milk. Always store shoes on well-fitting trees while they are still warm. Cover with a protective film of petroleum jelly if storing for any length of time. The shoes should then be warmed before wearing to make the leather more flexible.

Suede Brush with special wire brush. Use a soft rubber brush and a little soap and water to remove dirt or mud. Leave to dry away from the heat and then brush to restore the nap.

Steam from a kettle should raise the nap on neglected suede. Rubbing gently with fine sandpaper followed by brushing should remove shiny patches. Special suede cleaner will restore the colour.

Proofed suede should be brushed with a soft clothes brush. All suedes should be sprayed with protective spray before first using.

See also REFERENCE TABLES—Shoe sizes.

Smell removal

Clothes

Hanging clothes in the open air on a fine day will dispel any cooking smells clinging to the fabric.

 HANDY HINT

To remove perspiration odour, add a little vinegar to the rinsing water and then rinse clothing again in clear lukewarm water.

Hang the clothes in the fresh air to dry if possible. An alternative is to soak the soiled garment in a solution containing laundry borax 1 teaspoon borax to 568ml (scant 1 pint) warm water. Then wash in warm, soapy water to which a few drops of ammonia have been added, and rinse thoroughly.

Stain removal

Stain removers

Keep various stain removers in the house, ready to use in an emergency.

Stain removal chart

Stain	On washable fabric	On non-washable fabric
Adhesives: *clear*	Dab with acetone or non-oily nail varnish remover. Launder.	Dab with acetone or non-oily nail varnish remover. Dry clean.
contact	As above.	As above.
epoxy resin	Dab with lighter fuel if synthetic, cellulose thinner if natural fibres.	Dab with lighter fuel if synthetic, cellulose thinner if natural fibres.
latex	If still wet, wipe off with damp cloth. If dry, use liquid grease solvent.	If still wet, wipe off with damp cloth. If dry, use liquid grease solvent.
Beer	Soak in lukewarm water then launder. If dried onto whites use bleach, onto coloureds use borax solution.	Blot and wipe with damp cloth. If dried, sponge with acetic acid solution (2 parts to 5 parts water). Wipe with damp cloth.
Beetroot	Rinse in cold water. Soak in borax solution for 20 minutes. Launder.	Obtain professional treatment.
Bird droppings	Launder thoroughly.	Wipe off deposit and use aerosol grease solvent.
Blood	Sponge with salt water solution then soak in enzyme detergent. Launder.	Wipe off surface deposit. Sponge with cold water to which a few drops of ammonia are added. Wipe with water.
Candle wax	Scrape off surface deposit. Put white blotting paper over stain and use warm iron on top to melt wax into paper. Use grease solvent for last traces. Launder.	Scrape off deposit and use blotting paper treatment. Clear traces with aerosol grease solvent.

Stain	On washable fabric	On non-washable fabric
Chewing gum	Use a polythene bag of ice-cubes to harden the gum. Crack it off in pieces. Use liquid grease solvent, then launder.	Use ice-cube and cracking treatment, then grease solvent.
Chocolate	Scrape off deposit. Launder using enzyme rather than ordinary detergent. If still marked, use borax solution.	Scrape off deposit. Use aerosol grease solvent. Sponge area with clean warm water.
Coffee and tea	Soak in a borax or enzyme detergent solution. Launder.	Sponge with borax solution, then with warm clear water. Use grease solvent to clear traces.
Creosote	Dab with lighter fuel or eucalyptus oil. Launder. Use glycerine to soften old stains first.	Obtain professional treatment.
Dye	Soak in enzyme detergent solution. Treat remaining marks with a dye stripper if white, with methylated spirit and ammonia if coloured. Launder.	Dab with enzyme detergent solution, then methylated spirit and ammonia. Obtain professional treatment if unsuccessful.
Egg	Sponge with cold salt water then wash in enzyme detergent solution. Clear traces of dried yolk with grease solvent.	Scrape off deposit. Dab with strong solution of washing-up liquid. Wipe with damp cloth.
Fruit juice	Rinse thoroughly in cold water. Wash in enzyme detergent solution.	Sponge with cold water and blot dry. Sponge any traces with borax solution, then clear warm water.
Grass	Rub marks with methylated spirit, then launder.	Obtain professional treatment.

STAIN REMOVAL CHART: Grease and oil

Stain	On washable fabric	On non-washable fabric
Grease and oil	Scrape off deposit. Use a grease solvent or, on really bad marks, a paint stripper. Launder.	Spread talcum powder on small marks, leave 5 minutes then brush off. Repeat treatment until all grease or oil is gone. Brush well.
Hobbies: *artist's paints*	Sponge with cold water, soak in enzyme detergent solution. Launder.	Sponge with cold water and blot dry. Dab remaining marks with white spirit.
model-making cement	Scrape off deposit. Use liquid grease solvent. Launder.	Scrape off deposit. Use liquid grease solvent. Sponge with warm water. Dried stains need professional treatment.
plasticine	Scrape off deposit. Dab with liquid grease solvent. Launder.	Scrape off deposit. Dab with liquid grease solvent. Sponge with clear water.
Ice-cream	Wipe off deposit. Soak in enzyme detergent solution. Launder.	Wipe off deposit. Treat with liquid grease solvent, then with methylated spirit if any colour remains. Sponge with clear water.
Ink: *ball point*	Scrub with warm soapy water. Launder.	Obtain professional treatment.
felt-tipped	Dab with methylated spirit. Launder.	Dab with methylated spirit. If this fails, obtain professional treatment.
permanent	Sponge with cold water and launder. Professional treatment may be necessary.	Sponge with cold water. Professional treatment probably necessary.
washable	Hold under running cold water then launder.	Sponge with cold water repeatedly until removed.

Stain	On washable fabric	On non-washable fabric
Iron mould and rust	Rub marks with lemon juice, rinse in cold water. Or use a proprietary rust remover.	Use proprietary rust remover.
Jam	Launder. If this does not remove all stains, soak in enzyme detergent solution, then re-launder.	Scrape off deposit. Sponge area with a solution of washing-up liquid.
Make-up	Wipe off deposit. Soak in ammonia solution. Launder.	Wipe or brush off deposit. Apply aerosol grease solvent. Remove colour traces with methylated spirit.
Milk	Rinse in warm water, then launder in warm water. Very hot water will set the stain. Remove any traces with grease solvent.	Sponge with warm water. Apply grease solvent.
Nail varnish	Wipe up deposit. Dab with acetone or non-oily nail varnish remover. Apply grease solvent then launder.	Wipe up deposit. Dab with acetone or non-oily nail varnish remover. Apply grease solvent. Remove colour traces with methylated spirit.
Paint	Scrape or wipe off deposit. Emulsion paint should come out with normal laundering following a soak in cold water. Oil-based paints should be dabbed with white spirit or paint stripper, followed by laundering.	Scrape or wipe off deposit. Sponge emulsion with cold water. Treat oil-based with white spirit or paint stripper. Have delicate fabrics cleaned professionally.
Paraffin	Apply grease solvent, then launder.	Wipe up as much as possible. Apply grease solvent.

Stain	On washable fabric	On non-washable fabric
Perfume	Rinse in warm water. Launder.	Sponge lightly with warm water and blot dry. Have delicate fabrics cleaned professionally.
Perspiration	Sponge with a weak solution of ammonia, rinse and launder. Whites can be bleached.	Sponge area with solution of 5ml white vinegar to 250ml warm water.
Scorch marks	Bad marks cannot be remedied. Sponge light marks with borax solution, then sponge with warm water. Launder.	Bad marks cannot be remedied. Rub light marks with glycerine solution. Sponge with warm water. Repeat if necessary.
Shoe polish	Use grease solvent. Launder.	Scrape off deposit. Use aerosol grease solvent. Remove colour traces with methylated spirit.
Tar	Dab with eucalyptus oil or tar remover. Launder.	Dab with eucalyptus oil or proprietary tar remover.
Urine	Rinse in cold water then launder. Use hydrogen peroxide solution on stubborn marks that remain.	Sponge with warm salt water. Rinse with clear warm water and blot dry.
Vomit	Scrape off deposit. Rinse under running cold water. Soak in enzyme detergent solution. Launder.	Scrape off deposit. Sponge with warm water containing a few drops of ammonia. Rinse with clear water and blot dry.
Wine and spirits	Rinse in warm water. Soak in borax solution. Launder. Use hydrogen peroxide solution on stubborn marks that remain.	Sponge with warm clear water. Sprinkle talcum powder on stain and leave to absorb it.

Warning notes

Check the list given here before using certain products to make sure you will not damage your fabrics.

- *Ammonia* causes certain dyes to bleed.
- *Acetone* and non-oily nail varnish remover damage acetate fabrics, like Tricel.

● *Enzyme detergents* harm non-fast colours, flame-resistant or rubberised fabrics, metal fastenings, silk or wool. Do not soak rayon in an enzyme solution.

● *Hydrogen peroxide* damages nylon. Hydrogen peroxide with added ammonia damages wool.

● *Methylated spirit* damages rayons and Tricel.

▲ WARNING ▲

As most stain removers are poisonous, many of them give off fumes and some are flammable, store them well out of the reach of children.

Zips

Mending zips

Metal zips Sometimes break at the bottom with one of the teeth becoming dislodged so that the slider is only attached to one side. If this happens, unpick some of the stitching holding the bottom of the zip in place, prise off the bottom stop on the damaged side and ease the slider back into place. Carefully close the zip and sew over the bottom teeth just above the damage.

Make a new bottom stop by sewing the straight metal eye of a hook and eye across the teeth above the stitching. Restitch the bottom of the zip in position (**a**).

If the top stops should come off, they too can be replaced by a straight metal eye, in this case bent around the tape above the teeth and sewn in place (**b**).

Nylon zips These may pull apart in the centre if there is too much strain on them. If the teeth are undamaged, run the slider up and down to interlock them once again.

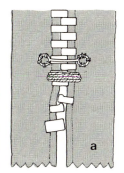
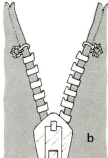

Shortening zips

If you have to buy a zip which is too long, simply sew across the bottom teeth, attaching a metal eye at the required point and cutting off the surplus tape. Open-ended zips should be shortened at the top by removing the extra tape and teeth and making new top stops with metal eyes as described.

For skirt and trouser zips which will have a waistband sewn across the top, just cut away any excess tape at the top after insertion. Replace the top stops as described.

★ HANDY HINT ★

If a nylon zip seems stiff, run a piece of soap over the teeth. Lubricate a metal zip by running a lead pencil up and down the teeth.

CHAPTER 9

SOFT FURNISHINGS

Bedspreads•Blankets•Curtains•Duvets
Loose covers•Pillows•Sheets
Table linens•Towels

Bedspreads

There are many different types of bedspread available: simple, throw-over covers which reach to the floor, often fringed or braided; smaller coverlets which are used on top of a valance or floor-length cover; neat, tailored designs with box-pleated corners; and frilled bedspreads, possibly with quilting in the centre panel.

Fabrics

Any fabric which is reasonably crease-resistant and can withstand the constant handling and folding that bedspreads receive, can be used. The following are most popular:

Candlewick A cotton tufted fabric, hard-wearing and crease-resistant. It is easily machine washed, but a large cover can be very heavy when wet.

Nylon and Terylene Their lightness makes them easy to wash at home and they drip dry very quickly.

Tapestry weave These bedspreads are usually the throw-over kind with fringed edges. Intricate designs are produced by weaving different colours together. They may be made from a variety of fibres, so check before washing. Some may need to be dry cleaned.

Lace Lace or lace-like fabrics may be used on their own or over a plain-coloured bedspread to match the decor of the room. Again, check the care label before washing or dry cleaning.

Indian fabrics Usually hand-woven, heavy, thick cotton woven in strips of thinner, patterned cotton. The dyes are usually not colour-fast and they tend to fade in bright sunshine. Dry cleaning is recommended.

Quilted and patchwork bedspreads Both take care and patience to make, but the results can be stunning. A quilted spread can be made reversible and can be washed if synthetic wadding is used.

Fake furs These make exotic throw-over bedspreads. They are usually machine washable but check on the care label.

Blankets

Nowadays blankets are available in a wide variety of colours and textures. Traditional blankets are made by normal warp-and-weft weaving to produce either 'solid' blankets or a cellular type. A lighter, more lacy cellular blanket is produced by a type of knitting. All cellular blankets should be used with a 'solid' – though not necessarily thick – covering on top, to benefit from the insulation provided by the trapped air.

Wool is now an expensive item but pure wool blankets generate a lot of warmth for very little weight and will last for years. Pure merino is regarded as the luxury quality, and although it is not necessarily hard-wearing, it produces very soft, light, warm blankets.

Blankets are also available in synthetics, with acrylics and nylon being widely used on their own or in blends. For those who are allergy-prone, synthetics provide a useful alternative to wool. They are easy to wash, dry quickly and are mothproof. See Sheets and pillowcases for blanket sizes.

Washing blankets

It is probably easier to have blankets dry cleaned, especially if they are wool; but they can be washed at home. Follow the manufacturer's instructions carefully. Blankets can be washed in a machine or by hand.

Washing by hand

1 Make up a plentiful supply of warm, sudsy water, using soap flakes rather than synthetic detergent, and possibly a fabric conditioner. In hard-water areas, if you do not use a fabric conditioner, do add water-softener to the water.

2 Move the blanket about in the suds and knead gently.

3 Make sure it is thoroughly rinsed. A dull, lifeless blanket often owes its sad appearance to poor rinsing.

4 The blanket will be very heavy when wet; hang it over two lines about 90cm (3ft) apart if possible.

5 Ease the damp blanket back into shape and if necessary, brush pile while damp.

Storing blankets

Any blankets not in use should be stored in a polythene bag with moth repellent if they contain wool. Even a small amount of wool in a mixed fibre blanket will make it vulnerable to moths.

Blankets, electric

Electric blankets provide a cheap and easy way of keeping warm in bed. Use them correctly and there should be no problems.

All electric blankets sold in the United Kingdom have to meet the relevant British Standard.

Overblankets

Overblankets can be left on all night and set to different temperatures to suit the user. They take about half an hour to warm up and then control the heat of the bed all night, according to the room temperature.

Some overblankets can be tucked in, but most are just laid loosely over the bed. They come in single or double sizes. The control unit has a pilot light to indicate whether the blanket is on, and the two sides of the bed can be controlled independently.

Prevention of overheating Electric overblankets have a built-in cut-out that comes into operation if they overheat or if creasing or a heavy weight on top creates a 'hot spot'.

Manufacturers recommend that you do not use more than one supplementary cover or you may produce excessive heat that operates the cut-out.

 ★ HANDY HINT ★

If you like the weight of covers, it is probably best to use an electric underblanket combined with conventional top blankets.

Underblankets

These are the most widely sold variety in the United Kingdom; they are cheaper than overblankets, but are *not* designed to be left on overnight.

Underblankets are made to fit standard single and double bed sizes and may have a fixed temperature (i.e. on or off only) or a choice of up to three heats. As with overblankets, a pilot light in the control box shows when the current is on, and double blankets may have dual control.

The underblanket may come supplied with tapes, or merely have holes into which you fit your own tapes. These are tied underneath the mattress to hold the blanket in position and prevent it from moving when you turn over.

An electric underblanket is usually put directly on top of the mattress or mattress cover and below the under-blanket and sheet. You can put a sheet directly over an electric blanket, but without a barrier you can often feel the coils of wire that produce the heat.

▲ WARNING ▲

Nearly all electric underblankets carry instructions that you should not lie on them when the current is on. It is the tendency to ignore this instruction that has caused the majority of accidents.

Extra low voltage (ELV) blankets

These special blankets are designed for extra safety, particularly for the elderly or sick. They can be left on 24 hours a day, seven days a week, without danger, and can also be lain on when the current

is on. They have a very low voltage so are cheap to run and very safe, even when a person is incontinent.

They do not provide such a high temperature as conventional electric blankets, but are a much better buy for an elderly, forgetful person.

Cleaning and servicing

It is usually possible to wash electric blankets at home provided you remove the switch and lead assembly – but always check manufacturer's instructions, and follow them carefully. Unless specially recommended by the manufacturer, do not dry clean an electric blanket; the cleaning solvents could damage the insulation. Every blanket should be checked and, if necessary, serviced every two years, and the manufacturer will report when the blanket has reached the age and stage at which it should be replaced rather than repaired.

★ HANDY HINT ★

For speedy service, send your electric blankets off to the manufacturer for checking during the late spring or summer.

Store your blanket in a cool place and fold it as little as possible.

Continental quilts (duvets)

A continental quilt is a large, fabric bag filled with down, down and feathers or a synthetic fibre. Also known as a duvet, it has for many years been the standard form of bedding in many European countries and is now very popular elsewhere.

A continental quilt is used in place of a top sheet, blankets and traditional quilt or eiderdown. It can weigh as little as one-fifth of conventional bed coverings, while being just as warm, or more so, as it moulds itself to your shape.

Deciding on a quilt

Before buying, it is best to try one out, perhaps borrow one from friends. For some people they are the ideal form of bedding, while others hate them. The only way to find out is to sleep under one for a few nights.

Types of filling

The secret of the continental quilt lies in its filling and in the air trapped in this, which acts as an insulator. The traditional filling is down which, unlike feathers, has no stiff quill and is also considerably lighter.

The best and most expensive down is from the eider duck. Duck down is used and also mixtures of down and feather, feather and down – containing a larger proportion of feathers. Synthetic fibres are washable and cheaper than down or feathers, but do not always mould to the body as well as the natural fillings.

Choosing a quilt

The warmer you wish your quilt to be, the higher must be its *Tog* rating, the warmth being measured in inter-nationally recognised units called Togs. The minimum rating for a quilt is 7.5 Togs and the higher the number, the warmer your quilt will be.

Some quilts can have 'cold spots' along the lines where they are stitched, so choose a quilt which has internal dividing walls between the channels, so that the thickness of the quilt is almost uniform.

Sizes

To be effective, a quilt must drape over the sides and foot of the bed so that no draughts can get in.

Recommended width Allow an overhang of at least 23cm (9in) on both sides and at the bottom, but this width must also take in the bulk of the sleeper, so it is best to go for an extra wide quilt if you or your partner is large. The same applies to length.

It may be preferable to choose two single quilts for a double bed, especially if one person is a restless sleeper and tends to monopolise the bedclothes, or prefers a different degree of warmth.

Length Most quilts are 2m (6ft 6in) long. Extra long ones of 2.2m (7ft 2in) are recommended for people who are over 1.83m (6ft).

Quilts are available for single beds, small double, standard double and also various larger sizes as well as for bunk beds and cots.

Cleaning and care of quilts

An outer cover must always be used on a quilt to protect it from surface dirt. Polyester/cotton covers are the most usual. They are easy-care and wash and dry quickly. Generally, quilt covers can be obtained in ranges to match or mix with fitted bottom sheets, valances and pillowcases to give a co-ordinated appearance to the bedroom.

Washing Washing is not suitable for down and feather fillings unless specifically stated. Some manufacturers offer a cleaning service, otherwise they should be taken to a specialist dry cleaner.

 WARNING

Do not use a self-service dry cleaning machine in a launderette to clean your continental quilt. Toxic fumes may remain in the filling. The cambric casing may also be damaged.

Synthetic quilts These are washable, though they may lose some of their warmth and softness through lumping of the filling. Follow the manufacturer's instructions.

Routine care An occasional airing outside over a clothes line or balcony will benefit the quilt, as will a good, regular shake every day.

Curtains

There are various points to bear in mind when choosing curtain fabrics, in addition to the overall colour in relation to the decor of your room.

Choosing a fabric

Curtain material must hang well. Look at the fabric draped before you buy it and find out whether it is washable or needs dry cleaning, whether it is shrink-resistant and whether it will fade if exposed to strong sunlight.

Make quite sure that any pattern is printed correctly on the grain of the fabric. Crooked patterns can spoil the final effect.

It may be necessary to sew weights, or strips of weights, into the hem of curtains of lightweight fabric.

Linings

These are used for various reasons.
● They help the curtain to drape better.
● They protect the curtain fabric from light, dust and dirt, which damage it and make it wear out more quickly.
● They keep light out and provide a little more insulation. One type of lining has metal insulation which helps to prevent heat loss.

 HANDY HINT

If you keep to a neutral colour for your curtain linings throughout the house, the windows will have a more uniform look from outside.

Some curtain tapes are now designed to provide attachment for removable linings, which can be taken out and washed regularly. In other cases, the lining can be hooked on to the runner.

Interlining This gives curtains extra body, helping them to drape better and showing the fabric to its best advantage.

The usual fabrics for interlining are *bump* and *domette*, although *flannelette sheeting* is also suitable. Bump is rather like a very thick flannelette sheet and is fawn or white in colour. Domette is similar, but less fluffy than bump. The extra weight of the interlining means that you need particularly strong tracks from which to hang the curtains.

For estimating curtain quantities, tracks, rods, poles and pelmets, and ready-mades see HOME DECORATION – Curtains.

Eiderdowns and quilts

Old-fashioned eiderdowns have now been almost completely replaced in the shops by quilts filled with polyester. There are still a few filled with down and feathers, and quilts thus labelled must contain at least 51 per cent down. (If they are labelled in reverse – i.e. feather and down – this standard does not apply.)

Quilts filled with polyester are light, warm and easy to wash. The heavier the filling the warmer the quilt.

Cleaning quilts

Down and feathers Like pillows, down and feather and down-filled eiderdowns should not be washed or dry cleaned unless it is absolutely necessary. If it *is* necessary, take to a professional cleaner or 're-maker' who will add extra filling.
Synthetic These quilts are too large for domestic washing machines, and it is better to use the bath to provide free movement which will not disturb the filling. Because quilts are available in many different covering fabrics, it is important to follow washing instructions carefully.

Polyester-filled quilts can usually be dry cleaned, but it is important to air them thoroughly for at least 24 hours after cleaning to allow dangerous fumes in the dry cleaning chemicals to disperse. Never iron a quilt of this kind, as the filling will compress.

Loose covers

Loose covers are secondary covers fitted over the original upholstery of armchairs and settees. Almost any upholstered furniture, with the exception of pieces covered in velvet or leather, can be fitted with loose covers.

They are an excellent way of extending the life of shabby furniture, although you should not regard them as a cheap form of re-upholstery because they will not disguise lumpy padding or sagging springs.

Other benefits of loose covers are that you can remove them easily for cleaning, you can vary the decor of a room by having two sets of covers in different fabrics and you can replace worn panels more easily than on attached covers.

Loose covers can be made-to-measure; it is best to obtain estimates from several firms as prices vary greatly. It is also possible to buy stretch, all-purpose covers, which are designed for chairs and sofas made in most of the conventional styles. These covers fit closely and when well-made of a good quality material can transform an old suite. Cheaper makes do not always fit satisfactorily, so make sure that they can be returned if you find they are not suitable. (See also HOME DECORATION – Cushion covers.)

★ **HANDY HINT** ★

If you are replacing existing loose covers, the simplest way is to unpick these and use them as a pattern for cutting the new material.

If you have chosen a large, repeating pattern, make sure that the large, central motif comes in the middle of the back of the chair and the cushion. The pattern must also match up on each arm and on the back, so you may have to allow for some wastage in the fabric.

Pillows

There is nothing to quite equal a down pillow; it is worth its high price because of its comfort and durability.

Other choices include a mixture of down and goose or duck feathers, which are firm and hard-wearing; polyester-filled pillows, which are light and warm, but lack resilience; and pillows made from latex foam which have more spring than down or feather. Man-made fillings may be the best choice for people who are allergy-prone.

★ **HANDY HINT** ★

When buying a pillow, compress it firmly between both hands. A good one will return to its original shape.

Cleaning pillows

If they have become badly stained, pillows may occasionally need washing. Avoid washing feather and down if possible, as this disturbs the oil around the feathers. For other pillows:

1 Make up a warm solution of soap flakes and knead the pillow gently by hand.

2 Rinse it in three changes of warm water and, if possible, spin dry for two minutes to remove some of the water.

3 Hang the pillow up by two corners and shake periodically while drying.

4 Once it has stopped dripping, it can be dried off in a large tumble dryer. (*A polyester-filled pillow should not be put in a dryer.*)

Latex pillows which have been stained should be sponged clean with a soapy cloth, rinsed with a cloth wrung out in clean water and patted dry with a towel.

Sheets and pillowcases

Sheets

Cotton This has now become something of a luxury, but wears well provided it is of good quality. Union (mixed fibre) sheets combine the durability of linen and the warm finish of cotton.

Most sheets now on the market are in blends of *half cotton* and *half man-made fibres*, the most common being cotton-modacrylic and cotton-polyester. These sheets can combine the pleasant feel of cotton and the easy-care qualities of man-made fibres, though some do show a slight tendency to 'pill' – develop little balls of fluff – in wear. Washed in strict accordance with the manufacturer's instructions, they dry adequately smooth without ironing.

Linen Now a luxury item that few people can afford but some are lucky enough to inherit. It is made from flax and is one of the strongest natural fibres.

 ★ HANDY HINT ★

When buying linen sheets, hold them up to the light to check their authenticity. If it is genuine linen, then the fabric should appear uneven and thicker in places. Non-linen yarns will be uniform.

Bedding sizes

Bed size	Flat sheets	Fitted sheets	Blankets
Small single 90cm × 190cm (3ft × 6ft 2in)	180cm × 260cm (6ft × 8ft 6in)	90cm × 190cm (3ft × 6ft 2in)	180cm × 240cm (6ft × 8ft)
Standard single (100cm × 200cm) (3ft 3in × 6ft 6in)	180cm × 260cm (6ft × 8ft 3in)	100cm × 200cm (3ft 3in × 6ft 6in)	180cm × 250cm (6ft × 8ft 3in)
Small double 135cm × 190cm (4ft 6in × 6ft 3in)	230cm × 260cm (7ft 6in × 8ft 6in)	135cm × 190cm (4ft 6in × 6ft 2in)	230cm × 250cm (7ft 6in × 8ft 3in)
Standard double 150cm × 200cm (4ft 9in × 6ft 6in)	275cm × 275cm (9ft × 9ft)	150cm × 200cm (4ft 8in × 6ft 6in)	250cm × 280cm (8ft 3in × 9ft 3in)
Kingsize 180cm × 200cm (6ft × 6ft 6in)	275cm × 275cm* (9ft × 9ft)	180cm × 200cm (6ft × 6ft 6in)	250cm × 300cm (8ft 3in × 10ft)

*These are standard bedding sizes. It is possible to obtain larger sheets for kingsize beds, but only at some specialist bedding centres. Or you can make your own.

Flannelette sheets Made of a soft, lightweight fabric with a cotton base. They are hard-wearing and warm, so are often used for children and old people.

Modacrylic-polyester The blend of these synthetic fibres feels more pleasant than nylon. If synthetics are disliked, look for sheets that are at least half cotton.

1. *Join the two edges and seam together 1.6cm ($\frac{5}{8}$in) in. Trim one edge 6mm ($\frac{1}{4}$in).*

★ **HANDY HINT** ★

Cotton-polyester sheeting can be bought by the metre (yard) to make your own sheets in widths of 1.7m (5ft 9in) and 2.3m (7ft).

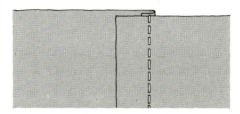

2. *Press turnings to one side, keeping the larger on top.*

Nylon These sheets can be brushed or have a smooth finish. They are inexpensive but not necessarily everyone's choice as they are slippery, non-absorbent and can be very hot in warm weather.

Sheets are also available in satin finishes and synthetic fibres.

Fitted sheets Can be bought in man-made fibres and in cotton polyester blends, and are a great aid to bed making. The disadvantage is that wear is concentrated in the same area.

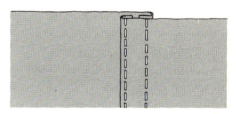

3. *Turn this under 6mm ($\frac{1}{4}$in) and machine stitch close to the fold.*

Repairing flat sheets

It is almost always the middle of the sheet which wears out first. When sheets are showing signs of wear, but before they become too thin or are in holes, cut them down the middle. Join the two outside edges together with a flat fell seam Figs, 1, 2, and 3. Hem the new edges. The life of the sheet will be doubled.

Pillowcases

These are made in much the same choice of fibres as sheets. The housewife style has a simple tuck-in and the Oxford style has a fabric trim or frill. The standard size is 50cm × 70cm (20in × 28in).

Sheets and pillowcases are now made in an exciting range of colours and prints. Many collections are co-ordinated so that patterns can be mixed with plain, and curtain fabrics and valances are frequently available in matching colours and designs.

Table linen

Table cloths

These are not used as much as they once were, as so many modern tables have easy-clean, wipeable finishes. However, a pretty cloth can add a look of freshness to even simple family meals and a grander cloth can make an elegant setting for a special occasion.

Table cloth sizes A table cloth should overhang the edge of the table by about 25–30cm (10–12in). A larger overhang can be uncomfortable or even dangerous, as the cloth might be pulled right off the table.

For a large square or oblong table, measure the length and width and add the recommended overhang (above) on all sides. Choose a polyester and cotton sheeting as near to the required width and length as possible, allowing about 7.5cm (3in) extra on every side. Turn up and tack a 2.5cm (1in) hem all round, mitreing the corners, and machine stitch.

To cover a *round* table, you will need a square of cloth, each side of which measures the diameter of the table plus the overhang required.

1 Fold the cloth into four and lay it on a flat surface.

2 Attach a soft pencil or chalk to one end of a piece of string that measures the required radius of the cloth.

3 Pin the other end of the string to the

point of the fold and, keeping the string taut, mark a quarter-circle on the top layer of cloth.

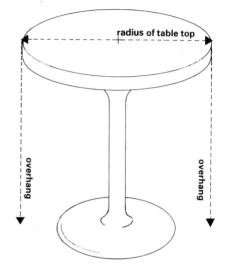

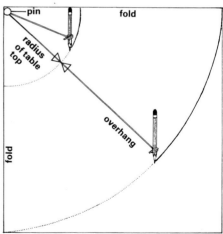

4 Cut carefully round the chalked line.

5 Finish the cloth with a narrow hem, slashed so that it will lie flat (**a**).

6 Cover with bias binding (**b**).

Keep any leftover fabric to make matching napkins.

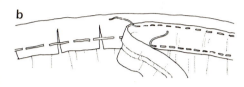

Table napkins These can match or contrast with table cloths and are often sold in sets. Families eating two or three meals together every day will probably need clean napkins daily, so a good supply is needed. Use a contrasting napkin ring for each member of the family.

★ **HANDY HINT** ★

Deep coloured paper napkins can 'bleed' on to pale cloths if they get wet, so take care not to use a bright red paper napkin to wipe up a spill on a white cloth.

Table linen fabrics

Acrylics Easy-care, often in coarser weaves and bright checks.

Cotton Reasonably hard-wearing and easy to launder.

Cotton-polyester Easy-care, but napkins not very absorbent.

Pure linen Hard-wearing, top quality and expensive.

Linen-polyester Easy-care and cheaper.

Rayon and rayon-cotton Inexpensive.

Tea towels and kitchen towels

Tea towels

Linen tea towels are available in traditional white with coloured borders and also in an innumerable variety of printed designs, many of which are decorative enough to use as wallhangings. Linen is excellent for drying as it is absorbent and leaves no trace of fluff on glass. Tea towels made of cotton or towelling are also absorbent, but do leave fluff.

Some tea towels are made in a blend of cotton and man-made fibre, but these are not as satisfactory as natural fibres, being less absorbent.

Tea towels should, ideally, be washed after each using, as they can harbour and pass on germs.

Roller towels

These are available in several varieties of towelling. When buying, make sure the towel size is right for the particular roller attachment you have.

Towelling can be bought by the metre, so it is very easy to make your own roller towels the exact size and colour you want.

Like tea towels, roller towels should be laundered frequently.

Towels

Most towels are made of fabric called *terry towelling* (sometimes called Turkish towelling), and have a woven cotton foundation into which are woven cotton loops. This gives the soft, absorbent pile so efficient for drying oneself after washing.

Friction towels, which are rougher, have the same cotton foundation, but the loops are made of linen.

Buying bathroom towels

Always buy the best quality you can afford – they have to stand up to very hard wear.

 HANDY HINT

Buy towels which look bulky, and have long, dense, finely-packed loops woven into the construction of the towel.

There should be a selvedge on both sides, or a double hem so that they will not fray when washed.

Buy towels with a well-known brand name or the brand name of a good store.

Fabrics for towels

As well as pure cotton, which is the best fabric for absorbency and durability, towels are available made of a cotton/polyester foundation with cotton loops. This is claimed to make the towel more hard-wearing without affecting the absorbency. However, all cotton/polyester towels will prove to be less absorbent.

Pure cotton towels shrink between 8-12 per cent after repeated laundering, but cotton/polyester shrinks less.

Smoothly woven linen These 'hucka- back' towels make useful, easily washed, quick drying hand and guest towels.

Towel sizes

These can vary from manufacturer to manufacturer – the names 'bath towel' or 'hand towel' do not indicate a standard size. When ordering by post, make sure the sizes are what you want – too small a bath towel can be an irritation. Bath sheet normally indicates a really large towel, which will wrap easily round you or be suitable for taking to the beach.

Care of towels

Make sure you have adequate towel rails in your bathroom – install a heated one if possible. Sharp hooks can tear towels, so use rails or rings.

Laundering Wash towels before you first use them. The addition of a little fabric softener plus, if possible, tumble drying, will make them soft and fluffy. Towels should not be ironed.

 HANDY HINT

Wash new dark coloured towels separately for at least six washes as the colour is apt to run into other washing.

Worn towels Worn edges on old towels can be bound with bias binding or cotton tape. Wash and dry the tape first to shrink it. Large towels that have become worn can be cut into small pieces to make flannels or hand towels. Bind with pre-shrunk tape in matching or contrasting colours.

CHAPTER 10

MOVING HOUSE

Do-it-yourself removals•Hiring a van
New neighbourhood•Packing
Planning•Unloading

New house

You can minimise the work and worry of moving house by careful planning and attention to detail at both the new and old home.

Once you have signed and exchanged documents and, about four weeks later, money on completion day, you may move in immediately. But there are some jobs which will be easier to attend to if the house is empty.

Central heating

If you are having a new central heating system installed the job will be quicker and easier if the house is empty.

 HANDY HINT

Consult the engineers on the siting of radiators, but take into consideration the size and shape of pieces of furniture that you will want in the various rooms.

Damp

If there is a damp problem this should be dealt with by experts before you move.

Re-roofing

This should be organised to be done in the summer months – the house may be without a roof for some time while the work is in progress.

Re-wiring

Your personal surveyor or the building society will have told you if this is necessary. It can be a complex procedure and will mean that the electricity is cut off while the work is being done.

 HANDY HINT

Before re-wiring starts, decide where you will need electric points. It is almost impossible to have too many, and the work will be cheaper if it is all done at once.

Rubble

Any rubble left by previous owners, or caused by building work and alterations, can be cleared by a contractor, or sometimes the local council will remove it for a fee. A skip can be hired from the council or an independent building firm.

Finding out day-to-day details

The surveyor's report and estate agent's description do not tell you everything you will want to know about your new house.

You should come to an agreement with the vendor and get him or her to list the 'fixtures' that will be left in the house and what will be removed. This should cover such things as curtain rails, television aerial, carpets, curtains, light fittings, storage heaters – even garden sheds, stocks of fuel, etc. A similar agreement should be reached between you and the buyer of your old house.

Measure all rooms accurately in the new house, not forgetting alcoves, so that you can plan where the furniture will go. It is sensible to make basic plans as suggested in KITCHEN SENSE.

Measure doors, corridors and staircase dimensions and consider the floor strength when planning where to place heavy items such as a freezer.

Check the following items

Locations of	● sewage/septic tank/ cesspit covers.
	● mains water stop-cocks, inside and outside the house.
	● gas taps, pilot lights.
	● mains electricity switches and meters.
Access to	● cold water tank.
Details of	● heating oil storage tank, filling procedures.
	● starting, running and closing down central heating.
	● fuel type for solid fuel appliances (including any special procedures).
Find out	● when chimneys were last swept.
Check	● suitability of existing gas/electricity supplies for your equipment.
Names and addresses of	● oil supplier, coal merchant, chimney sweep, recommended local joiner, electrician, plumber, central heating engineer, window cleaner, decorator, etc.

New neighbourhood

Get to know your new home area well before you move in, if possible.

What you will need to know

1 Find out about schools and arrange for the children to attend.

2 Register with a doctor and dentist.

3 Locate emergency services such as hospital casualty department.

4 If you have a pet, find out the name and address of the local vet.

5 If the new house has no telephone, locate the nearest public one or try to make arrangements to use a neighbour's in case of difficulties during moving.

6 Find out early closing day and ask about milk, newspaper and other deliveries. It is often useful to have groceries delivered during the first few weeks in a new house.

7 Find out about local transport.

8 Find out the day when the dustbins are emptied and laundry delivery and collection.

9 Check with the library or town hall about recreational facilities, sports, tennis courts, swimming baths, clubs and interest groups, as well as day and evening classes.

10 Find out if the local garage services your make of car and sells the relevant spare parts and, if not, which is the nearest garage that does.

Old house

Removal

Start arranging removal estimates at least six weeks ahead. It is sensible to get three professional estimates as they may vary considerably. An estimator usually needs about three days' notice to come and assess the volume. Before he comes, list what will be moving with you and what will be left behind. You must accept the successful estimate *in writing* before the removal firm can organise your move, insurance, etc.

▲ **WARNING** ▲

Do not add things after the estimate has been accepted or the removers will be entitled to charge more.

The estimator must know exactly what is going, including contents of drawers and cupboards, lofts, sheds and so on. Do not forget bicycles, prams and similar items. Fragile and valuable items should be noted individually.

Once he has seen everything, he should be able to tell you how long packing and loading should take, how long the journey will be and the time required for unloading.

Packing up

Some people like to leave everything to the removal firm; others prefer to pack certain items themselves. In terms of insurance, it is sensible to have break-ables packed professionally, since if you do not, the removers' insurance will not cover breakages. If you own valuable jewellery – take this with you, sep-arately. It is not usually covered by removers' insurance.

You may be able to have a consign-ment of tea chests in advance, so that you can start some of the packing.

Books These are best packed by you. Try to obtain robust cardboard boxes in advance of moving day (most moving firms will supply them if asked). If you have to use tea chests never fill them more than a little under half full, as otherwise the weight will be too much to carry.

The larder/storecupboard The contents are also best packed by you. Try to use up as much as possible during the week before the move. You may decide that it is more sensible to give or even throw away packets and jars that are nearly empty.

 ★ **HANDY HINT** ★

When packing up larder items, re-member to keep back some 'instant' foods and drinks for use on removal day. Items such as coffee, tea, long-life milk, biscuits, etc.

Plants If you are moving any *garden plants*, lift them as late as possible, leaving a good ball of soil round the roots. Wrap the root ball firmly in layers of damp newspaper or straw and put the whole plant in a polythene bag or sack, tying the stems, if they are long, within a tripod or wigwam of canes to prevent breakage.

Large house plants should also be staked for travel, wedged (in their pots) into a suitable box, watered lightly and covered with a polythene bag.

Small house plants can be fitted closely together in a shallow box and watered and covered in the same way. Try to find a box deep enough to take the whole height of the tallest plant, and cover it with a lid or with cling film to prevent damage.

Planning your packing

Rather than pack up one complete room, start packing items you will not need at all during the time of upheaval.

If blankets, curtains and rugs are to be cleaned before packing, get this done in good time.

Stereo equipment, record players and loudspeakers, as well as radios and electrical equipment, are best packed in their original boxes, so that there is no possibility of moving parts becoming damaged. If you have not kept the original boxes, consult your local dealers about the best way of packing and whether they can supply boxes.

The best way to pack

It is important to know what is in each box, case or drawer. Do not rely on lists on odd bits of paper or stuck to the outside of boxes. You will need a robust notebook devoted to the removal and nothing else. As you finish packing each container, note the contents and mark the container with a prominent identifying letter or number.

If some boxes are going into storage be sure that they are packed separately from those which are going with you.

Do not fill every container right up to the brim.

Have only one category of item in each container, rather than filling up the corners with miscellaneous objects.

If removers are going to do most of the packing, make sure that you have a general inventory, or you will not know the contents of individual boxes and trunks in case you need to make an insurance claim.

Removal day – preparation

Make a large day-by-day chart for the week before removal day and on it write the approximate times for meter readers and connections at your new and old homes. Add reminder lists. The following suggestions may be helpful.

Vital necessities

Items which you will not want to pack will include:

Sheets, towels, blankets
Clothes and shoes
Toys, school books and games equipment
Basic cooking utensils
Clothes-mending kit
Writing paper and envelopes
Address book
Items for the journey

New address notifications

These should be sent to:

Banks
Savings accounts
Credit card firms
Mail order firms
Store/business accounts
Insurance companies
Driving licence centre
National insurance
Tax office
Solicitor
Accountant
Clubs and societies
Television rental firm
Service contract engineers

Magazine subscription departments
Electricity, gas and water authorities
Arrange:
Letter forwarding service by Post Office
Installation of telephone if necessary
Cancellation of standing orders for rates, etc.
Reading of meters
To turn on electricity, water and gas in your new home, and to turn off these supplies in your old home, if necessary.

● *Clear* all outstanding accounts.

● *Turn off* night storage heaters two days before you leave if you are taking them with you, to allow time for the bricks to cool.

● *Arrange parking* with the police if you live in, or are moving to, a restricted or no parking zone.

● *Cancel* milk and newspapers.

● *Meal planning* should include simple, quickly-prepared food for removal week. Even if you disapprove of 'convenience' foods, now is the time to take advantage of their ease of preparation. (See FOOD AND NUTRITION.)

● *List* everything that is to accompany you on the journey, from valuables to a bottle of water for the dog, including important documents and any regular medication needed by one of the family.

● *Clear* the freezer (it is a good idea to run down the contents over the previous weeks), defrost and clean it (see KITCHEN SENSE – Freezers).

● *Clear*, defrost and clean the refrigerator (see KITCHEN SENSE – Refrigerators).

● *Remember* any clothes being dry cleaned, shoes mended, library books to be returned.

Removals – do-it-yourself

If you think of doing your own moving, work out carefully what it will entail in time, effort and hidden costs. If you possess lots of heavy furniture, precious items, etc. – *don't*.

Hiring a van

Names of hire firms can be found in the telephone directory yellow pages. Make sure what the hire fee covers – beside the cost of van hire, there will be VAT, petrol, insurance, mileage and perhaps other extra costs.

Size of van With an ordinary driving licence the size of the van is limited to $2\frac{1}{2}$ tonnes. To cost a move, you will have to work out the capacity of the van, to assess the volume of furniture you want to move, and to work out the number of journeys it will take to move the furniture from one place to another. This is not an easy calculation to make if you are not a professional, and you should over-estimate rather than under-estimate, as you will probably not be able to load the van as closely as a professional removal firm could do it.

If you need a van larger than $2\frac{1}{2}$ tonnes you could consider hiring one with a professional driver.

Loading and unloading

You will need at least three fit people to handle furniture, and for very heavy and unwieldy pieces four lifters are needed. No good piano should be loaded by amateurs, but should be moved separately, by professionals, which would also add to the expense.

Removal day

Be completely ready as early as possible. If the van has not arrived within half an hour of the stated time, ring to check that there has been no mistake in the date.

Take the head of the team through the house showing what is to be moved. Have all breakable objects laid out on a table for easy packing.

Station someone by the door to check items as they are removed and if possible tick them off.

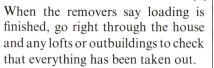

★ **HANDY HINT** ★

When the removers say loading is finished, go right through the house and any lofts or outbuildings to check that everything has been taken out.

Give the removers the address of the new house and, if possible, a sketch map. Confirm arrival arrangements and if overnight stays are involved, give your telephone number in case of emergency. Make a pre-move plan of the house and colour-code furniture and rooms to give to the removers.

The journey

You will have already made arrangements for travel for the family.

Picnic basket If the journey is a long one, the picnic basket should include hold-in-the-hand snacks, plenty of fruit and, if the weather is cold, a thermos flask of hot soup or coffee. Don't forget a damp flannel or pack of wet tissues.

Survival kit For arrival in the new house, the kit should include: the new keys, lavatory paper, electric light bulbs, fuses and fuse wire, plugs and adaptors, first aid kit, a self-seating plug, basic tools such as screwdriver and spanner, torch, alarm clock, matches, washing-up mop and detergent, tea-making and coffee-making equipment, can-opener, cutlery, crockery, kettle, saucepan, frying pan and of course all toiletry requirements and those items listed under *Vital necessities.*

Unloading and checking

When the van arrives, show the head remover where each room is and indicate roughly where large, heavy pieces of furniture are to go. Do not begin unpacking or cleaning, but give all your attention to the removal operations.

If you have tea chests to unpack yourself, do this when the men are having a break, or after all the big pieces of furniture are in.

Finally, check that the van is empty (get right into it, and look on the floor for tiny items like drawer knobs or handles that might have come loose). Then sign the agreement and pay the bill. If the firm has a stated policy on the acceptance of gratuities, adhere to it.

Claims

Claims for loss or damage should be made within a few days.

CHAPTER 11
MONEY MATTERS

Assurance•Banking•Buyers' rights
Calculators•Income tax•Insurance
Mail Order•Mortgages

Assurance

Life assurance can be regarded in two ways: as a means of providing money for your dependents in case of your death, or as a way of increasing personal savings by investment.

There are three basic types of policy: term, whole-life and endowment. Any policy offered by a company should fall under one of these headings, even if it is given a different name.

HANDY HINT ★

The difference between assurance and insurance is that the former covers an event that is bound to happen, such as dying or reaching a certain age, while the latter covers something that only might happen, such as damage to your car or house.

Policies best for assurance

Term assurance This is the simplest kind of life assurance and provides the most cover for the least money. It protects your dependents by providing money if you die *within a specified number of years*. If you die after the specified term has ended, your family receives no money, even though you have paid all the premiums.

Convertible term policies can, whenever the holder can afford higher premiums, be converted into *whole-life* policies that will pay a sum to the dependents whenever the holder dies.

Decreasing term assurance is usually linked with a mortgage to protect its repayment; the insurance decreasing as the mortgage does.

With *family income benefit* the dependents receive regular fixed amounts instead of one lump sum to help replace the income lost on the death of the breadwinner.

Whole-life assurance This costs more than term assurance because the payment of the amount assured is made on the death of the policy holder, whenever that occurs.

With or without profits If you take out a whole-life policy 'without profits' your family will only get the assured sum. If you choose a 'with profits' policy, the premium will be higher but the profits the company has made during the time you have been paying the premiums will be added to the sum paid to your dependents.

Policies best for investment

Endowment assurance This type of policy provides you with a certain sum of money within your own lifetime. Premiums are paid over a specified period of time and should you die within that time, your dependents will be paid the sum assured. It can be combined with a mortgage.

Premiums are fairly high, but it is a good way of ensuring some capital when you want it – say on retirement.

With or without profits terms apply to endowment assurances also.

Annuities The sum gained at the maturity of an endowment policy can be used to buy an annuity. You pay the company a lump sum in return for a fixed income of regular payments.

You can only gain on annuities by living longer than the company has anticipated.

★ **HANDY HINT** ★

Always choose an insurance broker who is a member of one of the established broker bodies.

Payment of premiums This varies from company to company. Although it is usually calculated as an annual payment, arrangements can be made to pay quarterly or even monthly instalments by bankers' order or direct debit.

The amount of the premium may be influenced by the state of your health and any record of hereditary disease. Withholding relevant information may render your policy void.

Assurances generally qualify for tax relief; and after some time you may be able to take out a loan on your policy or use it as security for a loan.

Banks and bank accounts

Opening an account

When you decide to open a bank account, the bank will only need some simple details such as the name and address of yourself, your employer and two referees. Your employer can count as one referee – to verify that you are who you say you are and, very important, that you are a reliable person.

Current accounts

With a current account the bank provides the customer with his own personal cheque book, so that bills can be paid by cheque.

If there is not enough cash, the manager may honour the cheque if he thinks you are a reliable customer, but you will receive a note from the bank asking you to get your account straight. **Statements** Every so often you will receive a statement of your account (both current and deposit), usually every six months, but on request this can be more frequent.

Deposit accounts

Unlike a current account, this type of account pays interest on the money deposited in it. The rate paid is linked to the base lending rate and therefore varies. Cash can be drawn out immediately in an emergency, providing you go to the branch which holds the account, but you will lose interest on your deposit. If, however, you give the bank seven days notice of your intention to withdraw, you can receive both money and interest.

Budget accounts

Some of the larger banks offer a budget account scheme. Customers tell their bank manager what the regularly recurring bills are – anything from school fees to heat, light and telephone – and work out what the annual total comes to. The bank then agrees to make the money available and pay the bills as they arrive. The customer has to meet the annual outgoing in twelve monthly repayments to the bank, plus a service charge to cover overheads. This arrangement can prevent difficulties in paying several large bills which may all arrive at the same time.

Giro accounts

Most banks operate a credit transfer system, known as bank giro, which will pay bills direct on your behalf. Local rates, gas and many other bills have special giro forms attached to them. Fill them in, sign them and make out a cheque to cover the entire amount. The bank will then issue the individual payments, at no extra charge, and accept the cheque in settlement.

Joint accounts

If you are married, both husband and wife can have a separate cheque book for the same account. This means that if your partner is away or sick either of you can draw cash from the joint account.

Running a joint account does mean that you must be particularly careful to ensure that you do not both draw large sums at the same time without making sure that the money is there to meet them. It is sensible to check with each other at regular intervals and keep cheque stubs up to date.

Cheques and cheque books

When you open a bank account you will receive a cheque book containing consecutively numbered cheques. Each cheque also carries the number of your account and the code number of the branch of the bank where your money is deposited. Keep a record of these numbers away from your cheque book – they must both be quoted when you pay money into your account through another branch or by bank giro.

The clearing process The person to whom you send a cheque takes it to his bank, which forwards it to the bank's head office. From there it is forwarded to the head office of *your* bank, who send it to your branch, where the amount is debited from your account. This process can take from two or three days to a week.

A bank may refuse to pay out on one of its customer's cheques because:

● There is not enough money in the account.

● The customer has 'stopped' the cheque (see Stopping cheques).

● The cheque is post-dated, that is the date on the cheque is later than the date on which it is paid in.

● The cheque has been filled in wrongly – the amount in figures perhaps differing from the amount in words.

When this happens the cheque is said to be dishonoured, or to 'bounce', and it is returned to the payee, who has to chase up the person who originally issued the cheque (the drawer).

Stopping cheques If you lose your cheque book or a particular cheque goes astray, or if you wish to withhold payment for some reason, you can stop cheques by ringing your bank and quoting the number or numbers of the cheques which should not be honoured. You should then confirm this in writing.

If you lose a cheque paid to you, tell

the drawer immediately, so that he can tell his bank to stop it. Another cheque, marked 'duplicate', can be issued to save confusion.

Cheques paid out and guaranteed by a cheque card cannot be stopped.

Bank charges These vary from bank to bank. It is a good idea to find out how your charges are calculated. In some cases keeping a certain balance in credit in your account means either that there are no charges or they are smaller.

Overdrafts and loans

An overdraft This means that the bank agrees to let you run up debts for an agreed period. Interest is calculated on the amount of money you have borrowed for the exact period that your account is overdrawn. It is usually less expensive than a loan for short-term borrowing.

Loans The bank agrees to allow you to borrow a sum of money for a one or two year period or sometimes more. You are committed to pay an agreed rate of interest for the whole of that period as if you had permanently borrowed the total sum involved. Repayment is normally by monthly instalments and interest charged is generally at a higher rate than for overdrafts.

Credit cards

Most bank managers will offer their customers extended credit by means of a credit card which allows you to buy goods immediately. This card is free and the bank pays out to the supplier as soon as you have completed the transaction. You have your account debited some six

weeks later, when you receive your monthly statement. Don't confuse this type of card with cards such as American Express, where you pay an annual fee to use the card, and must pay the debt incurred in full when the bill is received.

▲ WARNING ▲

Do not confuse credit cards with *bank cards* which are issued by the bank to act as a kind of guarantee against your cheque.

Bank cards

With a bank card, goods up to the value of £50 can be paid for and the same amount of money can be drawn in cash at banks other than your own, both in the United Kingdom and most European countries. The amount drawn on a cheque that is backed by a bank card is immediately debited to your current account.

Some banks issue *cash cards* which can be used to draw money, 24 hours a day, from a cash dispenser in the outside wall of the bank.

Bills

Most people worry if bills are not paid before a reminder notice is sent. It is important to take a disciplined approach to bill-paying.

Organising your bills

If you can obtain an old filing cabinet or desk with several drawers, you will find it easier to keep a check on your bill-paying.

As the bills come in, keep them together in a drawer or file, and deal with them once or twice a month. When you have paid them, file them away in case there are any queries. Keep your receipts in case you need to complain or return goods. Cheque stubs can be useful if a bill is presented again after you have paid it – you can then quote the number and date of the cheque by which you made the payment.

Paying your bills

You may find that sitting down for half an hour each month to write a few cheques and keeping a record of payments and receipts on cheque book stubs is enough to keep track of monthly transactions.

Standing orders and direct debit If you have regular payments to make, it is sensible to arrange for your bank to pay them by a regular standing order (do not forget these when you are making up your accounts). Bills which may vary from time to time can be paid by direct debit, which means the company you are paying can debit your account for different sums. (See also Giro account earlier in this chapter.)

Budgeting and economy

A budget is the only sure way of working out in advance where the money is going to go.

Where the money goes

Work out how much money there will be to budget with. Perhaps you have two incomes, also possible salary rises, bonuses, overtime or freelance earnings, but these last items should only be included when they are absolutely definite.

Remember if you are budgeting from, say 1 January and your rise does not apply until 1 June, you will only get six months of it on the year's total income.

 WARNING

Your budget should include a sum for emergencies – from repairs to unexpectedly necessary journeys.

Work out the annual or six-monthly total of all the bills and add them up. You will have to make an allowance for inflation. Subtract this figure from your income and see if you are left with a credit balance. If not, you will have to organise economies and the way you do this all depends on your own preferences. Whatever you decide on you must stick to it. It is what is going to stop you overspending.

 HANDY HINT

To help stay within your budget, do not carry more cash with you than you can afford to spend.

You may find it will help to make up some weekly and monthly charts, as suggested on the following page, to help you keep track of your accounts.

Chart for weekly expenditure

	Mon	Tue	Wed	Thurs	Fri	Sat	Sun	Weekly Total
Grocer/greengrocer								
Milkman/baker								
Fishmonger/butcher								
Laundry/cleaner								
Chemist								
Newsagent/bookshop								
Off-licence								
Gas/electricity								
Telephone/postage								
Fares								
Car								
Clothing								
Children's expenses								
Pets								
Entertainment								
Personal expenses								

Grand Total

Chart for monthly expenditure

Today's Date	Comments	Invoice Date/ Final Demands	Date Bill Paid and Method	Monthly Total
Mortgage				
Rent				
Rates				
Gas				
Electricity				
Other fuels				
Telephone				
Repairs & renewals				
Savings				
Insurance				
Hire purchase				
Credit cards				
TV rental/licence				
Subscriptions				
Medical				
Holidays				

Grand Total

What to pay when

Some bills have to be paid on a specific day at regular intervals – like the rent or mortgage and fares. Bills for rates, fuel and telephone usually give a few days grace, followed by a reminder notice. In general these cannot be moved and in your budget plan you should write down in which months they are due and how much each is likely to be. You will now be able to spot the black months with heavy outgoings.

Other large items of fixed expenditure such as life assurance premiums, car insurance, television licence, road tax and medical insurance will also fall due on a particular date, but it may be possible to move some of them – consult the relevant companies about this.

Spreading the load You can probably break some of your large payments up into smaller ones, usually monthly rates and insurances can be paid this way. Or you can open a budget account (see Banks and bank accounts).

Keeping accounts

If you do not keep accounts you will not know how your budget is panning out. You can either itemise every penny you spend – it sounds a chore but you will soon get used to it – or merely keep totals under rough headings.

★ **HANDY HINT** ★

Try to bring your accounts up to date every week. It is easier to make up for one week's overspending than for one month's.

Bulk buying

Bulk buying can be a way of saving both time and money. It is a good way of building up long term stocks, and commodities which you use often and in large quantities, which can be bought more cheaply and quickly in one trip.

Storing the bulk

Before you work out what is cheapest and where, you must be sure that you have adequate space to store your purchases. Non-perishable goods keep best in a dry place where the temperature is fairly constant.

Where to shop

Once you have organised your storage space you must decide where to do your shopping.

'Cash and carry' stores often give substantial discounts, but check first that your local supermarket is not just as competitive overall. Even small local shops may be prepared to make reductions for quantities.

When looking for the lowest prices, talk to neighbours, look in the local paper and check supermarket prices.

What to buy

The question you must ask yourself when bulk buying is: 'Am I buying this because I need it or because it's cheap?' There is no point in buying anything, however good a bargain, if it is not what you really want and will not be used regularly.

★ **HANDY HINT** ★

Before buying food in bulk, buy a small quantity to test it – the family may hate it. Even if they enjoy it, do not overdo the buying – eating endless quantities of the same food soon puts people off it.

Don't think, either, that because your store cupboards are bursting, it means you can all eat twice as much as usual. Keep up all your usual economical habits or you will find that you are not saving at all.

Stocktaking Control your stocks sensibly. Make a list of the items you think you require and then work out carefully how much you actually need during, say, three or six months. To get the maximum price reduction you may have to buy quite a large quantity of goods, so stick to things you know disappear at a regular rate.

Group bulk buying Among a group of people, this means that you can buy smaller quantities, still at the low price. However, it takes a little organisation to make the project work smoothly.

Items for bulk buying

Household basics: Lavatory paper, kitchen paper, foil, cling film, light bulbs, fuses, cleaning products, washing-up liquid, dishwasher powder and rinse aid, polishes, bath cleaner, soap, shampoo, toothpaste, detergents (which should be stored well away from food as their smell transfers easily), fabric softener, bleach.

Canned foods (bearing in mind the maximum good condition storage life of different foods – see FOOD AND NUTRITION – Store cupboard): Fruit, vegetables, spaghetti, baked beans, sardines, soups, etc., pet foods.

Bottled goods Sauces, pickles, jam, honey, oil and vinegar, wine, mixes, spirits.

Dried foods Pulses, grains and cereals, dried fruit in airtight containers.

Frozen foods (these will keep in a refrigerator for three months if the frozen food compartment has a 3-star marking, for one month if it has a 2-star marking. In a freezer food will keep for longer – see FOOD AND NUTRITION – Freezer, use): Frozen vegetables, fruit, meat, fish, convenience foods – beefburgers, fish fingers, sausages, etc.

Buyers' rights

When you are shopping, you should know your rights when things go wrong – even more essential is to know them beforehand, so that you can avoid problems.

Nowadays the law protects the shopper in many ways but if, for instance, you buy a dress that says 'dry clean' and wash it, you cannot complain to the seller if it shrinks.

Sellers' law simplified

The law protects the shopper in a number of ways. Further information can be obtained from the Office of Fair Trading.

● All goods sold must be 'of merchantable quality', that is, fit to be sold and not damaged in any way.

● They must be 'fit for purpose' – that is, function as they are supposed to do – a typewriter must type, wood-working glue must stick wood.

● The goods must be 'as described' – if the box says 'floral pattern' and contains a geometric design, you have cause for complaint.

These three conditions apply to all goods sold and cannot be negated or limited by a guarantee, even if you have signed it.

★ **HANDY HINT** ★

You should always sign and send off any guarantee that comes with something you buy, as it cannot take away your common law rights but may give you some additional benefits.

Although ultimately the manufacturer is responsible for his products, the shopkeeper is penalised for errors, even if he was not aware of them.

Unsolicited goods The British Unsolicited Goods and Services Act 1971 has made a lot of difference to the method of selling by which traders send unordered goods to your home and then demand money for them. If you now receive goods in this way and do not want them, you can:

Either keep them for six months, making sure they are not used or damaged in that time. After that, if the sender has not collected them, they legally become your property.

Or write to the sender saying you do not want the goods. If he fails to collect in 30 days, they become your property.

Do not be alarmed if the sender calls and demands money. If you did not order the goods and do not want them, he can be fined for asking for payment.

The Trade Descriptions Act 1968 This makes it a criminal offence for any seller to misdescribe the products he sells, in any way – verbally or in writing. The Act also applies to services, but it is harder to prove that a service is wrongly described.

Price marking Also covered by this Act and, unless there is a genuine reduction, which means that the goods must have been sold at the higher price for at least 28 days during the past six months, dramatic 'reductions' cannot be displayed.

The Weights and Measures Act 1963 This means that weight or other indication of quantity must be marked on the packaging of anything you buy. The only exceptions are milk bottles and small packets of certain foods. Some specific foods such as salt, sugar and butter must be sold in what are called 'prescribed quantities'.

The British Food and Drugs Act 1955 This lays down that all food and drink must be correctly described on its packaging and also specifies certain standards of hygiene in shop premises and the way food is stored.

All packaged foods must show a list of the ingredients they contain in order of weight.

Descriptive labelling

Labelling on goods can indicate whether they are a suitable buy for you.

A British Standard number shows that the manufacture is up to a standard laid down for that particular item. *The British Standard Kitemark* means that random tests are made on the product from time to time to ensure that standards are being maintained.

Electrical goods must meet certain safety standards automatically; look for electrical and gas safety labels when you buy.

Making a complaint

It is important to make sure that you know exactly what your complaint is about and that you have genuine grounds for making it.

First contact the shop where you bought the goods, since it is legally the responsibility of the shopkeeper to see that all his goods meet the conditions laid down in the Sale of Goods Act. The shop must give you back your money if any of these conditions are not met. They may offer you a credit note, but you do not have to accept this.

▲ WARNING ▲

If you inspected the goods thoroughly before buying them, the shop does not have to give a refund if the fault should have been obvious at that time. You are also not entitled to a refund if you did not check that what you were buying was fit for the required purpose.

The same conditions apply when you are buying second-hand, though it is obviously harder to prove. It helps if you have a witness when buying second-hand goods.

Complaining about services This is more difficult. The best precautions you can take are to check the small print before you have any work done and to make sure that you keep the receipt afterwards. Take up any complaints quickly in writing to the head office of the firm and be sure to keep copies of all correspondence.

▲ WARNING ▲

Never send in original bills or receipts as these may be valuable evidence that you need at a later stage. Have photo-copies made and send these to the firm if they demand them.

If you cannot get satisfaction by complaining directly, consult a consumer advisory centre or the Citizens Advice Bureau. Sometimes a trade association will be prepared to help – some have agreed codes of conduct with the Office of Fair Trading and do their best to ensure that customers get satisfaction from their services.

If you want action taken about a trader, consult the Trading Standards Officer or the Public Health Inspector at your town hall.

It is their job to investigate consumer complaints and if necessary take action to prosecute.

By making such a complaint you will also be helping other consumers. For instance, it is in the interests of the community to report bad food caused by dirty conditions or poor storage.

Calculators

An electronic calculator can help in checking your annual budget, adding up your day-to-day expenditure, working out 'best buys' or bulk-buying, or the amount of paint needed for a room or the length of fabric needed for furnishing.

Choosing a calculator

There is a vast range of price and size, but the main points you should look for are ease of operation and a certain minimum of technical features, such as a 'floating' decimal point, what is called 'full flow arithmetic' and a 'clear last entry' key which means you do not have to start again at the beginning if you make a mistake.

A percentage key is useful, particularly for working out VAT, and so is a memory key, which enables you to do several operations and then store the result and follow up with more operations using the stored information.

Covenants

The word covenant basically means a binding agreement. It is generally used to refer to a deed drawn up for paying money or a clause in a contract for house purchase.

Money covenants

A deed of covenant is a method of legally paying money, tax free, to a charity or an individual.

Charities Would-be donors sign a form which commits them to pay a sum of money regularly on a particular date for a term of not less than seven years, or until death if that is sooner.

The sum will be described as 'such sum as will, after deduction of income tax at the standard rate, amount to X pounds'. This means that the donor actually pays the X pounds, but the charity can claim back from the tax collector the amount of money that the donor has paid on that sum.

In most cases donations to charities are made through a banker's order.

Gifts to individuals The principles are basically the same as with charities, but a solicitor should draw up the deed of covenant. It is also necessary to make arrangements with the tax inspector, who will need to approve the details.

 ★ **HANDY HINT** ★

Look into the effects of taxation on the recipient carefully to make sure that other rights are not complicated.

Gifts to students These may be covenantable, but this must be checked with a solicitor.

Credit

Most people use credit facilities at some time or another. It is important to shop around for the best rates and choose an arrangement that is best suited to your life style and your finances.

Bank loans

One of the most accessible institutions for getting credit is your bank, particularly if you keep your account straight and only overdraw after making a special arrangement. Basically the bank manager will ask four questions.

Why do you want credit? Work out exactly what you need credit for. The bank manager will probably feel that redecorating the house before putting it up for sale is a more acceptable reason than merely wanting a holiday.

How much credit do you need? There is no point in asking for more than you need. Calculate carefully how much you will require to complete your scheme, and if your calculations seem sound, the bank manager will have more confidence in you.

Will you be able to pay it back? This is something you must also work out carefully – and it will help if you have a clean record at the bank, have paid off any overdrafts promptly and have not asked for too many of them.

What guarantee can you offer? If there is no obvious asset to which the bank manager can relate the loan, you may be asked to deposit the proof of ownership of saleable goods – such as savings certificates, house deeds – with the bank, or certain life assurance policies.

Different types of loan Banks operate different types of loan at different rates of interest. You are likely to get better interest rates than with a finance company or money lender.

Finance companies

Finance companies offer various types of credit which operate in slightly different ways. Rates of interest charged are high.

▲ WARNING ▲

Be wary of pitfalls when signing a contract. Make sure you read and understand the small print. Check what will happen if you fall behind with your payments or want to sell or exchange the goods.

Hire purchase When you undertake a hire purchase agreement, you are agreeing to hire goods from the finance company for a fixed sum for a fixed period, after which you will have the option of buying the goods for a nominal sum, usually by paying the last instalment.

The goods do not belong to you until this final payment is made. For this reason it is not usually possible to buy goods on hire purchase if they have a poor resale value (such as clothes and soft furnishings).

If you fall into arrears with the hire purchase payments, the company will have the right to take back the goods, though it may be necessary for them to get a court order before doing this if you have paid more than a certain proportion of the total price.

Credit sale If you enter into a credit sale agreement the goods are yours from the outset. If you fail to keep up with payments the finance company cannot take away the goods, but it can sue you for debt. You do not have the right to terminate this type of agreement.

Personal loans Finance companies may give you a loan, if you agree to pay it back at a fixed rate, over a fixed period. Personal loans are usually given for buying large items, such as central heating, garages, cars and so on, but are more expensive than loans from building societies or banks.

In certain cases, such as a loan on a home extension or other major improvement, it may be possible to claim tax relief on the interest paid.

Credit cards

Some banks and credit card companies issue cards which can be used to make purchases in shops, garages, restaurants and so on displaying the card symbol. There are two types: those issued by banks (Access, Barclaycard) are free to use and you can repay your debt over several months; the other type (Diners Club, AmEx) involves paying an annual use fee and also settling the account in full when the bill comes in. All cards supply you with free credit for up to about six weeks, but interest rates are high if you make a large purchase and pay it off gradually using a bank credit card. Credit cards can also be used for drawing money from a bank and for air and rail fares, car hire and so on.

Debt

Unemployment may mean payments cannot be kept up, a large unexpected bill could arrive, or a family on a tight budget could find themselves getting behind with bills. In any of these cases, take action as soon as possible.

Different courses of action

Once you realise that you have money problems, try to sort yourself out before creditors start to pursue you.

Work out what all your debts are and what you can afford to pay on a weekly or monthly basis. Then write to your creditors explaining how much you can afford to pay and why you cannot stick to your original commitments.

You may find it easier to take your problems to your bank manager. Explain your commitments and your income. You should be able to come to an arrangement whereby you pay off a certain proportion of your debts every month, leaving yourself with a tight, but manageable, budget.

If your creditor takes you to court, you will appear on a blacklist and have difficulty getting future credit.

Know your rights

Do not be frightened by threatening letters from your creditor if you are behind with payments. He is committing an offence if he puts pressure on you beyond asking for payment.

Do not send money through the post except by cheque or postal order. If these are lost, you can stop the cheque or reclaim the value of the postal order by taking the counterfoil to the issuing post office. In other cases, money lost in the post is your responsibility, unless your creditor has specifically asked for it to be sent in this way.

If you take goods to be repaired, cleaned or serviced, the company you take them to has the right to hold the goods until you have paid for the work.

Loans for gambling are against the law and the borrower has no legal obligation to repay his creditor.

Wives' household debts
A husband can be held liable for his wife's debts if these are incurred for household goods and services, and are considered to be reasonable and appropriate to his means.

Shopkeepers, however, have no valid claim against the husband if he can prove that he paid his wife an adequate housekeeping allowance and that she managed it incompetently.

Estimates

An *estimate* is an approximate judgment regarding delivery, services or goods. A *quotation* gives you the cost of providing the service or the goods at current prices.

What an estimate covers
An estimate should cover the nature of the work to be done, give information on the materials to be used and an idea of what quality of finish will be applied. It should also include the date by which the work will be completed and the price to be charged. Estimates cover all the services related to the home, and care and maintenance of major equipment.

How an estimate is prepared
The consumer can set out the terms under which the work is to be done and get it agreed in writing by the supplier of the services.

More commonly, the supplier prepares an estimate for the consumer. In general terms, he is bound by the figure in his estimate. However, traders cover themselves by saying on the estimate itself that the figure quoted is an approximate one and is subject to fluctuations in the cost of labour and materials. This allows the price to be varied within reasonable limits.

 ★ **HANDY HINT** ★
Deal with well established and reputable firms. Before asking for an estimate find out whether it is free or how much the charge will be.

Making a complaint
If something goes wrong, the Trade Descriptions Act will help protect your rights. You can sue the supplier in the County Court which deals with claims up to £1000. A simple, low-cost procedure enables you to take all the steps yourself (see Small claims).

Filing

A home filing system is invaluable for keeping household paperwork under control. Allow for expansion, so that changes do not mean starting again from scratch.

What needs to be filed
Subject headings which would help:

Bank Statements, cheque stubs, correspondence.

Bills Outstanding regular bills, receipts, notes of bills paid in instalments or by banker's order.

Building society and other savings Savings books, statements, dividend slips, share certificates.

Car Insurance and test certificates, servicing and repair details and receipts.

Credit card account Statements and counterfoils.

Education Correspondence with school, school notices, reports, receipts if any.

Employment Contracts and payslips for any staff employed such as a cleaner or babyminder.

Guarantees Domestic appliances, etc.

Hire purchase agreements

Household expenses Divided into heat/light, rates, repairs, etc.

Holidays Brochures, deposit receipts.

Income tax Assessments, correspondence.

Insurance Policies, renewal notices, correspondence.

Medical Health cards, vaccinations, etc.

Mortgage Payments, any loans.

Subscriptions Clubs, magazines, etc.

What to file in

There are a number of specially designed home files on the market which will hold enough paperwork for most households' needs. These can range from carrying cases containing a dozen or so suspended files to fan-type expanding wallets which are cheaper though less durable.

Filing cabinets These will take up more space, but are useful if you have a study

or permanent work corner. Secondhand ones are usually good value and can be painted to fit in with your decor.

Income tax

This complicated subject is understood mainly by the government department which administers it and by professional accountants and accounts offices.

If you have any doubts or queries, get in touch with your tax office, who will be able to help with your problem.

Self-employed

If you are self-employed you can offset some of your expenses against tax, but it is wise to take professional advice as there are a number of snags to avoid. All self-employed people need the help of an accountant and it is helpful to retain professional advice annually.

Tax return forms These are fairly complicated and must be filled in each year (up to April 5). Your local office of the Department of Inland Revenue can help you and explain the basic tax situation.

Insurance

The main aim of insurance is to protect you and your family from suffering financial loss as the result of some misfortune.

Insurance can cover death, bad weather, holiday illness, motor accident, fire in the home, flood damage, burglary and many other problems.

Some insurance is necessary by law (motor), some advisable in view of the cost of replacing articles (jewellery) and some sensible (life insurance).

Household

There are two kinds of household insurance – building and contents – though both can be combined in a householder's package policy, which can also be extended to cover extras such as a boat, horse, bicycle, etc.

It is a good idea to link building and contents insurance to the rate of inflation. Many major insurance companies now offer this facility.

Building insurance When a building society, bank or insurance company lends money for house purchase, it will insist on the building being insured. The policy covers the building and any outbuildings against such perils as fire, lightning, explosion, flood, subsidence and vehicles or aeroplanes hitting the house. These 'insured perils' are listed at the beginning of the policy and include accidental damage to fixed glass and washbasins, and to underground pipes.

If the house cannot be lived in after one of these perils has occurred, the policy will pay loss of rent or cost of other accommodation during the repairs.

> ## ▲ WARNING ▲
> The building must be insured for its full rebuilding cost plus an extra 20 per cent for clearance of debris and architect's fees. It is not enough to insure for the market value only.

Contents insurance The contents of your home are covered against the same perils, but not accidental damage. If the house is shared or sub-let, any theft must be accompanied by forcible entry if it is to be covered by the policy.

There are three levels of contents cover:

● *'Indemnity'* The company pays for the replacement value after deduction for age, deterioration or wear and tear.

● *'New for old'* This costs about 25 per cent more and provides a new replacement whatever the condition of the article.

● *'All risks'* This includes loss or accidental damage occurring anywhere. You can take out 'all risks' cover on specified items such as jewellery or cameras and you *must* insure for the full value. This is the most expensive type of insurance.

> ## ▲ WARNING ▲
> Important documents, house deeds, etc. are not insurable and should be lodged with a bank or solicitor.

Personal insurance

Health insurance A number of companies have special policies to cover costs incurred because of ill health, including private medical fees and loss of income. They sometimes undertake to pay a lump sum in the event of serious injury.

Travel insurance This can cover last-minute cancellation expenses, loss of baggage, illness or injury.

Unusual policies It is possible to take out

insurance policies to cover unpredictable events – such as rain at a garden party – and also to protect something unusual. Dancers may insure their feet or legs and pianists their hands.

Restrictions and problems

Restrictions Check the terms of any policy to see if there are restrictions, such as the age of a driver in a motoring policy; leaving the house unoccupied in a household policy and non-insurance of clothes at laundries and dry cleaners. Always read the small type very carefully.

WARNING

False statements, including failure to tell the insurance company if you have a criminal record, non-payment of premiums or failure to report previous claims, could invalidate your insurance cover.

Problems First consult your broker or company. The next resort is to go to the British Insurance Association which has information offices in most large towns.

The Motor Insurers' Bureau will provide compensation for bodily injury due to a motor accident, when there is no other effective insurance in force.

Mail order

Mail order is a good way to shop if you live a long way from shopping centres. It is also a convenient way of buying a very wide range of goods which you would sometimes have to search fairly hard to find locally.

Types of mail order

Book and record clubs This is one of the most popular forms of mail order because you buy the goods by filling in a form which appears as an advertisement in a newspaper or magazine, and often agree to pay so much in return for a set number of books or records a year. There can be problems when you want to stop the goods arriving and they continue to do so, or when they do not arrive at all.

If you have difficulties, write to the consumer relations department of the company and state your problem. If that does not work and the company is a member of the Mail Order Publishers' Authority, write to the Authority. (For unsolicited goods, see Buyers' rights.)

Catalogue mail order You choose what you want and the agent sends away for the goods. If anything is wrong with the goods the agent will deal with the mail order company and send the goods back if necessary.

If everything is in order, you pay for your mail order purchases by weekly instalments. This is a form of hire purchase, covered by the Consumer Credit Act.

The prices you pay may not necessarily be the lowest, but you can offset this against the cost of travelling to the nearest shopping centre.

Small ads mail order These are the advertisements placed in newspapers and magazines. You send the money and they send the goods by post or carrier. It may not be the cheapest way of shopping, but it can be very convenient.

When you order goods in this way, write to the address in the advertisement and set out clearly what you are ordering, where you saw the advertisement, the date, your address and refer to the fact that you are enclosing a cheque or postal order, plus its amount. Keep a copy of the advertisement and pin it to a copy of the letter. Keep the cheque or postal order counterfoil as well.

You should get delivery within 28 days or sooner, but if the goods do not arrive within 28 days, write again. If that does not produce results, write to the advertisement manager of the magazine or newspaper in which you saw the advertisement. He will take it up with the company and can stop more advertisements being placed if there is a backlog of unfulfilled orders.

The Newspaper Publishers' Association has set up a repayment scheme for people who lose money to mail order companies that go out of business; to prove your claim, you will have to produce all the details outlined earlier.

However, if you think the goods do not match up to their description, either in words or pictures, contact the consumer protection department at your town hall or civic centre, as it may be a case for prosecution under the Trade Descriptions Act.

Society and club mail order Some clubs and societies offer products related to their special interest – for example, motoring or gardening – and sometimes these are good value. If you do not get delivery of the goods you have ordered and paid for within 28 days, write to the secretary of the club with details.

Store catalogues Some department stores send catalogues to account customers and anyone else who asks for them. Some chain stores do the same for customers living overseas.

Usually you pay the whole account at once, unless you have an easy payment account with the store. When you order, make a note in the catalogue of when you sent the order, your cheque number and other details. If you are ordering for someone else, let the person know what it is, so that you have a check on whether it has arrived and is what you specified.

Whichever kind of mail order it is, the goods are covered by consumer legislation just as if they had been bought in shops. If they are faulty, damaged or dangerous, not what was described or the wrong quantity, you can take the matter up with your local consumer advice centre or with the consumer protection department; just as you can with goods bought in shops.

Complaints

If you do have problems, write to complain, giving the date when you sent the order, what you ordered, how you paid for it and your complaint. Keep a copy of your letter, date it and write your name and address in capital letters. That way you prove your purchase and give the information needed so that the company can check their records. It is also information that you will need if you have to take the matter further than the company.

Mortgages

A mortgage is the loan agreement between a house or flat owner and a money lending institution which enables the owner to buy his property. Mortgages can be arranged through building societies (most in this country are), local authorities, banks or special mortgage brokers. If using the latter, be sure that the company is a reputable one before entrusting any money to it.

Mortgage loans are repaid over prefixed time spans, which can vary but are usually 15, 20 or 25 years, and interest paid varies depending on the length of the loan. Building society interest rates are fixed by a consortium of the societies and are standard, although they vary from year to year. Local authority mortgages tend to have a higher rate of interest than building societies, but they will lend up to 100 per cent of the purchase price, whereas a building society usually asks for at least a small percentage to be paid in cash. You can obtain tax relief on the interest you pay on your mortgage.

Check your lending institution for information on different types of mortgages and any other special requirements they may have before you buy your property.

Rates

The rateable value of a property is intended to represent the rent that it would fetch if let to a tenant in the ordinary way.

Adjustments are made if the dwelling is altered or improved – i.e. by adding a sunroom or central heating.

The rateable value is the yardstick used for calculating how much money you will have to pay. For instance, if the rateable value is £300 and rates are 50p in the pound, you would pay £150 – if rates were £1.50 in the pound, you would pay £450.

The money raised is spent on managing the district and its services, providing such items and services as roads, police, fire service, refuse disposal, education, etc.

Paying rates

The local authority sends you a bill, generally twice a year. However, arrangements can usually be made to pay rates in 10 equal instalments, by cash or banker's order.

Appeals If you feel your rates are too high, you can lodge an appeal. The local authority must let you see the valuation list, so you can check whether you are paying more than your neighbour in a seemingly identical home.

Savings

If your budgeting works out well and leaves you with a surplus, or if you have an unexpected windfall, it is sensible to put the money into a savings scheme which will give you interest.

Some savings schemes are index-linked and will top up your savings by the amount you have lost because of the rise in the cost of living. However, you must leave your money in the scheme for a number of years before the addition is made to it.

Building societies

These generally run three systems:

● A share account offers the lowest rate of interest, but is convenient as money up to a certain amount can be withdrawn on request.

● A build-up account is for regular saving and attracts higher interest.

● A subscription account has the highest rate, but you are committed to regular payments for several years.

Government (post office) savings

Savings bank This pays a small rate of interest. A fixed sum can be withdrawn immediately, but larger sums take a little time to clear.

Savings bank investment account The money must be left for more than a month, but accrues more interest.

National savings certificates Each unit costs £10 and the value builds up at the end of the first year and then at four-month intervals. The yield is completely tax free.

Index-linked certificates (now called People's bonds!) After they have been held for one year the money you get back will be increased each month in line with price rises since buying.

Save as you earn This is an index-linked savings scheme whereby you save a fixed amount every month for five years and each of the sixty contributions is adjusted in line with any change in the Retail Price Index which has occurred. The final amount can be drawn out at the end of the five-year period, or can be left in for another two years, when it will qualify for a tax-free bonus equal to two of your monthly payments.

Payment can be made by deduction from pay, if your employer runs a SAYE scheme; by banker's standing order or in cash at a post office or by Girobank standing order. The maximum monthly payment is £20 and the minimum is £4.

Small claims

If you wish to claim against someone who has sold you faulty goods or given you bad service, you can do so in the county court. Such an action is relevant if the amount you are claiming is £1000 or under. You need no legal knowledge, or a solicitor, to take this action.

Making a claim

First ask for a form from the court office (the address will be in the telephone directory). The form is simple to fill in, needing only names and addresses, the amount of the claim, with brief details of its nature, and whether you want to have the case heard by an arbitrator.

Arbitration If the sum you are claiming is not more than £100 you can ask the registrar of the court to settle your case by arbitration. If the sum is higher and both parties agree, he can order arbitration and then the case is heard in private. It is very informal and the arbitrator carries just as much weight as an award given by the court in public.

CHAPTER 12

KITCHEN SENSE

Cookers•Dishwashers•Microwave ovens
Mixers•Refrigerators•Toasters
Washing machines

Basic kitchen plans

If you are lucky enough to be able to plan a kitchen from scratch, you can have everything the way you want it. When you have to adapt a room that already has certain immovable fixtures, the task becomes more difficult.

Preparing a basic plan

1 Draw the ground plan of your kitchen to scale on a large piece of graph paper.
2 Mark all doors and windows and also any places where you hope – planning permission allowing – to make doors or windows.
3 Draw, in scale, shapes of any fixtures such as a sink, boiler, or existing equipment like the cooker or washing machine that you do not want to move.
4 List all the items that you want on the floor of your kitchen.

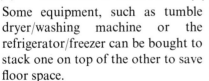

★ **HANDY HINT** ★

Some equipment, such as tumble dryer/washing machine or the refrigerator/freezer can be bought to stack one on top of the other to save floor space.

5 Measure and draw out squares in the same scale as the plan on another piece of paper to represent your equipment, then move them around on your plan to see how the various combinations look.

Take into account the way you will be using the equipment, the way doors open and the importance of being near the appropriate services, such as water, gas and electricity.

Most kitchen unit and equipment manufacturers now build to a range of standard sizes, so you can allow space for items you do not yet have.

Planning the work flow

Experts claim that a perfect kitchen layout runs: work surface, cooker, work surface, sink, work surface. It is certainly helpful to have a scheme which allows you to put hot dishes down next to the cooker and to have ample room around the sink. But the important point is that your layout works for *your* way of preparing and cooking food. It will also be dictated by the shape of your kitchen. Your main working surface should be as close as possible to where you keep your utensils and ingredients. A well thought out kitchen plan will save you time and energy.

Safety in the kitchen

Be sure to keep electrical equipment and water as far apart as possible, even at the risk of making slightly more work for yourself.

Choose kitchen equipment carrying the standard safety mark, to minimise risk. Keep potential hazards like poisonous chemicals out of the reach of children and store sharp knives and choppers on a magnetic rack or wooden holder mounted on a wall out of harm's way.

Guard against fire and keep a small chemical extinguisher or asbestos fire blanket hanging near the cooker. See also HOME SAFETY.

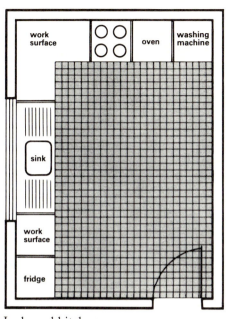

L-shaped kitchen

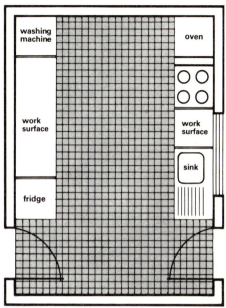

Corridor kitchen

U-shaped kitchen

Galley kitchen

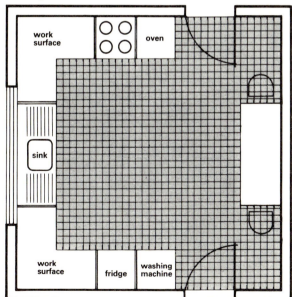

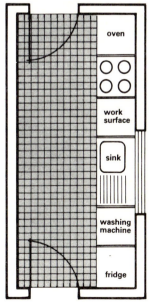

Built-in units

If you are reasonably certain that you will be staying in your house for a few years, it is worthwhile investing in matching, built-in units. A modern fitted kitchen is easy and labour saving and when you eventually have to move, will add to the value of your home.

Types of built-in units

To arrange for a professional firm to fix a range of purpose-built, matching units is very expensive. An alternative is to buy self-assembly kits, put them together and fit them yourself. This, of course, does need a certain amount of do-it-yourself experience.

New on the market is a range of matching doors which can be fitted to existing cupboards to unify the appearance of the kitchen. These are available in standard sizes and can also be made to measure.

★ HANDY HINT ★

If you want to install units gradually, make sure that the manufacturers intend to keep your range in production for some years ahead.

What to allow space for

You will need to allow space for crockery and glass, cookware, pots and pans, cutlery, baking equipment, larger equipment, such as mixers, blenders and mincers, kitchen cleaning materials, tea towels and so on. You may also need space for a pedal bin and vegetable rack. Dry stores, jams and so on are better kept in wall cupboards above the work surfaces. See also HOME IMPROVEMENTS – Cupboards.

Coffee makers

If you drink a lot of coffee, then a coffee maker of some kind is a must. There are various types on the market which infuse the ground coffee by different methods.

Types of coffee maker

Percolators These are filled with water up to the required mark and the coffee put into a basket. When the water boils it passes up a centre tube and drips down through the coffee, turning off automatically when the coffee is ready. They incorporate a device to keep coffee hot.

Filter types In these, the water is heated and drips into a separate serving jug, usually of glass, passing through the ground coffee which is placed in a filter. Most models can make anything from two to eight or ten cups.

Vacuum machines These pass the water from the bottom half of the coffee maker to the top, and then the made coffee is sucked back down by a vacuum process.

WARNING

It is particularly important to use a BEAB approved model which has a safety cut-out to prevent overheating if the container boils dry.

Excellent coffee can be made with a simple filter which fits into the mouth of a heatproof glass jug. This is known as the jug method.

Cookers

A cooker is an expensive piece of kitchen equipment that should last for many years. Even if you are restricted to one particular fuel, there is still a wide range to choose from.

A basic cooker consists of a hob, usually with two to four rings or burners. Most models also incorporate an eye-level or below-hob grill.

Electric cookers

These may have radiant rings or solid discs on top. The former heat up more quickly and retain heat for less time, so that you waste less fuel. Some radiant rings incorporate a duplex element, and can be adjusted so that only the centre coils of the ring heat up, thus saving fuel when you are using a small pan. Some cookers have ceramic hobs, made from a smooth sheet of durable glass ceramic which conceals the radiant heating elements. The position and size of the elements is marked on the surface of the hob. They are easy to clean, but you should avoid using abrasive materials which may scratch the surface.

Electric ovens are always thermostatically controlled so that precise cooking temperatures can be achieved. Most incorporate an automatic timer which can be set to turn the oven on at a certain time and also turn itself off.

Fan-assisted ovens Some ovens are fan-assisted, which means that they maintain the same temperature throughout. The fan circulates the heated air and prevents the normal situation where the top oven shelves are hotter than the lower ones. These ovens are useful when batch baking or preparing several casseroles for the freezer, but some people prefer a variation in temperature, to cook different types of dishes simultaneously. Fan-assisted ovens are more economical to use and easier to keep clean than conventional types.

Cleaning oven linings Most electric ovens have easy-clean linings which cut down or eliminate the chore of oven cleaning. Continuous cleaning linings stay clean provided the oven is used at a minimum of 190°C (375°F) for at least an hour a week. These linings are sometimes fitted only on the sides and back of the oven, so that top and floor may still have to be cleaned conventionally. (See also CLEANING THE HOUSE – Oven cleaners.)

Electric grills For economy, some cookers have the advantage of a half-grill facility. Many grill compartments also double as a small auto-timed oven.

Gas cookers

These are more easily controlled than electric cookers and give at the turn of a tap an instant increase or reduction in heat. On most models there are large and small hob burners to accommodate pans of different sizes. The oven is thermostatically controlled.

Formerly, gas cookers had a small pilot light always burning in the oven.

This made it inadvisable to fit them with automatic timers, as food left in them would become slightly warmed and are liable to breed harmful micro-organisms. Today, with the invention of electronic spark ignition, there is no pilot light and the oven can be lit either at the press of a button or by a pre-set automatic timer.

Like electric ovens, gas models may come with easy-clean linings.

Buying a gas or electric cooker

Whichever you buy, look for clear, easy to operate controls, a good range of shelf positions and a plate-warming rack or drawer. Some people also find a rôtisserie useful.

Oven doors *Drop-down* doors are useful for standing a dish on while you baste or stir, but take up space in a small kitchen. *Side-opening* doors can usually be supplied to open on the more suitable side for the design of your kitchen. *Glass panels* in the oven door, or glass inner doors are useful, in conjunction with an inner light, to see how food is cooking.

 WARNING

If your oven temperature is consistently too high or too low, contact your local service agent, gas or electricity board, to adjust the thermostat.

Oil-fired and solid fuel cookers

These generally have two large, solid cooking plates on top, on each of which you can place two or three pans at a time. They have covers which keep in the heat when not in use. One plate gives quick boiling, the other is for simmering, but it is essential for full efficiency to have pans with flat, machined bases to make the most of the heat.

These cookers usually have two ovens, one hot and one slow. New owners may take time to adjust to them, but the advantages of having constant heat at any time of the day or night makes this type of cooker well worth considering, especially if you have a large, living-kitchen layout. Domestic water can be heated by such cookers and they give a gentle background heat in the kitchen. Storage space is, of course, necessary for the fuel.

Microwave cookers

These are compact little cabinets in which food is cooked by microwaves (electromagnetic waves). These act on the molecules in the food, which vibrate against each other. Cooking is by time not by temperature, and is usually done very quickly. Although they look like ovens, microwave cookers carry out all the functions that one would normally associate with the hob: boiling, pot-roasting, steaming, poaching, melting.

 WARNING

Aluminium foil and stainless steel, or dishes decorated with gold or silver should not be used in the microwave cooker. They reflect back the waves, and could damage the cooker.

They do not brown foods, although manufacturers have devised ingenious ways of solving this problem. Special leaflets supplied with the cookers show how to use microwaves efficiently. They are certainly clean, safe and simple, and can be plugged in to any 13 amp outlet. One of their greatest uses is for cooking frozen food by thawing and heating it in a fraction of the time normally taken.

Split-level cookers

The main advantage of these is that you can site each unit where it suits you and the kitchen layout best. The eye-level oven means that you do not have to bend to remove or check the food inside. It is safer in a home where there are children or elderly people. It is also possible to mix fuels – that is, to have an electric oven with a gas hob or vice versa. However, a split-level hob means one less working surface, unless it has a shut-down lid.

Wall-mounted grills and mini ovens

These can be useful in a small kitchen, provided that large quantities of food do not need to be cooked at one time. A hob will also be needed for boiling if this is the only form of cooker in use. There are several brands of excellent small cookers also available.

Cooker hoods

Cooker hoods may be ductless or ducted. Both types consist of a metal canopy which is fitted 60–90cm (2–3ft) above the hob or 40–60cm (1ft4in–2ft) above an eye-level grill. Some types are not suitable for fixing above gas grills.

The hoods come in various sizes, from about 50cm (1½ft) wide to about 90cm (3ft). They are usually about 15cm (6in) high and 50–55cm (1½ft–1ft9in) deep, from wall to front of the unit. It may be possible to install one either between or beneath fitted units. Most models incorporate a light to give direct lighting to the cooker hob.

How they work

Cooker hoods remove the cooking smells from the kitchen by taking air from above the cooker and filtering it. The cleaned air is released back into the kitchen or out through a duct in the wall.

Foam and aluminium filters absorb grease, while charcoal traps smells and steam. The air is driven through the cooker by a fan which may be operated at different speeds, depending on the amount of steam.

Ductless hoods These work by absorbing, filtering and recirculating the air from cooking smells, but they do not have an air outlet for direct extraction from the house.

The absorbent materials used may have to be changed more frequently than for ducted hoods.

Ducted hoods These filter the grease out of the hot air and it is then driven through ducts to the outside of the house.

Maintain the efficiency of your cooker hood by washing the aluminium mesh sheet or foam pad regularly. If your hood has an activated charcoal or carbon filter, the manufacturer's leaflet will recommend how often this should be replaced.

Installation

All cooker hoods must be earthed and are usually run off a 13 amp plug fitted with a 3 amp fuse. In some cases fittings must be done professionally.

If you are fitting a cooker hood with a fan in a room with a chimney or fuel-burning appliance which does not have a balanced flue, it is essential to ensure that there is an adequate air inlet so that you do not create a down draught or draw fumes down the flue.

Cupboards

The more cupboards you can comfortably fit into your kitchen, the more organised you will be.

Types of cupboard

Cheap cupboards can often be picked up at auction sales etc., stripped down and repainted (see REPAIRS AND MAINTENANCE – Furniture).

Self-assembly units are cheaper than those sold as fitted units and, when in place, can look equally attractive.

More expensive cupboards from fitted ranges can be a mass of ingenious designs intended to maximise space. If your budget permits, you will certainly find it helpful to buy units fitted with racks that swivel out so that you can store items in awkward corners, with pull-out wire baskets for holding utensils, cans and possibly vegetables. Some of these cupboards are fitted with special

cantilevered shelves on which equipment such as a large mixer can be swung up for use, and down and away for storage. Some firms make these fitments separately so that you can install them in home-made or cheaper units.

Shelf depth This should not be too great, particularly if you are trying to make the most of a limited amount of space.

Wall-mounted cupboards These should not be fitted too near to the cooker. They should be fixed at least 38cm (1ft3in) above the working surface and not be more than 23–30cm (9–12in) cm depth.

See also HOME IMPROVEMENTS – Cupboards.

Dishwashers

A dishwasher uses water heated to a far higher temperature than human hands can stand. It uses temperatures up to 65°C (140°F) which kill most germs. It also needs a strong detergent, and therefore tends to produce cleaner washing up than that done by hand in a sink.

A dishwasher can cope with a large quantity at one time and so normally only needs to be used once or twice a day or after entertaining.

Choosing a dishwasher

A dishwasher needs a water supply and an electric socket as well as the drainage system. Most run off the cold water supply and are of a size to fit into a row of standard kitchen units, though there are also small models to fit on top of a work top or draining board. Large models usually take 12 international place settings, table models take four to six.

Check on the number of place settings (glass, cup and saucer, soup plate or sweet dish, dinner plate and side plate plus cutlery) that it will hold. Make sure that your glasses and crockery will fit into it. The revolving spray arm can knock against very large plates and long stemmed glasses can be difficult to fit in. Before you settle on a model, check whether any of the interior racks are movable to take extra large items.

Controls Most models have several wash cycles of different lengths and heats, including a cold rinse. When a few dirty items are to be left in the dishwasher until a full load has been collected, a 'bio' cycle for hardened food deposits is helpful and also a cooler wash for more delicate items.

Detergents Special dishwasher detergent must be used according to the manufacturer's instructions. You will also require a rinse aid liquid to prevent smears and streaks, and, in some models, household salt to activate a water softener.

What you can wash

Most modern crockery is dishwasher proof. Silver and stainless steel cutlery can be put into the dishwasher, though not together. Bronze cutlery cannot be washed in the dishwasher and neither can bone, ivory or wooden handled items (with the exception of some specially designed wooden handled ranges now available).

Most glass is safe, but lead crystal or delicate engraved pieces should not go in. Dishes with gold trim may not be suitable for dishwasher cleaning. Some pots, pans and casseroles can go in, but unglazed casseroles will crack. In general such items take up too much space and the machine cannot remove burnt-on food deposits efficiently.

Advantages

Dishwashers save time spent at the sink, use less hot water, clean thoroughly and more hygienically, and can store dirty crockery out of sight before it is switched on.

Disadvantages

A dishwasher takes up space in the kitchen. More crockery and cutlery may be needed as there is a tendency to be economical and only operate the machine once full. You will find detergent, rinse aid and water heating are quite expensive.

Food preparation machines

What a mixer can do

Depending on the power of the mixer, it will be able to perform a wide range of tasks. These include: whisking, whipping, kneading, mixing, creaming, beating and rubbing in – all jobs which are tedious and time-consuming.

On many mixers the bowl automatically rotates, and can be left to itself while you can carry on with preparing the remaining ingredients.

Food mixers

Before buying a food mixer, decide what jobs you want it to do, and the amounts that you want it to cope with. If possible try to watch a demonstration, look at the instruction book and check that the controls are easy to use and the handle comfortable. In large table models, check which attachments are available, which ones, if any, are included in the basic price, and what jobs they are designed to do. Some food mixers are extremely noisy.

Table mixers

These tend to be rather heavy, and should be kept in one place on a worktop for convenience. One type has an arm which overhangs the mixing bowl and various powered attachments can be fixed to it. The other type has a central spindle in the base of the machine, onto which the beaters fit. Choose the appliance that is most suited to your particular cooking requirements.

Attachments Attachments available for table mixers include blenders, grinders, mincers, slicers/shredders, juice extractors, potato peelers, can openers, bean slicers, pea hullers and cream makers.

It would be sensible to learn first how to make full use of your basic mixer and then gradually add those attachments which seem most useful to you.

Electronic mixers These have miniature controls inside and automatically adjust the strength of the motor to the task in hand. They give a greater precision and control over a wide range of mixing jobs.

Hand mixers

The simplest kind of electric beater is a small, hand-held type powered by a battery and with a pair of rotary beaters. Mains-operated hand-held mixers have smaller, less powerful motors than table models and fewer speed control settings. They are generally used with a bowl and stand, but whether these are supplied with the mixer depends on the make and/or price. Hand mixers can usually do most of the same basic beating, creaming and whipping as table mixers.

Normally there will be wire beaters for light mixtures, heavier metal ones for stiffer mixtures and a dough hook for kneading. These hooks will not deal with large quantities and some types of bread.

Rinse the beating end immediately after use as it becomes difficult to clean if left. Store small, hand-held beaters carefully, preferably on their own hooks.

Blenders

A blender or liquidiser is a useful buy for making soups and purées, and for anyone who has to prepare invalid or baby food.

Types of blender

Blenders come in a variety of types and materials, as well as sizes. Some share the basic motor onto which they fit with a small grinder for nuts, coffee, spices and so on. Both the blender and grinder in this type of machine can be washed, as the motor is housed in a completely separate unit. The motor runs at only one speed.

The more elaborate and expensive blenders may have a choice of several speeds, though only two or three are generally needed.

Blades Cheaper blenders may have only two cutting blades, others have four or six, all fixed in the base.

★ **HANDY HINT** ★

Check the position of the blades, as in some models they are set too high to deal with small quantities.

Goblets

These vary in size and shape, but should never be filled more than two-thirds full. They are generally made of plastic and have a plastic lid with a removable piece in the centre through which food can be dropped while the maching is running. It is sensible to choose a goblet that has a handle.

Always clean the goblet very thoroughly. The best way is to squirt a little washing up liquid inside, quarter fill with warm water and switch on the blender for a few seconds. Repeat with clear water, rinse and turn upside down to drain.

Food processors

Among the most advanced pieces of kitchen equipment on the market are food processors. These are powerful machines which perform a wide range of tasks, and are operated by simply changing blades to perform the appropriate function. This means that one machine does every job, and greatly simplifies your work in the kitchen.

Food processors vary in price, and are a good investment for family cooking and for freezer owners who need to prepare a lot of food in batches. Watch a demonstration in the store, and read the manufacturer's leaflet before making up your mind which one you wish to buy.

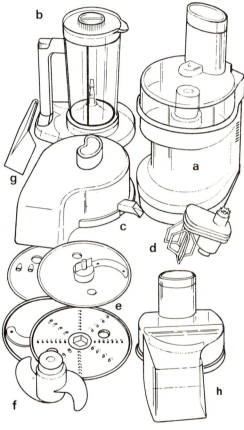

Food processor (a); blender attachment (b); juice extractor (c); whisk attachment (d); discs with various cutting faces (e); plastic blade for mixing dough (f); plastic spatula (g); special lid with ejector for preparing large quantities (h).

Freezers

Being able to store perishable food in a freezer for several months means fewer shopping trips, and a glut of fruit or vegetables from the garden can be stored away to be eaten when supplies are scarce and costly. You can take advantage of special offers and bulk buying, you can cook when you feel like it, and special occasions such as Christmas can be planned and catered for well in advance

Choosing a freezer

The type and size you select will depend on your family's needs and the space available to house it.

What size to choose A useful guide is to allow 57 litres (2cu ft) net freezer space per member of the family, plus 57 litres (2cu ft). About 25 litres (1cu ft) of space stores 10–12kg (22–25lb) of frozen food.

The *chest freezer* with top opening lid, ranges in size from about 120 litres (4½ cu ft) to 650 litres (23cu ft). The *upright freezer* with front opening, comes in sizes from 60 litres (2¼cu ft) up to 370 litres (13cu ft). Combined refrigerator/ freezer models are also available.

Chest freezers These take up more space than uprights, but are more economical to run. Movable baskets help to store different groups of food separately.

Refrigerator/freezer These models have less freezing space but again, take up less room than a chest type freezer.

Upright freezers The shelves and sliding baskets allow food to be stored in a more organised and more easily accessible way.

Siting the freezer

A freezer will operate efficiently in a cool, dry and well ventilated place. Spare bedroom, hallway, even the garage can be used if there is not room in the kitchen. If you do site it in the garage, make sure it is lockable. Site the freezer near to an electric socket and tape the switch to avoid it being inadvertently turned off.

Operating the freezer

Exterior lights may indicate that the freezer is on, when the freezer temperature is on fast-freeze setting, or if the temperature inside rises above normal.

Only freeze food which is in perfect condition and prepared correctly (see FOOD AND NUTRITION – Freezer use). Use specially designed packing material and mark with labels giving the date of freezing, the food and the quantity. Keep the freezer well packed – it is wasteful to freeze only small amounts of food.

Defrosting the freezer

Freezers require little day-to-day maintenance but must be defrosted occasionally. Defrost chest freezers about once or twice a year, uprights two or three times.

★ **HANDY HINT** ★

As a guide, defrost your freezer when the ice on the sides of the cabinet is more than 12mm (½in) thick.

---

1 Switch off the electricity.

2 Remove all the frozen food and wrap in newspaper, blanket, insulated container or even an old sleeping bag to keep cold. Store temporarily in a cool place.

3 Leave the door or lid of the freezer open and allow to defrost.

4 The process can be speeded up by placing bowls of hot water inside the cabinet and by helping to loosen the melting ice with a wooden or plastic spatula (never a metal object as this may damage the lining of the cabinet). Old towels placed at the base of the cabinet can help to mop up the water.

5 When all the ice is melted, wipe over the inside of the cabinet with a solution of bicarbonate of soda and hot water, not detergent.

6 Dry out thoroughly.

7 Switch the freezer on, and replace the food immediately.

Insurance

Freezer insurance can be obtained to cover loss of food through breakdowns and failure of the power supply. Frozen food should last for about 24 hours if the freezer is reasonably full and the door not opened. Fill spaces with newspaper or towels to keep the temperature down.

See also FOOD AND NUTRITION – Freezer use.

Kettles

Standard electric kettles

Most types hold 1.7 litres (3 pints) and take about four minutes to boil when full. Smaller and larger kettles are also available to suit your needs. Switch off immediately the steam starts to emerge from the spout and vents. A kettle left boiling will create condensation in the room and there is the risk that the water may boil away and the element be damaged.

BEAB safety-approved kettles have a built-in safety device which prevents overheating if the kettle boils dry or is switched on when empty.

Automatic electric kettles

These have a built-in thermostat which switches the kettle off automatically once it has boiled. With most types you simply set the kettle to boil by depressing a switch (some models have a light to show when this is done). The kettle will switch itself off and, in more sophisticated models, will switch itself on again when the water has cooled for a while.

Most automatic kettles hold 1.7 litres (3 pints) and high speed models are included in most ranges.

Energy conscious people will be glad to know of a new type of automatic kettle which can boil as little as a cupful of water. Designed like a jug, with a side handle to protect hands from steam, this kettle is fully automatic, easy to clean and holds 1.7 litres (3 pints).

Kitchen utensils

There are literally hundreds of kitchen tools and gadgets on the market. When buying, start with the basic utensils and add extra items as you can afford them.

Basic list of kitchen utensils

Baking
Baking sheet or Swiss roll tin
Bun tins
Cake tins, large and small
Flan dishes or rings
Loaf tins
Mixing bowls, including some with lips
   for easy pouring
Piping equipment
Sandwich tins
Rolling pin, pastry cutters and board
Roasting tin and trivet
Wire cooling tray

Cutting and opening
Apple corer
Carving set
Can opener
Chopping board
Corkscrew
Crown cap opener
Garlic press
Grater/shredder
Kitchen knives, assorted
Knife sharpener
Mincer
Potato peeler
Scissors
Screw-top jar opener

Cookware
Gratin dishes
Individual ovenproof dishes
Pie dishes
Pudding basins
Range of casserole dishes, flameproof
   and ovenproof
Soufflé dishes

Pots and pans
Deep fat fryer
Double boiler
Frying pan

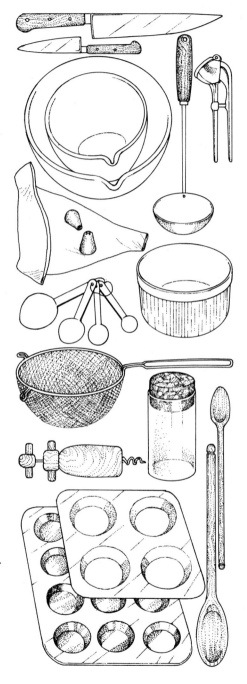

Omelette pan (optional)
Pressure cooker
Saucepans, assorted
Steamer or steaming attachment
Wok
Stirring and beating
Kitchen forks
Kitchen spoons
Ladle
Perforated spoon
Potato masher
Spatulas, wooden and rubber
Tongs
Whisks and beaters
Wooden spoons
Storage
Airtight plastic boxes and tins
Bread bin
Freezer containers (if necessary)
Herb and spice jars
Storage jars
Straining
Circular strainers with handles
Colander
Sieves
Weighing and measuring
Kitchen scales (showing both metric
    and imperial measures)
Measuring jug
Measuring spoons
Miscellaneous
Fish slice
Kettle
Jelly mould, ring mould

 ★ HANDY HINT ★

Many supermarkets sell off ceramic pâté containers once the contents are finished. Such dishes make very inexpensive, ovenproof casseroles.

Refrigerators

Choosing a refrigerator

A 90–120 litre (3½–4½cu ft) model is usually adequate for a family of two or three. A larger 140–170 litre (5–6 cu ft) type will be needed for a larger family. Make sure that whatever you choose will fit into your kitchen.

Look for versatile shelving, adjustable racks and make sure that tall bottles can be accommodated. Check that the refrigerator door will open conveniently.

Refrigerators are available both with and without a freezer compartment. Which you choose may depend on whether you own a freezer and if so, where the freezer is situated. If it is in the garage, for instance, some frozen food storage may be useful in the kitchen. Self-defrosting refrigerators are available and save work.

Noise A certain amount is inevitable with the usual type of compressor refrigeration unit. Absorption type units are silent, but are only available in sizes under 140 litres (5 cu ft). Absorption types (gas) refrigerators also cannot reach very low temperatures so are not suitable for storing frozen food.

Installation A 13 amp power point is needed near to the refrigerator. Place tape over the switch to prevent it being turned off by mistake.

Defrosting a refrigerator

When the ice is 6mm (¼in) thick, the refrigerator needs defrosting. There are four basic methods: manual, push-button, accelerated defrost and completely automatic defrost, depending on the type of refrigerator.

 HANDY HINT

Refrigerators work better and are more efficient if there is little or no ice on the frozen food compartments.

Manual

1 Remove all the food from the frozen food department and from the main cabinet of the refrigerator too.

2 Switch off the electricity or turn to the defrost position.

3 Place a drip tray under the frozen food compartment and, as the ice melts, the water will collect in the tray.

4 When all the ice has melted, empty the tray and clean out the refrigerator with a solution of bicarbonate of soda and hot water. Never use a detergent – it can leave a smell and taste.

5 Switch on again and return the food to the refrigerator.

Push-button When the button is pressed the refrigerator stops until the ice has melted and restarts automatically. As with the manual method, the frozen food should be removed and the drip tray emptied.

Accelerated defrosting This also has push-button control, but the walls of the

 HANDY HINT

Wrap the frozen food in layers of insulating material, such as newspaper, while the refrigerator is defrosting.

evaporator are heated. Check manufacturer's leaflet regarding removal of frozen food.

Fully automatic defrosting The food does not have to be removed. The unit cuts out automatically when defrosting is necessary and cuts in again when the ice is melted. The water is evaporated by the heat of the compressor.

See also FOOD AND NUTRITION Refrigerator use.

Sinks

Installing a new sink is quite expensive, so be sure you choose the right sink and have it fitted in the ideal location.

Types of sink

Stainless steel Most new sinks are stainless steel – choose 18/8 grade steel. These sinks are available in all shapes and sizes, and will fit into almost any unit or working surface. Stainless steel is the most expensive material for a sink, but is hard-wearing and easy to clean.

Glazed fireclay These traditional, deep sinks are very tough, but once chipped they should be discarded as they will be a trap for germs. Any china dropped into such a sink will break, so use a plastic bowl for washing up. A fireclay sink will not fit into a modern base unit.

Plastic Plastics such as polyester resin (reinforced with glass fibre) are used for making sinks as well as baths. Their main disadvantage is that they can be damaged by great heat.

Vitreous enamel On cast iron or sheet steel this is cheaper than stainless steel but is no longer widely available. Vitreous enamel sinks are unaffected by heat or strong chemicals and are easy to clean. Chips may be repaired with a proprietary bath renovator.

Double sinks Even if you have a dishwasher, there is a great deal to be said for having a double sink. All jobs requiring washing and rinsing can be done in sequence; one sink can be used for preparation and the other for clearing up, and two people can work side by side. Two sinks are more convenient if you have a waste disposal unit.

A double sink requires a mixer tap which swings from sink to sink.

Waste disposal unit

If you plan to have a waste disposal unit, the hole must be 9cm (3½in) in diameter – standard sized holes are only 4cm (1½in). A hole this size in a stainless steel sink can be cut, but only if it is in the middle of the sink.

A large hole may be fitted with a basket strainer while there is no waste disposal unit, and **plugs** of the right size are also available.

Slow cookers

An electric slow cooker is designed to cook food gently over a number of hours without it burning or boiling over. Models generally have a choice of two settings, enabling food prepared in the morning to be cooked all day on the lower setting, or ready by mid-day on the higher one. Automatic slow cookers can be set to switch down to the correct setting.

Slow cooking is ideal for soups, stews, casseroles, pot roasts and steamed puddings and will also tenderise cheaper cuts of meat. Slow cookers are usually made to hold either 2 litres (3.5 pints) in the family size, or 3.5 litres (6 pints) in the large size. Some are available with even greater capacity.

Convenience

A slow cooker can be left unattended while you are out shopping or at work. If you are delayed, the contents will not burn or dry up. A stew that was planned to be ready at three o'clock could successfully be left cooking until the evening.

Economy

A slow cooker uses only the same amount of electricity as a light bulb. However, the energy is used just to make one dish. If you were to load your cooker oven to full capacity, the cost per dish would probably still work out to be cheaper.

Safety, design and care

It is perfectly safe to leave a slow cooker operating unattended all day.

All models use glazed earthenware for the inner cooking dish, which is in some cases secured permanently in an outer protective casing, and in other cases sits in a metal lined heating base. A removable dish can be used for serving at table, refrigerator storage and crisping toppings under the grill, and can also be washed easily.

WARNING

Often, food has to be brought to boiling point before placing it in the slow casserole. Red kidney beans must be boiled for *at least* 10 minutes before slow cooking, or they cause very unpleasant side effects. Be sure to read the manufacturer's instructions carefully.

Toasters

Electric toasters

Electric pop-up toasters are generally less expensive to run than a cooker grill.

The majority of toasters will take two slices at one time, though some have a four-slice capacity.

Settings The degree of browning can generally be selected on a colour or number scale in advance. Some toasters have a heat-sensing device installed in one slot, which should be used if toasting only one slice of bread.

The degree of browning is generally affected by repeated use within a short period, as well as by the age and type of bread being toasted.

 WARNING

If the toast becomes lodged for some reason, never try to release it while the toaster is plugged in. Turn off, UNPLUG, allow to cool. Toast should then come out. If it sticks, release crumb tray and gently push it out.

Cleaning The crumb tray at the base of the toaster must be emptied regularly. Unplug the toaster before doing this. The crumb tray is released by a screw or latch mechanism.

Toasted sandwich makers These are very convenient for turning sandwiches into a hot snack. The hinged top closes onto the filled sandwich, which is placed on a non-stick hot plate. In a few minutes the sandwich is 'cooked', and the coated cooking surface can be wiped clean in a few seconds. Children can easily manage these toasters themselves if they are generally safety-conscious.

Toaster ovens These small appliances can be used as a grill or oven as well as a toaster. You simply place your bread on a rack or in a slot at the top, and turn the switch to 'toast'. Toaster ovens are very useful as supplements to your cooker, or for people who have little space and minimum cooking needs.

Washing machines

Decide how much you can afford, what your washing requirements are and where you will site your machine before making your choice.

Choosing a machine

Price Compare prices at shops and discount houses before buying. Remember to take the cost of delivery and installation into your calculations.

Capacity and type of wash List your average weekly wash and estimate its weight. Note any special treatment you need – for heavily soiled garments, for instance. Consider drying requirements. If you have no outside drying line, look for a machine with an efficient spinning action.

Space Twin tubs are usually about 750mm (2½ft) wide, 420mm (1ft4in) deep and 800mm (2ft8in) high. Automatics vary from 510mm (1ft8in) wide and 720mm (2ft4in) high to 660mm (2ft2in) wide and 900mm (3ft) high.

If you cannot fit a machine into your kitchen and have no utility room, a bathroom is the next best place. Electrical equipment in the bathroom must conform to the IEE wiring regulations.

Twin tub washing machines

Advantages
● They need no special plumbing and are relatively easy to move.
● Repairs are relatively cheap.
● It is easy to wash several loads needing different treatments.
● The spin dryers are very efficient.

Disadvantages
● You must stay with the machine for most of the washing, rinsing and spinning processes.
● You have to transfer the wet wash from the tub to the spin dryer by hand.
● Rinsing may not be totally effective.
● Fabric conditioner is awkward to use.
● Spinning needs to be timed if drying synthetic materials.
● Twin tubs are more expensive to run than automatic machines unless you are using the same water several times.

Automatic washing machines

In these machines, washing, rinsing, spinning and, in some cases, drying are all done in one drum. Most of the seven or more preselected programmes need no attention from you; the length and water temperature are automatically adjusted for different types of fibre.

In addition to basic programmes, there may also be 'optional extras' such as prerinse, extra spin or spin delay to avoid creasing.

Check that the controls are easy to understand – you may have to refer to the handbook at first. Check also that the washing powder and fabric softener dispensers are easy to clean and whether there is an outlet filter to check fluff, shirt buttons and so on. Check on the efficiency of the spinning action – the higher the rpm in relation to the size of drum, the more efficient it is.

Automatic machines are designed to be filled from hot and cold water supplies or from cold only.

Advantages
● They can be left alone, saving time and energy.
● They give excellent results.

Disadvantages
● They usually need to be plumbed in (though some can be used with tap connections).
● They do not always spin as well as twin-tubs.
● They are more expensive.

Tumble dryer Some automatic machines incorporate a heated tumble dryer in the door. This normally takes only about half the weight of a full load of clothes, but is very useful where space is at a premium.

See also CLOTHES CARE – Laundering.

CHAPTER 13

FOOD AND NUTRITION

Budgeting • Freezer use • Herbs • Meat
Seasonal food • Storage
Vitamins • Wine

ALL ABOUT FOOD

Budgeting

As the cost of food goes up and up, cutting costs becomes more and more necessary. Therefore, more time and effort has to be put into producing nourishing, attractive and cheaper meals.

Shopping

Be prepared to shop around for what you want. Street markets are often good and cheaper for vegetables, fruit and fish. Some foods may be cheaper towards the end of the day, but make sure they are still fresh!

Bulk buying can save money, but needs a bigger initial outlay and plenty of storage space. Avoid stocking up with anything the family is likely to get tired of. (See also MONEY MATTERS – Bulk buying.)

Growing your own

If you have room, vegetables and soft fruit grown in your garden are fresher and can be cheaper than shop bought produce. Concentrate on vegetables and fruits that cost most in the shops.

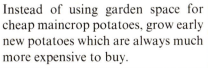

★ HANDY HINT ★

Instead of using garden space for cheap maincrop potatoes, grow early new potatoes which are always much more expensive to buy.

If your family is large and you have plenty of land, you can, of course, become self-sufficient in fruit and vegetables. You can freeze produce you cannot eat while still fresh. Tending a fruit and vegetable garden on this scale entails a lot of hard work as well as expenditure on tools, fertilisers, seeds, insecticides and so on.

Herbs are always useful to grow, outside or indoors, and add flavour and colour to simple dishes (see Herbs).

Making your own

Even if you cost in your time, it is cheaper to bake your own cakes and biscuits, to make your own yogurt and jam, chutneys, pickles and bottled fruit. You will also save money if you bake your own bread, buying flour in a 12.5kg (28lb) sack (or larger) rather than in small bags.

The real money-savers are wine and beer which, made from scratch using conventional ingredients, made with a basis of canned concentrates or made from one of the complete kits, will cost as little as one-fifth of the commercial varieties. (See also Wine.)

Good, cheap buys

● Beef – shin or skirt for stews.
● Pork – hand of pork, spareribs, liver for making pâté, belly of pork to flavour main meal vegetable dishes, or for Chinese cooking.
● Bacon – end cut joints and bacon bits.

● Chicken – boiling fowl for casseroles or cold with salad. Use stock for soups

● Mince – seasoned and flavoured with herbs, garlic, onion, for hamburgers, meat loaves, pies, spaghetti sauce.

● Offal, particularly the less popular cuts such as heart, oxtail, tripe, are both inexpensive and nutritious.

● Less popular game animals, such as rabbit and hare can also be reasonable to buy and make excellent casseroles or soups.

● TVP – Textured Vegetable Protein is made from soya beans. Reconstitute with water or stock and use to extend mince.

● Fish – coley is good for fish pies and kedgeree. Conger eel has close, white flesh. Mackerel is good grilled or baked in vinegar and served cold with salad. Sprats are a good buy and plaice is sometimes quite cheap. Monk fish makes an inexpensive substitute for shrimp.

The great cheap dishes

All over the world the great cheap dishes are made to a basic formula – a large portion of inexpensive, filling carbohydrate, enough protein for energy and some Vitamin C for general health.

Rice Plain long grain rice is best for most purposes. Brown rice has more flavour and nourishment but takes longer to cook. Use rice for risottos – using leftover meat – filling rice salads, and to accompany curries and stews.

Pasta Pasta is the satisfying main ingredient in macaroni cheese, spaghetti with meat or tomato sauce, tagliatelle or lasagne dishes.

Pastry Use as the base for economical savoury flans filled with egg, vegetables, bacon scraps, leftover ham, flaked fish and so on. It also makes pies and pasties satisfyingly filled with stewed, cheap meat, fish or vegetables.

Pulses Dried beans, peas and lentils are high in vegetable protein. Soak all pulses, except lentils, overnight before cooking. Add them to soups, vegetable dishes and meat and poultry dishes to make a meal go further.

Potatoes Layered with onion and bacon, or cheese and onion, and baked in the oven, potato dishes make excellent suppers. Savoury stuffed jacket potatoes are cheap yet filling.

Eggs Eggs are still one of the cheapest sources of protein. Try them hardboiled with cheese or onion sauce and plain rice, or make them into a curry. Serve them poached with cheese sauce and spinach or make hearty omelettes with a savoury filling.

Soups and stews Make filling soups and stews with the cheaper cuts of meat and all kinds of vegetables. Excellent cheap soups can be made in the blender, using leftover vegetables and a basis of stock.

 ★ **HANDY HINT** ★

The remains of the Sunday joint can provide the basis for several meals later in the week. Any leftover meat can be turned into risottos, pasta sauces, salad dishes or pies. The bones can be boiled with flavourings and bay leaves to provide a stock base for soups or sauces.

Soft cheeses

In addition to ripened soft cheeses, unripened soft cheeses are also widely available.

Cream cheese Often sold by weight in delicatessens. It is rich, smooth and has a high fat content.

Demi-sel and petit suisse These are similar cream cheeses imported from France. Both are delicious served with fruit and sugar. Demi-sel is slightly salted.

Curd cheese This has a lower fat content than cream cheese.

Cottage cheese A low fat curd cheese made from skimmed milk. It is sometimes sold flavoured with chives or pineapple. Because it is low in calories, cottage cheese can form part of a slimming diet.

Storing cheese

Buy only enough cheese for a few days – a week at the most – as it deteriorates fairly quickly once it has been cut.

Wrap cheese in greaseproof paper, foil or cling film and put into a polythene bag or container. Store in a cool place, or in the door or bottom shelf of the refrigerator. To get the best flavour, take the cheese out of the refrigerator at least an hour before you want to eat it.

Cooking with cheese

Hard cheeses, such as Cheddar, Gruyère and Parmesan, are the best for cooking. Cheese should never be heated more than is absolutely necessary as over-cooking makes it tough, stringy and indigestible.

 HANDY HINT

Grate leftovers of hard cheese and keep it in a polythene bag in the refrigerator or freezer. Use for sauces, sprinkling on gratin dishes and making sandwich fillings and spreads.

Common cooking methods

Baking Cooking food such as cakes, pastry, eggs, meat, fish or vegetables by dry heat in the oven without any liquid, though sometimes with a little fat. (See also Roasting.)

Boiling Cooking food in a liquid at a temperature of 100°C (212°F). The liquid bubbles and evaporates as steam.

Braising Cooking meat, poultry or fish in a covered dish on a bed of lightly fried vegetables with enough stock or water barely to cover (see Mirepoix). Vegetables such as leeks and celery can also be braised by cooking slowly in a covered dish with a small amount of liquid.

Frying Cooking food in hot fat or oil. Shallow frying uses a small amount of fat in a wide, flat pan. The food has to be turned over. Deep frying uses enough fat to cover the food entirely in a deep pan. 'Dry' frying uses no extra fat in a non-stick pan or griddle.

Poaching Cooking food in liquid just below simmering point 96°C (205°F). The food is only half covered with the liquid. Poaching is used for food that requires low temperatures or gentle handling, such as eggs and fish.

Pot roasting Similar to braising, but using very little liquid. The oven or top of the cooker can be used.

Roasting Strictly means cooking food in front of, or over, a fierce, glowing source of heat. Now applies to cooking meat or vegetables with some fat in an open dish in the oven.

Simmering Cooking food in liquid which is only allowed to reach 96°C (205°F).

Steaming Cooking food in the steam rising from boiling water. The water must not touch the food and the lid must fit well so that the steam does not escape.

 HANDY HINT

When boiling water for steaming gets low and needs topping up, always add boiling water. This keeps the steaming food cooking.

Stewing Cooking food in a small amount of liquid at simmering point in a covered casserole over low heat on top of the cooker or in the oven.

Sweating Cooking food very gently in melted fat to draw out its juices.

Common cooking terms

Au gratin Strictly means the forming of a thin crust of breadcrumbs or cheese on top of a dish which is browned in the oven or under the grill.

Baking blind Baking a pastry case without a filling. Prevent rising by lining the uncooked case with foil or greaseproof paper weighed down with uncooked dried beans, dry rice or bread crusts.

Barding Covering lean meat or breast of poultry with slices of bacon or pork fat before cooking, to prevent drying out.

Basting Keeping the surface of food moist by spooning over liquid or melted fat at frequent intervals while cooking.

Binding Adding a moist ingredient to dry ingredients to hold them together. For example, adding egg to a breadcrumb mixture to make a stuffing.

Blanching Treating food with boiling water to remove the skin from fruit, nuts, etc., to whiten some foods, to remove any strong or bitter taste. Also to prepare some foods for freezing. The food is either put into cold water, brought to the boil and drained immediately, or immersed in boiling water and then in cold water.

Bouquet garni A bunch of fresh herbs (parsley, thyme and bay leaf) used to add flavour when cooking casseroles, soups, sauces, etc. Discard before serving.

Breaded Food rolled or coated with bread crumbs before cooking.

Caramelising (1) Melting sugar in a minute amount of water in a thick bottomed saucepan until it turns rich brown. (2) Sprinkling sugar on top of a sweet pudding and browning under the grill.

Clarifying (1) Melting butter and straining through muslin. Heat gently without browning. (2) Clearing cloudy stock or broth with slightly beaten egg whites.

Coating Covering food with a thin layer, usually of flour, egg or breadcrumbs, and also melted chocolate, thick sauces, aspic jelly, etc.

Creaming Beating fat and sugar together with a heavy spoon or firm spatula until soft and creamy.

Croûtons Small cubes or shapes of fried or toasted bread used as a garnish for soups, etc.

Curing Preserving fish, meat or poultry by salting, drying or smoking.

Cutting in Combining fat and dry ingredients by cutting in with a knife.

Deglazing Detaching juices and particles, usually of meat, which have adhered to a pan in which the food has been browned or roasted. This is done by adding liquid to form a sauce.

Dice To cut into small, even cubes.

Dissolve Mixing a dry ingredient into a liquid to produce a solution.

Dredge Sprinkling food lightly with flour, sugar or other dry ingredients.

Dripping The fat obtained from roasted meat during cooking.

Fillet Boned fish or a special cut of boned meat.

Folding in Adding ingredients to a light and fluffy mixture, by folding in very gently with a metal spoon or knife blade, so that the air bubbles do not break down.

Garnish An edible savoury dish decoration.

Glazing Brushing a thin coating of liquid over food to give a shiny surface.

Grating Finely shredding foods such as cheese or vegetables.

Greasing Coating lightly with fat or oil to prevent sticking.

Hulling Removing the calyx from soft fruit.

Infusing Pouring boiling liquid over a substance and extracting flavour by leaving it to stand.

Kneading Working dough, usually bread dough, with the knuckles and heel of the hand to give a smooth texture.

Larding Inserting small strips of fat (pork or bacon) into the flesh of lean meat, poultry, etc. to keep it moist while cooking.

Macerating Steeping fruit in a marinating liquid, usually containing wine or liqueur, to give added flavour.

Marinade A blend of seasonings and liquids, often including oil, wine and herbs, in which meat is turned for some hours to tenderise and give it flavour.

Parboiling Boiling for only part of the time required to cook an item, and finishing off by some other cooking method.

Paring Peeling or trimming vegetables.

Purée To make food soft and smooth by rubbing through a fine sieve or food mill or liquidising in a blender.

Reducing Boiling liquid in an open pan to reduce the quantity and make it concentrated.

Refreshing Pouring cold water over cooked vegetables to preserve their colour. The vegetables are reheated before serving.

Rendering Extracting the liquid fat from meat by melting over a low heat, standing in a cool oven or boiling for some time in a saucepan of water. Let the water cool and the fat will set in a solid layer on the top. Scrape the bottom of the fat clean with a knife.

Roux A mixture of equal amounts of fat and flour cooked together to form the basis of a sauce.

Rubbing in Mixing fat into flour by rubbing lightly with the fingertips until the mixture appears like breadcrumbs.

Sautéing Frying lightly in a small amount of fat or oil, over fairly high heat, shaking the pan frequently during cooking.

Scalding (1) Pouring boiling water over food to clean it, remove skin or loosen hairs. (2) To heat milk to just below boiling point.

Scoring Making evenly spaced shallow cuts with a knife in the surface of food. This aids cooking, appearance, cutting and absorption of flavours.

Searing Browning and sealing the surface of meat quickly over a high heat. This prevents juices from escaping.

Seasoned flour Flour mixed with salt and pepper and used to coat food before frying.

Sieving Rubbing or pressing food through a sieve. A wooden spoon is used to press the food through.

Sifting Shaking a dry ingredient through a sieve to remove lumps.

Skimming (1) Taking off the surface of stocks, gravies or stews to remove excess fat. (2) Taking the scum from the top of the water in which food is simmering.

Sousing Pickling in brine or vinegar.

Stuffing A savoury mixture used to fill cavities in poultry, meat and vegetables before cooking.

Syrup A solution of sugar in water. Heavy syrup contains more sugar than light syrup. Used to sweeten foods.

Trussing Tying poultry and game into a compact shape before cooking.

Whipping or whisking Beating air rapidly into a mixture, either with a whisk or with a hand or electric beater.

Zest The finely grated rind of lemon or orange, minus the white pith.

Less common cooking terms

Bain marie A flat, open vessel half filled with water which is kept just below boiling point.

Court bouillon A flavoured stock in which fish, meat or poultry is cooked.

Dégorge Drawing excess bitter juices from vegetables such as aubergines and cucumbers. Usually done by sprinkling with salt and leaving for 20–30 minutes.

En croûte Food wrapped or enclosed in pastry before cooking.

Flambé A dish which has been flavoured with flamed alcohol.

Fricassée A white stew of chicken, veal or rabbit with cream or egg yolks added.

Mirepoix Finely diced carrots, onion, celery, ham, lightly fried in fat and used as a bed for braising meat.

Fish

Fish is a good source of protein. There are basically three types – white fish, oily fish and shellfish. *White* fish include cod, haddock, sole, plaice and turbot. *Oily* fish include herring, mackerel and salmon. *Shellfish* include crabs, lobsters, mussels, scallops, oysters and shrimp.

Fish chart

Type of fish	Cooking method	Season
Bass	Poach, bake	May-Aug
Brill	Poach, bake, grill	All year, best April-Aug
Cod and coley	Grill, bake, fry	All year, best Oct-May
Crab	Boil	Most of the year, best
Dab	Poach, bake, fry	All year
Flounder	Fry, grill	Feb-Sept
Haddock	Poach, stuff and bake, fry	Sept-Feb
Hake	Poach, stuff and bake, fry	All year, best June-Jan
Halibut	Poach, bake, fry, grill	All year, best Aug-April
Herring	Poach, grill, stuff and bake	All year, best June-Dec
John Dory	Poach, bake, grill	Oct-Dec
Lobster	Boil first, then grill or bake	Feb-Oct
Mackerel	Stuff and bake, grill	Oct-July
Mussels	Bake, boil, use in sauces, soups	Sept-March
Oysters	Eat raw, poach, grill.	Sept-April
Pilchards	Fry, grill	All year
Plaice	Fry, grill, bake	All year, best during May
Prawns	Boil	All year
Salmon	Poach, bake, grill	Feb-Aug
Scallops	Bake, grill, fry	All year
Skate	Poach or fry the wings only	All year
Sole, Dover	Fry, grill, bake	All year
lemon	Fry, grill, bake	All year
Shrimps	Boil, fry, grill, poach	All year
Sprats	Fry, grill	Nov-March
Trout	Grill, bake, poach	All year, best March-Sept
Turbot	Poach, fry, grill	All year, best March-Aug
Whiting	Fry, grill	All year, best Dec-March

Choosing fish

Fresh fish should have a pleasant smell and firm flesh. *Whole fish* should have bright, clear eyes, not sunken and dull. *Herring* and *mackerel* scales should shine. *Shellfish* should feel heavy for its size. *Frozen fish* should be hard. Do not buy if the wrapper is torn or if there is frost inside the packet.

Smoked fish [Cod, haddock, salmon, trout, eel, kippers and bloaters (both these last two are smoked herring)]. These fish, because of the smoking process, will keep longer in the refrigerator than fresh fish.

Canned fish (Salmon, tuna, herring, mackerel, pilchard and sardines). Cans of fish are useful to keep in the store cupboard.

Frozen fish Economic in the long run because frozen fish has very little waste. White fish, oily fish and shellfish are all available frozen.

Freezer use

Almost all fresh and cooked foods can be preserved by freezing. There are a few simple rules to be followed to ensure success.

● Freeze only fresh food of prime quality.

● Cooked foods should be freshly prepared and allowed to cool completely before freezing.

● Foods for freezing must be packed in containers or wrapped in foil or plastic to exclude all air. This avoids dehydration ('freezer burn'), loss of colour, texture or flavour, and prevents strongly smelling foods affecting others.

● Pack foods in quantities suitable for use at one meal.

● Interleave chops, fish fillets, etc. with foil or freezer paper, to make them easy to separate.

● Follow the freezer manufacturers' instructions when freezing down fresh food. (See also KITCHEN SENSE – Freezers.)

● Avoid placing fresh food in contact with already frozen foods.

Wrappings and containers

Freezer polythene bags and sheeting, freezer paper and foil will wrap awkward shapes. Fasten with special freezer tape.

Polythene tubs and cartons with tight fitting lids (yogurt and cream cartons can be used, with an airtight covering) should be used for liquids, sauces, etc. Foil dishes or basins and waxed paper containers are also useful.

★ **HANDY HINT** ★

Do label and mark clearly what each container or package holds and the date it was put into the freezer.

Freezer preparation

Vegetables must be blanched before being stored in the freezer. The time varies from vegetable to vegetable (see chart), but ranges from about 1 minute to 3. To blanch vegetables, put them into a wire basket and plunge into a saucepan full of boiling water [at a ratio

Freezer storage chart

Baking

Food	Packaging	Storage time
Bread, rolls, croissants	Polythene bags.	1 month
Cakes, scones, biscuits	Polythene bags.	6 months
Unbaked pastry	Foil or polythene.	6 months
Unbaked yeast dough	Greased polythene bags with space to rise.	2 months
Pies (unbaked)	Over-wrap with foil.	6 months

Dairy foods

Food	Packaging	Storage time
Whole eggs	Beat together with sugar or salt. Waxed carton.	6 months
yolks	Mix with sugar or salt as above.	9 months
whites	Pass through sieve, then as above.	9 months
Milk	Homogenised only, in waxed carton.	3 months
Cream	Double or whipping only. Add sugar.	3 months
Ice cream	In original container or waxed carton.	3 months
Butter	Overwrap with polythene or foil.	3 months (salted) 6 months (unsalted)
Cheese hard soft	Foil. Tubs or cartons. As above.	3 months 3 months

Fish

Food	Packaging	Storage time
White fish	Polythene or foil.	6 months
Oily fish	Polythene or foil.	3 months
Shellfish	Tubs or cartons. Fish must be *absolutely fresh.*	3 months
Oysters and scallops	Remove from shell, (save juices) wash and pack in tubs or cartons with juices.	3 months

259

Meat and Poultry

	Packaging	Storage time
Beef and lamb large cuts	Wrap closely in polythene or foil.	9 months
small cuts	Interleave with foil, etc. Wrap in foil or polythene bag.	6 months
Pork and veal large cuts	Wrap closely in polythene or foil.	4 months
small cuts	Interleave with foil, etc. Wrap in foil or polythene bag.	1 month
Offal	Polythene bag or container.	2 months
Minced meat and sausages	Polythene bag.	2 months
Bacon rashers	Overwrap with foil	1 month
Poultry and game (oven ready)	Polythene bag or foil.	chicken 9 months duck, goose, turkey 6 months

Made up dishes

Casseroles with bacon	Foil or polythene container.	3 months
Casseroles without bacon	Foil or polythene container.	6 months
Meat pies	Cook in foil dish. Wrap with foil.	2 months
Pâté	Foil or polythene bag.	1 month

roughly of 450g (1lb) of vegetables to about 3.5 litres (6 pints) of water]. When the water returns to the boil, start timing. End the process by plunging the vegetables into ice-cold water.

Fruit can be frozen in what is called dry pack, i.e. by itself, or in dry sugar or syrup. The addition of syrup or sugar helps to protect both colour and flavour. To pack fruit in a dry pack, sprinkle the fruit with sugar in the ratio of 100g (4oz) sugar to 450g (1lb) fruit. This method of freezing is particularly appropriate for berry or currant fruits. To make a syrup for freezing fruit, add between 225g (8oz) and 450g (1lb) sugar to 568ml (1 pint) water – depending on individual fruits – and boil only until the sugar has dissolved. Cool before using. Use a light syrup for fruit such as cherries and citrus fruit, a medium one for apples and peaches and heavy syrup for fruit such as rhubarb and red currants.

Always leave about 12mm ($\frac{1}{2}$in) headspace when packing fruit with sugar or syrup.

Fruit and vegetable freezing chart

Vegetables	Preparation and packaging	Blanching time in minutes	Storage time
Artichokes (globe)	Trim off coarse outer leaves, stalks, tops and stems. Add lemon juice to blanching water.	7	12 months
Asparagus	Wash, scrape stalks, trim to approx equal lengths. Divide up into thick, medium and thin stalks. Pack in rigid containers.	thin – 2 thick – 4	12 months
Aubergines	Wash well and cut into about 12.7mm ($\frac{1}{2}$in) slices with stainless steel knife. Pack in rigid containers.	4	12 months
Beans (broad)	Pick young tender beans. Shell and discard any blemished beans.	3	12 months
Beans (French and runner)	Wash and trim ends, leave whole or slice thickly or cut into pieces about 25.4mm (1in) long.	whole – 4 sliced – 3	12 months
Beetroot	Select young and small beets. Cook whole beets until tender, rub off skins and pack in rigid containers. Large beets should be sliced or diced after cooking.	none	6 months
Broccoli	Wash and trim stalks cutting away any woody stalks. Divide up into thick, medium and thin stems. Pack in rigid containers, sprig to stalk. Separate layers with polythene film or freezer paper.	thick – 5 thin – 3	12 months
Brussels sprouts	Trim and remove discoloured leaves. Cross-cut the stalks and wash in salted water. Can be frozen individually. Pack in rigid containers or polythene bags.	small – 3 large – 5	12 months
Cabbage	Trim outer coarse leaves. Wash in salted water. Cut or tear into shreds. Drain well and dry. Pack in rigid containers or polythene bags.	2	6 months
Carrots	Remove tops and tails. Scrape and wash. Leave small new carrots whole, but slice or dice larger carrots. Small whole carrots can be frozen individually.	whole – 5 sliced – 3	8 months
Cauliflower	Select firm white heads. Remove most of outer coarse leaves. Separate into equal sized sprigs. Wash in salted water, drain and pack in rigid containers. Add lemon juice to blanching water to retain colour.	3	8 months

Vegetables	Preparation and packaging	Blanching time in minutes	Storage time
Celeriac	Wash, trim, scrape and slice, dry and pack into rigid containers or polythene bags.	6	9 months
Celery	Best suited after freezing for use as ingredient in recipes. Remove outer coarse stalks and strings. Cut into 50 to 75mm (2–3in) lengths. Freeze hearts whole. Pack in containers or polythene bags.	hearts – 8 stalks – 4	12 months
Corn on the cob	Remove outer husks, trim ends and wash. Freeze separately and pack in polythene bags.	5 to 8 depending on size	12 months
Corn kernels	Remove outer husks, and scrape kernels off the cob. Wash, drain and pack in rigid containers or polythene bags. Can be added to other vegetables before freezing, e.g. peas.	5	12 months
Courgettes	Wash and cut into 25mm (1in) slices. Drain and pack into rigid containers interleaving layers with freezer paper or aluminium foil.	3	12 months
Leeks	Remove coarse outer leaves and trim root end. Wash well, leave whole or slice and pack into rigid containers or polythene bags. They freeze well in white sauce. Seal well to prevent cross-flavour in storage.	whole – 4 sliced – 2	6 months
Mushrooms	Wash and peel field mushrooms. Trim stalks. Leave whole or slice. Add lemon juice to blanching water – or sauté in margarine – dry well and pack in rigid containers without blanching.	whole – 4 sliced – 2	12 months
Onions	Use only for cooking after freezing. Peel, slice into rings. Pack in small rigid containers and seal well to prevent cross-flavour in storage. They freeze well in white sauce.	2	3 months
Parsnips	Choose young and small parsnips, scrape and wash. Cut into quarters or slices. Drain and pack into rigid containers or polythene bags.	3	12 months
Peas	Choose young sweet peas, pod and discard any blemished peas. Blanch in small quantities. Drain well and pack in containers or polythene bags.	1½	12 months
Peppers (red and green)	Wash, halve and remove seeds and stalk. Can then be sliced if preferred. Remove only tops and seeds if later to be stuffed. Freeze individually, whole or sliced. Drain and pack in polythene bags.	2	12 months

Vegetables

Vegetables	Preparation and packaging	Blanching time in minutes	Storage time
Spinach	Choose young tender leaves. Wash well in running water, drain and press out as much water as possible. Pack in rigid containers or polythene bags in portions or family mealtime quantities.	2	12 months
Turnips and swedes	Remove thick peel and cut into 25mm (1in) cubes. Pack in rigid containers or polythene bags.	3	12 months
Herbs – mint, parsley, sage, thyme etc.	Wash, drain and dry. Chop finely and freeze in ice cube tray. Wrap cubes in aluminium foil or polythene bags. After freezing and storage, colour and flavour may be reduced.	1	3–6 months

Fruit

Fruit	Preparation and packaging	Blanching time in minutes	Storage time
Apples	Peel, core and slice. Use ascorbic acid to prevent browning. Blanch (see vegetables) for two or three minutes for dry pack. Alternatively pack in dry sugar or medium sugar syrup with ascorbic acid. Pack in bags. Leave headspace in syrup pack.		9 months
Apple purée	Peel, core and slice, cook until tender and sieve. Add sugar and pack in tubs leaving headspace.		6 months
Apricots	Peel, remove stones and freeze in halves or slices in medium sugar syrup with ascorbic acid. Pack in tubs leaving headspace.		9 months
Avocados	Peel, remove stone and convert flesh to purée, adding 10ml (1 teaspoon) of lemon juice to each 500ml (1 pint) of purée. Season with salt and pepper and pack in tubs leaving headspace.		2 months
Bilberries and blackberries	Pick firm berries, remove stalks, wash and dry. Freeze as dry pack, individually, or as dry sugar pack or in heavy syrup. Pack in tubs leaving headspace.		9 months
Blackcurrants	Strip firm currants off stem, wash and dry. Freeze as dry pack individually for jam making, or in dry sugar pack or in heavy sugar syrup. Pack in tubs leaving headspace.		9 months
Cherries	Pick fully ripe, firm fruit, wash and dry. Remove stones and freeze as dry pack for jam making or in light sugar syrup. Pack in tubs leaving headspace.		9 months

FRUIT AND VEGETABLE FREEZING CHART: Citrus fruits

Fruit	Preparation and packaging	Storage time
Citrus fruits: lemons, oranges, grapefruit	Peel and remove pith and pips. Separate into segments and pack in tubs with medium sugar syrup leaving headspace. Alternatively wash, dry and freeze whole, especially Seville oranges for marmalade making.	9 months
Cranberries	Remove stalks, wash and dry. Freeze whole in dry sugar for sauce or sieve for purée, then pack in tubs leaving headspace.	6–9 months
Damsons	Wash, halve and remove stones. Pack dry for jam making in dry sugar, pack for cooking and dessert varieties in heavy sugar syrup. Pack in tubs leaving headspace.	9 months
Grapes	Seedless varieties of grapes can be frozen whole; otherwise halve, remove seeds and pack in a light sugar syrup leaving headspace.	9 months
Loganberries	Select firm berries, remove stalks, wash and dry and pack dry, individually or in dry sugar; pack in tubs leaving headspace.	9 months
Melon	Peel and halve the fruit to remove the seeds. Cut into slices, cubes or balls and immerse immediately into light sugar syrup. Alternatively sprinkle prepared melon pieces with lemon juice and pack in dry sugar. Leave headspace in cartons or tubs.	9 months
Peaches	Peel, remove stones and cut into slices. Immediately immerse in medium sugar syrup with ascorbic acid. If dry sugar pack is preferred, dip slices into ascorbic acid solution before sprinkling with sugar.	9 months
Pears	Peel, core and cut into quarters or slices. Immediately sprinkle with lemon juice to avoid discolouration. Then cook for about five minutes in light sugar syrup. Drain the fruit, cool and pack in tubs in medium sugar syrup with ascorbic acid leaving headspace. Freeze and store best as a purée.	6–9 months
Pineapple	Peel and core, then cut into slices, rings or cubes. Pack into light sugar syrup using any juice from the fruit. Leave headspace in tubs and cartons.	3 months
Plums	Wash, halve and remove stones. Pack dry or in dry sugar pack for jam making. For dessert use pack in heavy sugar syrup with ascorbic acid, leaving headspace in tubs.	9 months

Fruit	Preparation and packaging	Storage time
Raspberries	Select firm berries and wash only if necessary. Freeze individually or in dry sugar pack.	9 months
Redcurrants	Strip currants off stems, wash and dry. Freeze individually or dry pack for jam making. Alternatively pack in tubs leaving headspace with heavy sugar syrup for desserts.	9 months
Rhubarb	Select only young and tender stalks. Cut into 25mm (1in) pieces and lightly cook. Drain and cool and pack in dry sugar for pie fillings and jam making, or in heavy sugar syrup for dessert use, leaving head-space in tubs.	9 months
Strawberries	Remove hulls and wash only if necessary. Freeze individually or in dry sugar pack.	9 months
Tomatoes	Best frozen as a purée, otherwise wash, dry and freeze individually whole if to be used for cooking.	6–9 months

Herbs

Even the simplest dishes are much improved by the addition of carefully selected herbs, either fresh or dried.

Chervil, chives and parsley do not dry well and perennials such as rosemary and bay do not need to be dried. Chives, mint and parsley freeze well.

★ HANDY HINT ★

To freeze chives, mint or parsley, first chop them finely and then pack into icecube trays. Cover with water and freeze. Store in a polythene bag in the freezer. When needed, simply melt the ice and use in the usual way.

Sprigs of herbs can be fast-frozen in polythene bags.

Herb	Use with
Basil	Tomatoes, mushrooms, beef, Italian dishes.
Bay leaf	Soups, stews, fish, in bouquet garni.
Borage	Garnish for drinks, salads.
Chervil	Eggs, salads, potatoes, in fines herbes.
Chives	Eggs, cheese, vegetables, salads, in fines herbes.

Herb	Use with
Coriander	Leaves in salads. Seeds in curries, chutneys, puddings.
Dill	Cucumber, salads, coleslaw, fish.
Fennel	Fish, sauces.
Marjoram	Meat, sausages, tomatoes, in bouquet garni.
Mint	Lamb, potatoes, salads, drinks.
Oregano	Tomatoes, Italian dishes.
Parsley	Vegetables, eggs, fish, in bouquet garni and fines herbes.
Rosemary	Lamb, pork, chicken.
Sage	Stuffing for duck, sauce for pork, pork sausages.
Savory (Summer)	Beans, pulses, cucumbers, marrows, courgettes. Soups and stews. Salads.
Savory (Winter)	Beans, pulses. Soups and stews.
Tarragon	Chicken, fish.
Thyme	Poultry, roast meats.

Meat

When buying meat, value for money and choosing the right cut are most important. Usually the best quality meat, which is most expensive, comes from the hind part of the animal as the muscles there do less work. This meat has a fine grain and is suitable for frying, grilling and roasting. Poorer quality, cheaper meat, containing more gristle and tough sinews, has a coarser grain and needs the longer cooking methods such as stewing, braising and pot-roasting.

★ **HANDY HINT** ★
If you choose a roasting joint of pork, ask the butcher to score the rind to make good crackling and the carving easier.

Roasting
All the better cuts of meat, poultry and game roast well. Vegetables such as potatoes, parsnips, turnips and onions are excellent accompaniment if roasted in the same tin as the meat.

Basic methods of roasting
High temperature Roasting at a high temperature produces meat with an excellent flavour but a good deal of shrinkage. Only roast best quality meat at a high temperature as other cuts will become dry and tough.
Medium temperature For less expensive

Roasting chart

Meat	High temperature 220°C (425°F), Gas mark 7	Medium temperature 180°C (350°F) Gas mark 4	Thermometer
Beef	On the bone: 15 mins per 500g (1 lb) + 20 mins. Off the bone: 20 mins per 500g (1 lb) + 25 mins.	On the bone: 20 mins per 500g (1 lb) + 25 mins. Off the bone: 35 mins per 500g (1 lb) + 25 mins.	Rare: 60°C (140°F). Medium: 71°C (160°F). Well done: 77°C (170°F).
Lamb	On the bone: 25 mins per 500g (1 lb) + 15 mins. Off the bone: 30 mins per 500g (1 lb) + 25 mins.	On the bone: 35 mins per 500g (1 lb) + 30 mins. Off the bone: 45 mins per 500g (1 lb) + 45 mins.	Rare: 77°C (170°F). Medium: 80°C (175°F). Well done: 82°C (180°F).
Pork	On the bone: 30 mins per 500g (1 lb) + 30 mins.	Off the bone: 35–40 mins per 500g (1 lb) + 35 mins.	89°C (190°F).
Veal	On the bone: 30 mins per 500g (1 lb) + 30 mins. Off the bone: 35 mins per 500g (1 lb) + 35 mins.	On the bone: 40 mins per 500g (1 lb) + 40 mins. Off the bone: 45 mins per 500g (1 lb) + 45 mins.	82°C (180°F).

Poultry

Chicken	25 mins per 500g (1 lb) + 15 mins. Roasted at 200°C (400°F), Gas mark 6.	30 mins per 500g (1 lb).	
Turkey	Allow 15 mins per 500g (1 lb). For an average weight of 6kg (13 lb).	Allow 20 mins per 500g (1 lb). For an average weight of 6kg (13 lb).	
Duck	Allow 30 minutes per 500g (1 lb). Roasted at 190°C (375°F), Gas mark 5.		

Game

Venison	15 mins per 500g (1 lb) + 15 mins.	170°C (325°F), Gas mark 3 for 40 mins per 500g (1 lb) + 40 mins	85°C (185°F)
Rabbit	10–15 mins then reduce to 180°C (350°F) Gas mark 4 for 35–40 mins, or as chicken (above).		

roasting meat the outside of the meat will brown and the inside will have time to cook well and become tender without drying out.

Spit roasting Suitable for any cuts of neat shape such as trussed poultry and kebabs. If the spit is in the oven, use normal roasting times.

Roasting by temperature Using a meat thermometer which is stuck into the thickest part of the joint.

Roasting in foil This produces a moist, tender result, keeps the oven clean but does not allow the meat to brown. Remove the foil or fold back to expose the top of the meat for the last 30 minutes cooking time to brown.

Roasting in a closed tin This has a similar effect to roasting in foil. Remove the lid for the last 30 minutes to brown.

Roasting frozen meat Frozen meat on the bone cooks well from frozen, but it is useful to insert a meat thermometer to make sure that the meat reaches the correct temperature. However, there will be a great deal of shrinkage.

New Zealand lamb should be thawed before roasting for best results.

Roasting vegetables Prepare the vegetables as usual, cutting in pieces if necessary. Parboil for 10 minutes in boiling salted water. Drain well, place around the meat and roast for about one hour. Potatoes may need longer if the medium temperature is being used.

Roasting game Venison and hare must always be marinated before roasting, to help tenderise the meat. Rabbit can benefit from marinating too, or at least soaking. If you are roasting the saddles of rabbit or hare only, roasting times given in the chart still apply. Many game birds can be somewhat dry, so always make sure that the breast of any bird you roast is barded.

 WARNING ▲

Pork, poultry, game and boned and rolled joints should not be cooked from frozen.

Bird roasting chart

Bird	Temperature	Time per bird
Black grouse	220°C (425°F) Gas mark 7	40 minutes
Capercaillie	as black grouse	40 minutes
Grouse	as black grouse	40 minutes
Guinea fowl	as black grouse	40 minutes
Partridge	as black grouse	25–30 minutes
Pigeon	230°C (450°F) Gas mark 8	15 minutes
Plover	as black grouse	15–20 minutes
Pheasant	as black grouse	30 minutes
Ptarmigan	as black grouse	40 minutes
Quail	as black grouse	15 minutes
Snipe	as black grouse	15–20 minutes
Woodcock	as black grouse	15–20 minutes

Beef

Forequarter

Cut	Cooking method
1 Shin	Stew.
2 Clod.	Stew.
3 Neck	Stew.
4 Brisket	Braise, pot-roast, boil.
5 Foreribs	Roast.
6 Thin ribs	Braise, pot-roast
7 Back ribs	Braise, pot roast
8 Chuck and blade	Braise, pot-roast, stew
9 Top and thick ribs	Braise, pot-roast.

Hindquarter

Cut	Cooking method
1 Leg	Casserole, stew.
2 Top rump	Fry, grill, braise.
3 Topside and	Roast, pot-roast.
Silverside	Roast, boil.
4 Rump	Fry, grill.
5 Sirloin	Roast, grill.
6 Fillet	Grill.
7 Thin flank	Braise, boil.
8 Wing ribs	Roast, grill.

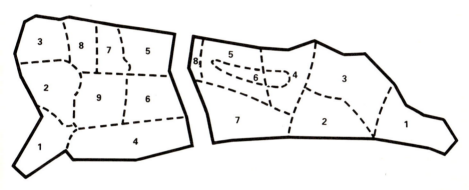

Pork

Cut	Cooking method
1 Leg	Roast.
2 Chump end	Roast, fry, grill.
3 Loin (including kidney)	Roast, fry, grill.
4 Belly	Roast, fry, grill, braise, stew.
5 Hand and spring	Roast, stew.
6 Blade bone	Roast, braise, pot-roast, stew.
7 Spare rib	Roast, fry, grill, braise.

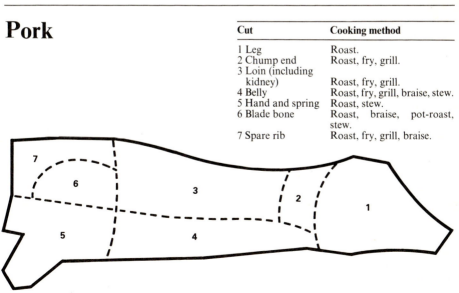

Lamb

Cut	Cooking method
1 Leg	Roast, braise, pot-roast, boil.
2 Loin	Roast, fry, grill.
3 Chump	Roast, fry, grill.
4 Best end neck	Roast, fry, grill
5 Breast	Roast, braise, pot-roast, stew.
6 Middle neck	Stew.
7 Scrag	Stew.
8 Shoulder	Roast, braise, pot-roast.

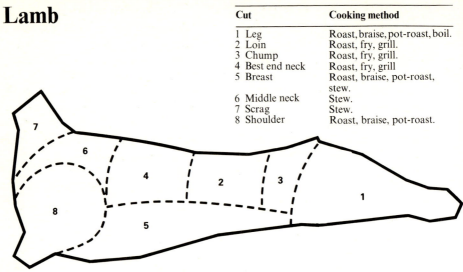

Veal

Cut	Cooking method
1 Knuckle	Braise, pot-roast, stew, boil.
2 Fillet	Roast.
Leg of veal: 1 & 2	Roast.
4 Chump chops	Fry, grill.
5 Loin	Roast.
6 Best end of neck	Roast, braise, stew.
7 Scrag end of neck	Braise, stew.
8 Shoulder without knuckle	Roast, braise, pot-roast.
9 Knuckle	Braise, stew, boil.
10 Breast	Roast, braise.

Menu planning

Whether you are planning for a family meal, for a dinner or luncheon party or for a buffet, the aim must be to make the food look as appetising as possible and to relate each course to the next one so that each complements the other.

Use of colour

Colour plays an important part in the presentation of food. However good each course may be on its own, it is a culinary disaster to serve a creamy asparagus soup followed by a creamy chicken casserole with rice and a creamy lemon syllabub, or a hearty oxtail soup with a rich brown stew and a chocolate mousse. Vary the texture and colour of the dishes, as well as the degree of richness or sharpness of each dish. Plan your meal round the main dish, making your starter and your dessert contrast with it and with each other.

Menu planning for the family

Planning menus for a week ahead may seem an unnecessary chore, but can save time and money. There is no need to stick too rigidly to your plan, but thinking ahead helps when it comes to using up leftovers or ensuring that meals are adequately balanced nutritionally, containing the necessary protein, carbohydrate, fat and minerals and vitamins for health. (See also NUTRITION.)

If you are out at work all day, plan to cook at the weekend and include some dishes that can be stored in the refrigerator and eaten later in the week. Flan cases can be filled with fruit or made into savoury quiches; stews, soups, pâtés, tarts and curries can all be prepared in advance and stored until needed. A freezer allows you to keep such dishes for a longer time before eating, but is not essential when cooking just a few days in advance.

Some ideas for menu plans

Working wife and mother If you are a working wife and mother, shopping will probably be done on Saturday. Everything in the menu plan can be bought then and stored without spoiling. A cooking session on Sunday afternoon can provide a few flan cases, stock from the turkey carcass, pâté or stew. Extra potatoes can be used for other meals and leftover vegetables added to a Spanish omelette for a nutritious and filling lunch or supper.

SATURDAY

Lunch:	hot dogs, fruit.
Supper:	grilled mackerel spread with French mustard, chips, peas.

SUNDAY

Lunch:	roast turkey with orange stuffing, roast potatoes, sprouts, fruit salad and cream.
Supper:	onion soup with garlic bread, jellied fruit flan.

MONDAY

Supper: cold turkey, savoury filled baked potatoes with fresh herbs, mixed salad, fresh fruit.

TUESDAY

Supper: onion soup with toast and pâté, apricot fritters.

WEDNESDAY

Supper: minced turkey cutlets fried in batter, mashed potatoes, peas and corn, fresh fruit.

THURSDAY

Supper: Spanish omelette, crisp green salad, apple flan with cream.

FRIDAY

Supper: pâté with baked potatoes, beetroot in yogurt, fresh fruit.

Working wife with no children Even on a fairly tight budget the occasional extravagance is included here – entertaining another couple at home is not difficult even when you are out all day. Easy but impressive dishes can be made on the day they are eaten, though soups and casseroles may be made in advance. Convenience foods help out a lot.

SATURDAY

Lunch: baked potatoes with cheese, celery.

Dinner: coq au vin or beef stew with potatoes, and green vegetable, mousse.

SUNDAY

Lunch:
(party) baked gammon with apricots and barbecue sauce, sauté potatoes, crisp green salad, fruit.

Supper: instant pizza (on bread), yogurt with honey.

MONDAY

Supper: cold gammon with savoury rice, green bean or tomato salad, apricot pie.

TUESDAY

Supper: eggs baked with vegetables and gammon pieces, salad, yogurt with cream.

WEDNESDAY

Supper: stuffed green peppers, raw mushroom salad, souffléed bananas.

THURSDAY

Supper: ratatouille with garlic bread, fruit, yogurt.

FRIDAY

Supper: **(dinner party)**	pork or lamb curry with rice, pickles and chutneys and raita, fresh fruit salad.

Mother at home The budget may be tighter, but more time can be spent on cooking, which can be done daily. Using leftovers imaginatively is a feature of this menu plan. The remains of a roast chicken can be used minced and also made into soup. Extra pancakes made one evening can be reheated in the oven or by steaming for the next day's lunch.

FRIDAY

Lunch:	fish fingers or sausages, peas, grated carrot salad with sultanas.
Supper:	smoked fish pie, broad beans or sprouts, fresh fruit.

SATURDAY

Lunch:	Welsh rarebit, celery, fruit.
Supper:	grilled liver with hot peanut sauce, rice, bananas in yogurt, sliced peaches.

SUNDAY

Lunch:	roast chicken, roast potatoes, cauliflower, fresh fruit jelly.

Supper:	thick vegetable soup, cheese straws, chocolate mousse or mould.

MONDAY

Lunch:	braised liver with mashed potatoes, broad beans, fresh fruit.
Supper:	devilled chicken legs, chips, salad, baked bananas.

TUESDAY

Lunch:	chicken soup with pasta shapes, cheese and pineapple chunks on toothpicks, plain yogurt with honey.
Supper:	egg curry, chutney, boiled rice, fresh fruit.

WEDNESDAY

Lunch:	minced chicken, mashed potatoes and peas, oranges.
Supper:	chicken and macaroni bake, boiled carrots, pancakes with lemon juice and brown sugar.

THURSDAY

Lunch:	vegetable casserole (in chicken broth), pancakes.
Supper:	salade niçoise, coconut flan.

Refrigerator storage chart

	Food	Packaging	Storage time
Dairy foods	Fats (butter, lard, margarine)	Keep in original wrappings	3–4 weeks
	Eggs, uncooked	Refrigerator door	2 weeks
	cooked	Refrigerator door (in shells)	1–2 weeks
	Milk and cream	Keep in bottle or original container	3–4 days
	Yogurt Soured cream	Keep in original container	1 week
	Cheese, hard	Foil or cling film	2–3 weeks
	soft	Keep in original wrappings	1 week
Fish	Fish, uncooked	On plate, loosely covered	1–2 days
	cooked	Foil	2–3 days
	smoked	Foil	3–4 days
	Shellfish	Cling film	1 day
	frozen	Original wrappings but check on packet	
Meat and poultry	Joints	On plate, loosely foil-covered	4–5 days
	Chops, steaks	On plate, loosely covered	2–3 days
	Minced meat/Offal	On plate, loosely covered	1–2 days
	Sausages	If prepacked keep in original wrappings. If not, or after opening, foil or cling film	2–3 days
	Bacon, cured Sliced meats	If prepacked keep in original wrappings. If not, or after opening, foil or cling film	1 week
	Poultry, uncooked	On plate, loosely wrapped	3–4 days
	cooked	Foil	3 days
	frozen	Follow instructions	
Vegetables and fruit	Vegetables, green	Polythene bags or crisper drawer	2–3 days
	Salad	Polythene bags or crisper drawer	2–3 days
	Fruit, hard	Polythene bags or crisper drawer	2 weeks
	Fruit, soft	One layer on tray, foil covered	1–2 days

Refrigerator use

A refrigerator which has a frozen food compartment will have a 'star' rating.
● One star – frozen food will keep for a week (ice and ice cream for one day).
● Two stars – frozen food will keep for one month (ice cream for one week).
● Three stars – frozen food will keep for three months (ice cream for one month).

Which refrigerator shelf to use

When storing food in the refrigerator it is important to remember that the temperature varies on different levels.

Store meat, cooked meat, made-up dishes, fish, cold desserts and jellies in the tray or in the shelf below the freezing compartment. The middle shelf or shelves should be used for cooked meat and made-up dishes. Use the bottom shelf or crisper drawer for vegetables, salads and fruit. Shelves inside the door are designed to hold milk, eggs, cheese, pâté, fruit juices and wines.

★ **HANDY HINT** ★

Let foods get completely cold then cover strong smelling foods well so that they do not flavour other foods such as milk, butter and cream.

Seasonal foods

Nowadays it is possible to buy virtually any food at any time of the year. This is because of modern freezing techniques, the growth of imports and the ease with which foreign foods can be air-freighted into this country. However, for economy it is sensible to buy fresh foods when they are in season and at their cheapest.

Spring best buys
(cheapest months)
Meat
Lamb, beef (April/June)
Fish
Whitebait (April)
Fruit
Rhubarb (May/June)
Seville oranges (February)
Vegetables
Spring cabbage (April/May)
Cauliflower (April)
Sprouting broccoli (March/April)
New potatoes (June)
Watercress (available all year)

Summer best buys
(cheapest months)
Meat
English beef (August/October)
English lamb (September)
Fish
Crabs (July/September)
Dover sole (June)
Herrings (May/September)
Plaice (August)
Scotch salmon (July)
Trout (June)
Turbot (June/August)
Fruit
Cherries (June/July)
Currants, red, white and black (July/August)

Gooseberries (June)
Loganberries (July/August)
Peaches (July/August)
Plums (August)
Raspberries (July/August)
Strawberries (June/July)

Vegetables
Beetroot (July)
Broad beans (June)
Courgettes (August)
Cucumber (June/July)
French beans (June)
Lettuce (June/August)
Marrow (August/September)
Radishes (June)
Runner beans (July/August)
Peas (June/July)
Sweetcorn (August/September)

Autumn best buys
(cheapest months)
Meat
English lamb (September/November)
Rabbit (September/January)
Scotch beef (September/December)
Venison (September/November

Fish
Haddock (November/February)
Hake (August/November)

Fruit
Blackberries (September)
Damsons (September)
Eating apples (September/October)
Pears (September/October)

Vegetables
Brussels sprouts (November)
Celery (September)

Leeks (October)
Onions (October/November)
Parsnips (November/January)

Winter best buys
(cheapest months)
Meat (Game)
Hare (October/March)
Grouse (October/December)
Partridge (November/February)
Pheasant (December/January)

Fish
Halibut (December)
Mackerel (December/March)
Scallops (February/March)
Sprats (January/February)

Fruit
Cooking apples (November/January)
Nuts (November/January)

Vegetables
Cabbage (November/January)
Carrots (November/February)
Cauliflower (September/June)
Celeriac (December/January)
Kale (November/May)
Potatoes (November/January)
Swedes (November/January)
Turnips (November/February)

Spices

In the past, spices were often used to disguise the taste of salted meat, which frequently became rancid during the winter when fresh meat was unavailable. Nowadays spices add subtle flavours to many different dishes. They also act as a stimulant to the appetite and digestion.

Spice	Use with
Allspice	Pickles, stews (use whole). Cakes, puddings (use ground).
Aniseed	Cakes, bread, salad dressing, shellfish.
Caraway	Cakes, bread, cheese.
Cardamom	Curries, sausages, some pastries, stewed fruit.
Cayenne	Smoked fish, tomato sauce.
Chilli	Curries, chilli con carne, Mexican dishes.
Cinnamon	Cakes, puddings, pies (use ground). Pickles, mulled drinks (use stick).
Cloves	Apples, ham, mincemeat.
Coriander	Curries, pea soup, pork, casseroles, cakes, apples.
Cumin	Curries, minced beef, beef loaf, pickles, chutneys, cream cheese, dips, cabbage, sauerkraut.
Fennel	Fish, sausages, bread, rolls.

Spice	Use with
Ginger	Pickles, preserves, confectionery (use whole). Curries, cakes, drinks (use ground).
Juniper	Pâtés, pork.
Mace	Potted meat, spiced wine, fish, milk puddings.
Mustard	Pickles (use whole). Commercially made mustards for beef, ham, sausages (use ground).
Nutmeg	Cabbage, potatoes, cakes, milk puddings, spiced wine.
Paprika	Goulash, salad dressings, on pale savoury dishes (as garnish).
Pepper (black and white)	In numerous dishes (use whole or ground).
Poppy seed	Bread, cakes, puddings, curries.
Saffron	Rice, Spanish and Italian dishes, saffron buns and cake.
Sesame	Bread, rolls, biscuits. Salads, cream cheese, vegetables, sweetmeats (use toasted).
Turmeric	Curries, pickles, rice.

HANDY HINT

To avoid ruining a dish, use cayenne and chilli peppers sparingly at first and taste, as they are very hot.

Store cupboard

A well stocked store cupboard is an insurance against emergencies. Most dry stores and cans will keep well in a cool, dry place.

Unopened packets of dry goods will keep well, but once the packet has been opened, it is best to transfer the contents to storage jars or canisters. These need not be absolutely airtight except if they are to be used for strongly-smelling goods, such as ground coffee, spices and herbs, or for foods which will absorb damp from the atmosphere, such as baking powder or salt.

Items which will keep for more than 6 months

Dried peas, beans
Macaroni, spaghetti
Pearl barley, rice
Ground rice, semolina, tapioca
Granulated, caster and loaf sugar
Golden syrup, treacle
Pickles, chutneys
Canned fish, fruit, meat, soups
Canned vegetables and tomato juice
Evaporated milk
Flavouring essences
Packet soups
Vegetable, yeast and meat extracts
Mustard and pepper

Items which will keep up to 6 months (unopened)

Flour, cake mixes
Dried yeast
Condensed milk (sweetened)
Dried herbs, spices
Curry powder and paste
Gelatine, jellies
Salt

Items which will keep up to 3 months (once opened)

Baking powder, bicarbonate of soda, cream of tartar
Honey
Dried fruits
Salad oil
Jam, mincemeat, lemon curd
Bottled sauces, vinegar
Cake decorations, such as silver balls, chocolate vermicelli
Bouillon cubes
Drinking chocolate, powdered milk drinks
Dried skimmed milk

Items which will only keep a short time (once opened)

Icing and brown sugar
Nuts, desiccated coconut
Block chocolate
Breakfast cereals
Tea, coffee, cocoa, instant coffee
Dried whole milk

Larder storage

Some houses, particularly those of the older type, have a ventilated larder, generally facing north, which provides excellent short-term storage for perishable foods.

Milk and butter will keep better if left in special porous containers which are soaked in water. These can be bought in most hardware and china shops quite cheaply.

The storage times given should be reduced in hot weather.

Food which will keep up to 3 weeks

Margarine, lard, cooking fat.

Butter keeps up to 2 weeks except in very hot weather.

Food which will keep up to 1 week

Hard cheese
Whole eggs
Root vegetables

Food which will keep for 2–3 days

Milk, cream, soft cheese
Egg yolks and whites, separated
Hard-boiled eggs
Bread
Bacon
Hard fruit

Food which will keep for 1–2 days

Raw meat and poultry
Cooked meat or poultry
Cooked made-up dishes
Cooked fish
Smoked fish
Green vegetables
Salads
Soft fruit
Fresh fish and shellfish should not be kept for more than half a day.

Some useful hints

● Wrap citrus fruit and apples in foil to prevent shrinking. Store in the refrigerator (for apples), the larder or cupboard (for citrus fruit).
● To keep lettuce fresh longer, put it unwashed into a lidded aluminium pan and store in a cold larder or in the refrigerator.
● Store a cut cucumber, end down, in a glass of water, covering the cut end with foil or cling film.
● Keep watercress fresh by immersing, leaves down, in water.

Wine

When buying wine from the supermarket or off licence, there is a wide range to choose from. It is usually true that the more you pay, the better the wine will be, but there are other considerations to take into account.

Types of wine

Red wines These are produced in most wine-making countries and are made from squeezed dark grapes, with the skin. They range from the most insignificant 'plonk' to some of the most magnificent and expensive wines made. They can be light and dry, heavy and dry or heavy and rich. Usually, red wines are served at room temperature (but cool room temperature). Better wines, such as old clarets and heavy Burgundies, should be opened at least 30–45 minutes before drinking to allow the wine time to 'breathe'.

White wines These are produced in more

northern climates than reds usually – England, for instance, produces white wines similar to those made in Germany. They are pressed from both white and dark grapes but without the skin. White wines can range from the delicate, semi-sweet fresh taste of the German Mosels and hocks, through the 'woody', more piquant taste of the greenish-coloured white Burgundies, to tart and dry Muscadets and Chablis. White wine should be served lightly chilled.

Rosé wines These are pink-coloured wines made mainly in Portugal and in France. Like red wines they are made from dark grapes with the skins, but for rosé wines, the skins are left in the fermenting liquid for less time. As a rule, rosé wines are not considered connoisseurs' tipples – with the exception of one, the French Tavel Rosé. Rosé wines should be served lightly chilled.

Sparkling wines These are wines made with a double fermentation (the second one causes the bubbles). Almost all are white, with one or two rosés. There is one sparkling red wine, the Italian Lambrusco. The most famous sparkling wine is made in the area of France called *Champagne*, although very respectable German (Sekt) and Italian (Asti Spumante) equivalents exist. Sparkling wine should be served lightly chilled.

Fortified wines These are wines which are either added to spirit (usually brandy) or have spirit added during or at the end of fermentation. The most popular fortified wines are sherry, made extensively in Spain around the city of Juarez, and port, which comes from Portugal. Sherry is usually served before a meal, or as a social drink; port is often served as a *digestif* after a meal.

Wines from different countries

French wines The cheapest French wines are imported into this country in large containers and bottled here; the best is bottled in the cellars of the vineyard where the grapes were grown. The main wine-growing areas in France are Bordeaux which produces red wine (claret), dry white (Graves) and the premier sweet wine in the world (Sauternes); Burgundy, which produces deep, heavy reds, light reds (Beaujolais, Fleurie), heavy whites (Montrachet, Meursault) and lighter, crisp whites (Chablis); the Rhône valley, which produces heavy rich red wines (Châteauneuf-du-Pape); the Loire valley, which makes mostly white wines (Vouvray, Saumur); Alsace, which produces German-type white wines (Traminer, Sylvaner); and Provence, which produces light white and red wines. You can tell the standard of a French wine from its label: the words *appellation contrôlée* indicate that the wine is what it claims to be and the strength and flavour are satisfactory. The words VDQS mean *vin délimité de qualité supérieure* and indicate a slightly lower, but still satisfactory and better than ordinary, standard.

German wines Most German wine is white, although some reds are produced, particularly around the Mosel. The three main wine-growing areas are the Rhine (hock), whose wines are bottled in a long, slim brown container; the Mosel, whose wines are bottled in a long, slim green container, and around the Kaiserstuhl in the southern part of the country. The 'A.P. number' on the label of German wines indicates that they have reached a good quality standard.

Italian wines Chianti is probably the most famous of the Italian red wines but others to look for are Barolo, Bardolino, Valpolicella and Barbaresco, all produced in northern Italy. Classical Chianti is produced in a tightly controlled area of Tuscany between Florence and Siena and can be recognised by the black cockerel symbol which is displayed on the neck of each bottle. Other Chianti must be produced in Tuscany. Italian white wines such as Soave are also produced in northern Italy, and the medium dry white wine Orvieto is produced around the hilltown of the same name, midway between Rome and Florence. On an Italian wine label, the sign of quality to look for is *denominazione di origine controllata*, which is the rough equivalent of the French *appellation contrôlée*.

Spanish wines The best Spanish wines are those from the Rioja district, which still constitute the best wine buys in the country. Spanish red wines are generally better than the whites which can be oversweet. Avoid Spanish wines claiming to be 'Sauternes' or 'Chablis' – they are mostly pale (although cheaper) imitations of the real thing.

Other countries Greece, Cyprus, Hungary, Yugoslavia, Portugal and Israel all produce large quantities of wine of varying quality, and the largest producer of wine in the world now comes from Latin America: Argentina. Some Argentinian and Chilean wine is beginning to find its way into this country and is worth looking out for. Excellent wines from California, Australia and South Africa are also becoming available – and appreciated.

★ **HANDY HINT** ★

Sometimes corks from wine bottles are difficult to reinsert. If this should happen, plunge the cork into boiling water, where it will soften and become manageable again.

Make your own wine

Even the cheapest shop bought wine is comparatively expensive. If you like to drink wine regularly, the cheapest way is to make your own.

From cans Cans of grape concentrate can be bought from specialist shops or large chemists. Results can be excellent.

From packs Packs of fruit juice concentrates, plus all the other ingredients needed to make up to 23 litres (5 gall) wine, are also available. Instructions are simple and in some cases the wine can be ready to drink in only three or four weeks.

From fruits, vegetables and flowers Wines can be made from many kinds of fruit, vegetable and flower, fresh or dried. The shops which sell wine-making equipment usually have a good selection of books to choose from that will help you.

Beer can also be made most successfully at home, using commercial packs or buying the ingredients separately.

NUTRITION

Balanced diet

Good nutrition means that all the body's requirements for its growth and repair are supplied, and that enough energy is generated to carry out these bodily processes and to make physical activity possible. By choosing foods from a wide selection, nutritional needs can be met without difficulty.

Foods for a balanced diet

Milk Supplies almost all the nutrients needed by the human body with the exception of Vitamins C and D and iron.
Cheese Hard cheese contains calcium and Vitamin A. It is more nutritious than soft cheese.
Eggs A good source of protein, iron and Vitamins A, B and D.
Meat Contains high quality protein, iron and B vitamins.
Fish Provides protein of the same quality as milk and meat. Fatty fish and fish liver provide Vitamins A and D. Minerals, such as iodine, are also found in fish.
Vegetables Particularly when eaten raw, are a major source of Vitamin C. Peas and beans contain protein and B vitamins. All vegetables contain minerals.
Fruit The most important source of Vitamin C, when eaten raw. Prunes and dried apricots contain Vitamin A.
Cereal More than a quarter of the protein, carbohydrate, iron and energy in the average diet is supplied by cereal products. Wholemeal flour contains more protein, iron, B vitamins and fibre than refined white flour.

Special nutritional needs

Babies Milk is naturally the most important food. Breast milk has special advantages, as it gives some protection from disease and contains the ideal balance of nutrients, while being non-allergenic and hygienic. Commercially produced baby milks, however, are now well formulated to contain the nutrient content of breast milk for babies who are not breast fed.

 WARNING
Do not add salt or sugar to baby food, even though it will taste bland to you.

Schoolchildren Active, growing children have high energy and nutrient needs, which should be supplied by regular, balanced meals, including plenty of protein rather than frequent snacks.
Pregnant and nursing mothers These have a greater need for carbohydrate, fats, protein, minerals and vitamins. A varied diet will usually ensure an adequate intake, but it is not wise to put on too much weight during pregnancy – your doctor will advise you.
The elderly Many people become less active as they grow older and their food intake should be reduced if they

are not to become overweight. One good meal a day can be supplemented with foods such as milk and cereal, eggs, bread, cheese and fruit, which need little preparation.

Those who are housebound should ensure a good intake of margarine, eggs and oily fish, which contain Vitamin D, as they will not get any of this vitamin from sunlight on the skin. Fruit, vegetables and unrefined cereals help to combat the risk of constipation.

★ **HANDY HINT** ★

As Vitamin C dissolves in water, cook vegetables and fruit in the minimum of water and for the shortest time necessary.

Calcium

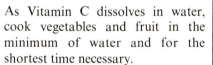

Calcium, with Vitamin D, is essential for making strong bones and teeth. The presence of Vitamin D ensures that the calcium is properly absorbed by the body.

Calcium not only builds bones and teeth, but is also needed by the nervous system and ensures clotting of blood. A deficiency can affect nerve cells and muscle fibres and cause cramp.

The body's ability to absorb calcium from the food is decreased by the use of chemical laxatives and by oxalic acid (found in spinach and rhubarb) and phytic acid (found in pulses, nuts, wholegrain cereals and bran).

Calcium deficiency can occur in pregnant and nursing mothers and old people. Too much calcium can encourage kidney stones and sometimes hardened arteries in the elderly.

Daily needs

Children from birth to 9 years	600mg
Children 9 to 15 years	700mg
Adolescents 15 to 18 years	600mg
Adults	500mg
Pregnant and nursing mothers	1200mg

Sources of calcium Cheapest sources of calcium are dried skimmed milk and processed cheese. Sardines, kippers, cabbage, broccoli, and sesame seeds also contain calcium.

Calcium foods

Calcium Chart

Type of food	Calcium mg per 25g	Weight average portion	Total mg calcium	Percentage of adult RDA (500mg)
Bread (wholemeal)	7	150g	42	8%
Bread (white, enriched)	23	150g	138	27%
Crispbread	22	75g	66	13%
Flour (white, enriched)	36	100g	144	28%
Flour (wholemeal)	9	100g	36	7%
Millet	88	50g	176	35%
Cheese (Cheddar)	200	50g	400	80%
Cheese (cottage)	20	90g	70	14%
Ice cream	35	50g	70	14%
Milk (dried whole)	220	25g	220	44%
Milk (dried skimmed)	315	25g	315	63%
Milk (fresh)	30	250ml	300	60%
Dried fish (whole)	750	7.5g	225	45%
Fish fingers	12	100g	48	10%
Herring (fillet)	29	110g	116	23%
Kipper (fillet)	29	100g	116	23%
Pilchards	60	50g	120	24%
Sardines	100	50g	200	40%
Tripe	35	100g	140	27%
Figs (dried)	50	50g	100	20%
Almonds	60	50g	120	24%
Peanuts	14	50g	28	5%
Sesame seed/paste	375	15g	225	45%
Milk chocolate	60	50g	120	24%
Molasses	125	25g	125	25%
Baked beans	15	100g	60	12%
Broccoli (cooked)	35	100g	140	27%
Cabbage (cooked)	14	100g	56	11%
Haricot beans	45	25g	45	8%
Kale	65	100g	260	50%
Turnips	14	100g	56	11%
Watercress	57	40g	91	18%

Recommended daily adult allowance 500mg

Fats and carbohydrates

Fats and carbohydrates together provide between 70 and 90 per cent of the total energy intake of the world's population.

Fats

These are the most energy containing of all foods and are found both in plants and in animals.

Saturated fatty acids are most frequently found in animal fats which are hard.

Unsaturated fatty acids tend to be vegetable fats or oils.

Fats are needed in the diet for growth and formation of skin, for the vitamins they contain and for their high energy value. They also make food more palatable and slow the process of digestion so that the eater feels satisfied for longer.

Carbohydrates

There are three kinds of carbohydrate: sugars, starches and cellulose substances. The first two are the principal source of energy in most diets. Cellulose aids the digestive process.

Sugars These include *glucose* (dextrose), the form in which sugar is present in the blood. Nearly all other forms of carbohydrate are broken down into glucose during digestion. Glucose is also found in fruit, plant juices and honey. *Fructose* occurs naturally in fruits, vegetables and honey. *Sucrose* comes from ordinary cane or beet sugar. *Lactose* and *galac-*

tose are present in milk and *maltose* in germinating seeds.

Starches These are found only in plants, mainly cereals and roots, and need to be cooked to be easily digestible.

Cellulose This substance forms the rigid framework of all plants. Two related substances are *pectin* found in fruits and roots, which make jam set, and *agar* extracted from seaweed, which can be used to make jellies.

Daily needs

Most nutritionists recommend 50–100g (2–4oz) of carbohydrate a day as a minimum. An excessive intake of carbohydrate, which is not balanced by taking increased exercise, can lead to obesity.

Calorie requirements Everyone requires a daily minimum calorie intake to continue functioning, but the amount varies, depending on the age, sex and type of life style of the individual.

Fats and carbohydrate foods

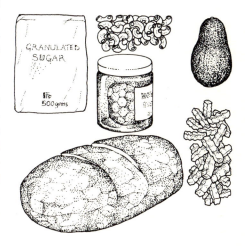

FOOD CALORIE VALUES

Food	Calories per 100g
Cereals	
Barley, pearl	360
Biscuits, sweetmeal	431
Cornflakes	354
Crispbread	318
Custard powder	353
Oatmeal	400
Rice	359
Spaghetti	364
Cheese	
Cottage cheese	114
Meat	
Liver, fried	244
Luncheon meat	313
Sausage, beef	299
Sausage, pork	367
Fruit	
Apples	46
Apricots, canned	106
Bananas	76
Dates, dried	248
Figs, dried	213
Peaches, canned	88
Pineapple, canned	76
Prunes, dried	161
Sultanas	249
Nuts	
Almonds	580
Coconut, desiccated	608
Peanuts, roasted	586
Preserves and sugar	
Chocolate, milk	578
Honey	288
Jam	262
Marmalade	261
Sugar, white	394
Syrup	298
Vegetables	
Beans, broad	69
Beans, haricot	256
Beetroot	44
Carrots, old	23
Lentils	295
Parsnips	76
Peas, fresh/frozen, raw	80
Peas, cooked	49
Peas, canned, processed	62
Potatoes, raw	49
Potatoes, boiled	76
Sweetcorn, canned	79
Turnips	18

Minerals

Minerals play an important part in keeping the body healthy, but as they are normally present in ample amounts in a balanced diet, deficiencies are not likely.

Important main minerals
Calcium, phosphorus and magnesium Used for making bones and teeth. For food sources see entries for Calcium and Vitamin D.

Sodium chloride (salt) All that is needed can be obtained from natural foods to which no salt has been added. Extra salt is needed after profuse sweating caused by physical activity.

Potassium Present in various foods such as fruit, vegetables and meat. Dietary deficiency is rare.

Mineral foods

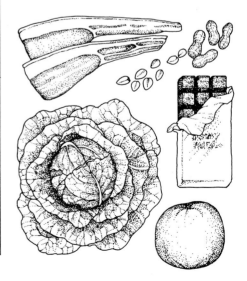

Mineral Chart

Sodium Chloride (salt)

Food	mg per 100g	mg per portion	
Bacon	2400	720	(30g)
Bread, white	1500	1500	(100g)
Butter, salted	600	120	(20g)
Cheese, Cheddar	1200	360	(30g)
Chocolate, milk	275	137	(50g)
Corned beef	4000	2000	(50g)
Cornflakes	2000	500	(25g)
Kippers	2000	1000	(50g)
Meat extract	14000	1400	(10g)
Yeast extract	9000	900	(10g)

Potassium

Food	mg per 100g	mg per portion	
Bread (brown and white)	150	150	(100g)
Cheese, hard	150	45	(30g)
Coffee, instant	5465	546	(1 tsp)
Fish, various	300	450	(150g)
Fruit, dried	1200	120	(10g)
Fruit, fresh	250	250	(100g)
Meat	300	300	(100g)
Potatoes, fried	1000	1000	(100g)
Green vegetables, cooked	200	140	(70g)
Green vegetables, raw	300	210	(70g)
Yeast extract	3140	310	(1 tsp)

Phosphorus

Food	mg per 100g	mg per portion	
Beef	156	156	(100g)
Bread, brown	240	240	(100g)
Bread, white	81	81	(100g)
Cheese, Cheddar	520	156	(30g)
Chicken	200	200	(100g)
Cod	242	242	(100g)
Eggs	218	109	(50g)
Milk	95	142	(150ml)
Oranges	24	24	(100g)
Peanuts, roasted	365	187	(50g)
Yeast extract	1900	190	(1 tsp)

Trace elements

These minerals are present only in tiny amounts.

Iodine Deficiency can lead to swelling of the thyroid gland, which is known as goitre. In some parts of the world, goitre is especially likely as the local soil and water lack iodine.

Fluorine Important in helping to prevent tooth decay, but excess amounts can produce mottling on the teeth.

Cobalt Part of the Vitamin B complex and deficiency can cause anaemia.

Zinc Present mainly in protein foods. Deficiency is seldom encountered.

Copper Deficiency is rare, though premature babies can develop anaemia if fed on cow's milk, which contains less copper than most foods.

Proteins

Proteins are essential 'building blocks' for the growth and replacement of hair, skin, nails and body tissues. An adequate supply of protein in the diet is therefore necessary for good health.

Quality

The quality of a protein is judged by the extent to which it can supply amino acids, from which all proteins are made up, and which form the building materials for the body.

Proteins from animal sources (milk, cheese, eggs, meat and fish) are well matched to human requirements.

Vegetable proteins, found in nuts and pulses, are of lower 'biological value' but when mixed at a meal (for instance beans on toast) improved protein values result.

Eating more than one protein food at each meal helps to ensure that any amino acid deficiency in one food is made up by the surplus in another.

★ HANDY HINT ★

Energy-giving foods such as fat and carbohydrate are needed by the body to prevent the protein being broken down to produce energy rather than for growth and repair.

Daily needs

The recommended amount of protein per day for a *normal adult* is 55–90g, or 1 gram per kilogramme of body weight (see table). A larger intake, however, is not dangerous to health.

Protein foods

PROTEIN VALUES

	g per 100 g
Cereals	
Barley, pearl, dry	7.7
Bread, white	8.0
Bread, wholewheat	9.6
Flour, white	10.5
Flour, wholewheat	13.3
Oatmeal	12.1
Rice, white	6.5
Rice, brown	7.5
Spaghetti	9.9
Dairy products	
Cheese, Cheddar	25.4
Cheese, cottage	17.0
Eggs (1 egg 6.0)	12.3
Milk, whole	3.3
Milk, dried skimmed	35.5
Milk, dried whole	25.0
Milk, evaporated	7.0
Yogurt (made with skimmed milk)	3.4
Yogurt (made with whole milk)	3.0
Meat	
Beef	18.5
Chicken	20.8
Lamb	16.0
Pork	15.8
Fish	
Cod (white fish)	17.4
Kippers	22.2
Mackerel	21.0
Fruit	
Apples (1 apple 0.5)	0.3
Apricots, dried	
(5 apricots, dried 2.0)	4.8
Avocados (½ avocado 2.0)	2.2
Dates (1 date 0.4)	2.0
Nuts and seeds	
Coconut, desiccated	6.6
Sunflower seeds	28.0
Peanuts	27.0
Almonds	21.0
Vegetables	
Beans, baked	5.1
Beans, haricot, dried	21.4
Beans, mung, dried	24.2
Beans, soya, dried	34.0
Beans, other, dried	21.0–24.0
Brussels sprouts	4.9
Lentils	23.8
Mushrooms	2.7
Peas, fresh	3.4
Peas, dried (whole or split)	24.0

Special needs

Babies and children They have much greater protein needs, in relation to their size, than adults, for growing.

Convalescents When the body has been damaged by a wound, surgery or infection, extra protein is needed for repairs.

Pregnant and nursing mothers They also need extra protein.

Vitamins

Each vitamin is different from the others and has its specific job to do in keeping the body healthy. Only small amounts of each vitamin are needed, and a normal balanced diet (see also Nutrition) should provide enough daily vitamins for everybody except, perhaps, pregnant and nursing mothers, small babies and old people.

 WARNING

Vitamins A, D, E and K are called fat-soluble vitamins and can be stored in the body's fat. It is important not to take excessive quantities of these, as you may do more harm than good.

Other vitamins are water-soluble and not retained in the body.

Vitamins are contained in various types of food – some foods contain more than one vitamin.

Vitamin A

Found in milk, cheese, eggs and liver

and in the form of *carotene*, a pigment which gives the colour to many yellow, orange and red fruits and vegetables, such as tomatoes and raw carrots. Ox liver and cod liver oil are also excellent sources of this vitamin. Vitamin A deficiency is shown by dry, rough and scaly skin, dull hair and long cracks in toe and finger nails.

Vitamin B

Comprises a group of some eight different types, which are water-soluble, so must be present regularly in the diet to avoid deficiency diseases. The most widely known ones are thiamin, riboflavin and niacin.

The B vitamins help to turn carbohydrate into energy, to immunise the body against infection and strengthen the red blood cells and nerve tissue.

Excellent sources are ox liver, wholemeal bread and flour, yeast and yeast extract, meat, cheese, fish, eggs, green vegetables, milk and pulses.

Vitamin C

Another water-soluble vitamin, without which a child's growth will be slowed down, wounds and fractures will take longer to heal and gums and mouth may become infected.

Vitamin C is found in green vegetables (as long as these are not wilted), fruit and potatoes (which are one of the principal sources of Vitamin C in the diet), blackcurrants, and then oranges, lemons, grapefruit and other citrus fruit. Brussels sprouts, cauliflower, cabbage and watercress are also rich sources of Vitamin C.

Vitamin D

This fat-soluble vitamin is of special importance to infants and children, as it plays a great part in forming strong bones, in conjunction with calcium.

The richest sources of Vitamin D are cod liver oil or halibut liver oil, oily fish, eggs, butter and cheese.

Sunlight on the skin can cause the formation of Vitamin D in the body itself. If children's bodies receive sufficient sunlight (avoiding, of course, any risk of sunburn), they will need less Vitamin D from their food.

Vitamin E

Prevents fats breaking down too quickly in the body and becoming harmful. It is also thought to prevent the destruction of other nutrients and is helpful in diseases such as cirrhosis of the liver, jaundice and diabetes caused by malabsorption of fat.

Vitamin E is found in wheatgerm oil, which is the best source, in nuts and nut oil and also rape-seed, safflower, sunflower and other oils as well as 'cold pressed' olive oil. Lettuce, cabbage and eggs also contain Vitamin E.

Vitamin K

Another fat-soluble vitamin which is essential to ensure correct clotting of the blood. Good sources are liver and green, leafy vegetables.

Vitamin P

One of the most recently discovered vitamins is found in oranges and other fruits. Lack of it can cause fragility of the capillaries.

REFERENCE TABLES

Metric measurements are here to stay. However, it is still sometimes necessary to translate them into and from the old imperial measurements, especially when you are dealing with such things as old knitting patterns, recipes, dressmaking instructions and so on.

When cooking, the simplest method is to invest in scales which show both metric and imperial weights. Other problems can be solved if you buy a ruler with metric measurements along one edge and imperial along the other. A tape measure graduated in inches on one side and centimetres on the other side saves complicated calculations. Even measuring jugs can be bought which show both scales of measurement.

The following section includes both exact tables and approximate conversions. Use the quick conversions carefully and preferably only for small lengths or quantities as the differences, when multiplied, can end up being quite large.

Area

Approximate conversions

10 square centimetres (sq cm) = $1\frac{1}{2}$ sq in
1 square metre (sq m) = $1\frac{1}{5}$ sq yd
1 square kilometre (sq km) = $\frac{2}{5}$ sq mile
(250 acres)
1 hectare (ha) = $2\frac{1}{2}$ acres

Exact conversions

Imperial	Metric
1 sq in	645.16 sq mm
1 sq ft	929.03 sq cm
1 sq yd	0.8361 sq m
1 acre	4046.86 sq m (0.4047 ha)
1 sq mile	2.590 sq km (258.999 ha)
Metric	**Imperial**
1 sq cm	0.155 sq in
1 sq m	1.196 sq yd (10.764 sq ft)
1 ha	2.471ˑacres
1 sq km	247.1 acres (0.3861 sq m)

Square yards and square feet to square metres

The usual abbreviations for square yards and square feet are sq yd and sq ft; square metres are generally shortened to m²—'metres squared'. This is helpful as a reminder that, when working out square measurements, you have to square figures, that is, multiply them by themselves. For example, an area 10m × 10m is 100m², not, as you might guess, 10. There are 144 (12 × 12) square inches in a square foot, 9 (3 × 3) square feet in a square yard and 10,000 (100 × 100) square centimetres in a square metre.

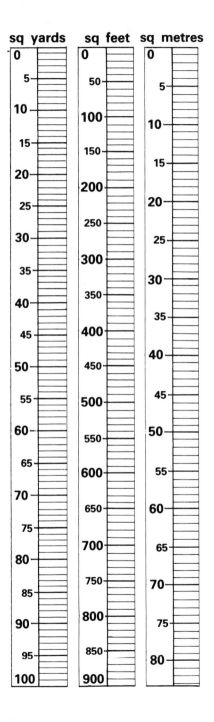

Length

Approximate conversions

1 metre (m) = 39 in
10 centimetres (cm) = 4 in
8 kilometres (km) = 5 miles

Exact conversions

Imperial	Metric
1 in	25.4 mm
1 ft	0.3048 m
1 yd	0.9144 m
1 mile	1.6093 km
Metric	**Imperial**
1 mm	0.0394 in
1 cm	0.3937 in
1 m	39.37 in
	3.2808 ft
	1.094 yd
1 km	0.6214 mile
	1093.6 yd

Converting inches to millimetres

The chart on the right runs from 0 to 1 metre (1000 millimetres), and should help you with at-a-glance conversions.

The chart can also be used for converting tenths of an inch found on, for example, school rulers. For example, to turn 4.2 inches into millimetres, look up ten times the amount in the inch scale, that is, 42. This will give you a reading of 1067mm, which is ten times the correct answer. Therefore the answer is 106.7mm.

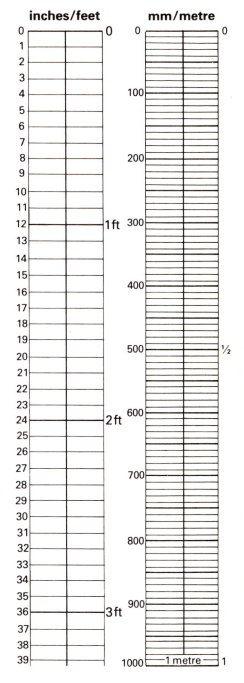

Converting inch fractions to mm

Inches are generally split into awkward fractions such as sixteenths, while metres are always divided into neat tenths, hundredths and thousandths. This chart gives the equivalent in millimetres of all the usual fractions of an inch.

Using the chart To find the metric equivalent of amounts smaller than 1 in, just look up the inch measurement in the appropriate column on the left of the chart and follow the line from it across to the right. This will bring you to the millimetre equivalent in the column on the right. For amounts over 1 in, look up the fraction as normal but to the millimetre equivalent add on 25.4 mm for 1 in, 50.8 mm for 2 in, 76.2 mm for 3 in, 101.6 mm for 4 in, 127.0 mm for 5 in, 152.4 mm for 6 in, and so on. Just multiply the number of whole inches by 25.4 to find how much to add on. Example: $2\frac{1}{4}$ in—$\frac{1}{4}$ in is 6.3 mm; 2 in is 50.8 mm, so the result is $6.3 + 50.8$, which comes to 57.1 mm.

inches	quarters	eighths	sixteenths	thirty-secondths	mm
0					0
				1/32	1
			1/16	2/32	2
				3/32	
		1/8	2/16	4/32	3
				5/32	4
			3/16	6/32	5
				7/32	6
	1/4	2/8	4/16	8/32	
				9/32	7
			5/16	10/32	8
				11/32	9
		3/8	6/16	12/32	
				13/32	10
			7/16	14/32	11
				15/32	12
1/2	2/4	4/8	8/16	16/32	13
				17/32	14
			9/16	18/32	
				19/32	15
		5/8	10/16	20/32	16
				21/32	17
			11/16	22/32	
				23/32	18
		3/4	6/8	12/16	24/32	19
				25/32	20
			13/16	26/32	21
				27/32	
		7/8	14/16	28/32	22
				29/32	23
			15/16	30/32	24
				31/32	
					25
1	4/4	8/8	16/16	32/32	25.4

Converting miles to kilometres

Converting miles to kilometres is fairly straightforward.

The nautical mile, used for measuring speed in knots (nautical miles per hour), is an internationally accepted unit used as part of the metric system, and so never needs to be converted.

Obsolete miles include the classical Roman mile of 1000 double paces ('mille' is Latin for 1000—hence the word). This was 1611yd; a modern mile is 1760yd. The more recently defunct Scots mile was 1976yd.

This chart has a logarithmic scale for extra accuracy with small distances. If you want to work out an amount greater than 100 miles or 160km, simply look up one-tenth of the figure you need to convert. For example, to turn 112 miles into km, look up 11.2 miles. The chart will give you a reading of 17.9km. Multiply this by 10 and you have the answer: 179km.

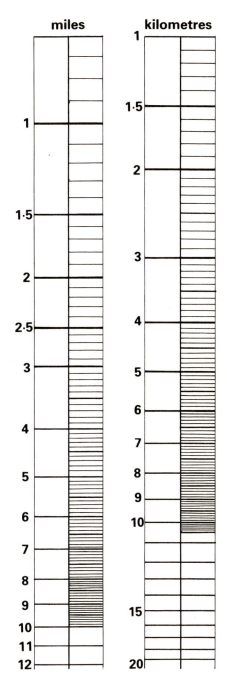

miles   kilometres

Imperial and metric fabric lengths

Under the old imperial system, the width of fabrics was measured in inches, and the length in yards, divided into fractions of an eighth. It was an untidy arrangement, though people were used to it.

Under the new metric system, fabric width is measured in centimetres, and the length in metres and centimetres. This table is for *length only*, since the imperial side is in eighths of a yard.

Strictly speaking, centimetres have been abandoned in the new metric system, which prefers millimetres, but centimetres are much more convenient for fabrics and so they have remained in use here. The system of writing the lengths is also non-standard: four and a half metres is written 4.50m, for 4 metres and 50 centimetres. In the normal metric method, as used for other measurements, the final 0 after the decimal point is dropped, so the same length of (say) metal rod would be 4.5m.

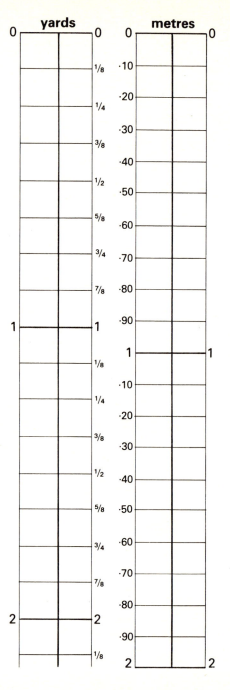

Measures of weight and capacity

Ounces, fluid ounces and pounds to grammes, litres and kilogrammes

A fluid ounce of water weighs an ounce, therefore an imperial pint (20 fl oz) weighs 20 oz. An American pint, however, contains only 16 fl oz and therefore weighs 16 oz (1 lb).

One millilitre weighs 1 gramme and one litre (1,000 millilitres) weighs 1 kg.

Conversion is quite easy. If you are going to be using American recipes you must remember than an American cup holds only 8 fl oz liquid, compared with 10 fl oz for an English cup.

When measuring dry ingredients by the cup, the weights will vary greatly, according to the item being measured. A cup of butter or syrup, for instance, weighs much more than a cup of breadcrumbs or grated cheese.

If you often wish to use American recipes, it is sensible to buy a set of U.S. cup measures (1 cup, ½ cup, ⅓ cup and ¼ cup). American teaspoons and table-spoons are also smaller than the imperial sizes.

If you have to deal with large quantities of liquid, such as oil or water storage tanks and petrol mileage in cars, the following table will help with your calculations.

Do not forget that a U.S. gallon is based on a 16 fl oz pint, not the imperial standard 20 fl oz.

weight measures				capacity measures				
kilogrammes	grammes	ounces	pounds	imperial pints	US pints	fluid ounces	millilitres	litres
	50	1				1	50	
		2				2		
	100	3				3	100	
		4	¼		¼	4		
	150	5		¼		5	150	
		6		1 gill		6		
	200	7				7	200	
	250	8	½		½	8	250	
0·25		9				9		0·25
	300	10		½		10	300	
		11				11		
	350	12	¾		¾	12	350	
		13				13		
	400	14				14	400	
		15		¾		15		
	450	16	1		1	16	450	
		17				17		
0·5	500	18				18	500	0·5
	550	19				19	550	
		20	1¼	1	1¼	20		
	600	21		pint		21	600	
		22				22		
	650	23				23	650	
		24	1½		1½	24		
	700	25		1¼		25	700	
	750	26				26	750	
0·75		27				27		0·75
	800	28	1¾		1¾	28	800	
		29				29		
	850	30		1½		30	850	
		31				31		
	900	32	2		2	32	900	
		33				33		
	950	34				34	950	
1	1000	35		1¾		35	1000	1
		36	2¼		2¼	36		

Atmosphere temperatures

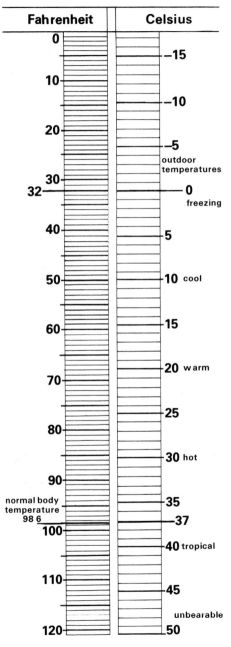

Fahrenheit	Celsius

Temperature

The usual measure of temperature for day-to-day purposes is the degree Celsius. It is written as °C and spoken of as degree C. This is the same as Centigrade but the old name has now been dropped.

To convert Fahrenheit to Celsius
Roughly: subtract 32, multiply by 5, divide by 9.

To convert Celsius to Fahrenheit
Roughly: multiply by 9, divide by 5, then add 32.

Body temperature
Normal body temperature in Celsius is 37° C (98.6° F). Half a °C variation from the normal is not anything to worry about, but more than one degree may be cause for concern.

Weather
On a hot day, the temperature may rise to 30° C or more, while 20° C is a warmish day. In a temperate climate, the temperature of a cool summer day or a mild winter day is about 15° C, but normal winter temperatures are about 5–10° C. 0° C is freezing, and any temperature below this is written with a minus sign, as − 5° C.

Room heating
The temperature different people find most comfortable varies a lot, but normally central heating is adjusted to give an even temperature of around 20° C.

Oven/Freezing Temperatures

Fahrenheit			Celsius
0			−17·7 deep freeze
water freezes 32			0
50			10
			20
			30
100			40
			50
150			60
			70
			80
200			90
oven settings 212 very cool	gas mark		100 water boils
			110
250	½		120
			130
			140
cool 300	2		150
warm			160
350	4		170
moderate			180
fairly hot			190
400	6		200
			210
hot			220
450	8		230
very hot			240
			250
500	10		260

Temperature range and conversion

The Celsius scale is based on the fact that water boils at 100° C and freezes at 0° C. If you are working in Fahrenheit, water boils at 212° F and freezes at 32° F.

Oven temperatures

The chart below provides a guide to the different markings you will find on oven controls. They are rough equivalents rather than exact conversions. If a recipe book gives its own conversion, it is sensible to use that stated temperature.

°C	°F	Gas mark
100	200	Low
110	225	$\frac{1}{4}$
120	250	$\frac{1}{2}$
140	275	1
150	300	2
160	325	3
180	350	4
190	375	5
200	400	6
220	425	7
230	450	8
240	475	9
260	500	10

Clothes sizes

The equivalents given in the following lists are standard, rather than exact, and clothes should, as before, be tried on for fit.

Hat sizes, which used to be given as the width, are now given as the circumference. glove sizes have not changed, but shoe sizes can now be found in a new system called Mondopoint (see Shoes sizes chart).

Men's clothes
Collar size, chest, waist, inside leg

in	cm
12	30
12½	32
13	33
13½	34
14	35
14½	37
15	38
15½	39/40
16	41
16½	42
17	43
17½	44
18	45
18½	46
19	48
19½	49/50
20	51
22	55
24	61
26	66
28	71

in	cm
30	76
32	81
34	85
36	91
38	97
40	100
42	107
44	112
46	117
48	122
50	125

Women's dresses

Size	Bust/hip in	Bust/hip cm
8	30/32	76/81
10	32/34	81/86
12	34/36	86/91
14	36/38	91/97
16	38/40	97/102
18	40/42	102/107
20	42/44	107/112
22	44/46	112/117
24	46/48	117/122

Hats

Old size	Metric size
5	41
5½	45
6	49
6½	53
7	57
7½	61
8	65
8½	69
9	73

Shoes

Shoes are difficult to measure accurately and should always be tried on before buying. The introduction of the international Mondopoint sizing system should help. This gives the length and width of feet in millimetres. Thus in a 230/85 the first figure is the length, the second the width across the widest part of the foot at the base of the big toe.

Shoe sizes

Mondopoint lengths in mm	UK sizes adults	European sizes adults	US sizes adults
210	2	35	3
	3	36	4
220			5
	4	37	6
230			
	5	38	
240	6	39	7
			8
250	7	40	
			9
260	8	41	10
270	9	42	
			11
	10	43	
		44	12
280		45	
	11		13
		46	
290	12	47	
			14
300			

Children's clothing

Clothing for children under one year is generally marked with the child's weight. Over one year the height is indicated. The age is not always included.

WEIGHT		HEIGHT		CHEST		AGE
lb	kg	in	cm	in	cm	
12	5.5	$24\frac{1}{2}$	62	$17\frac{3}{8}$	45	3 mos.
18	8	27	68	$18\frac{1}{4}$	46	6 mos.
21	9.5	29	75	$18\frac{7}{8}$	48	9 mos.
24	11	$31\frac{1}{2}$	79	$19\frac{5}{8}$	50	12 mos.
		34	86	$20\frac{1}{4}$	51	18 mos.
		36	90	$20\frac{7}{8}$	53	2 yrs.
		38	95	$21\frac{1}{2}$	54	3 yrs.
		$40\frac{1}{2}$	102	$22\frac{1}{8}$	55	4 yrs.

Cooking

Conversion to metric measurements

The metric measures in this book are based on a 25g unit instead of the ounce (28.35 g). When cooking always use *either* imperial *or* metric measurements.

If you want to convert your own recipes from imperial to metric, we suggest you use the same 25g unit, and use 600 ml in place of 1 pint, with the British Standard 5-ml and 1.5-ml spoons replacing the old variable teaspoons and tablespoons. These adaptations will sometimes give a slightly smaller recipe quantity and may require a shorter cooking time.

Note Sets of British Standard metric measuring spoons are available in the following sizes – 2.5 ml, 5 ml, 10 ml and 15 ml.

When measuring milk it is more convenient to use the exact conversion of 568 ml (1 pint).

For more general reference, the following tables will be helpful.

Metric conversion scale

Liquid		
Imperial	**Exact conversion**	**Recommended millilitres**
$\frac{1}{4}$ pint	142 ml	150 ml
$\frac{1}{2}$ pint	284 ml	300 ml
1 pint	568 ml	600 ml
$1\frac{1}{2}$ pints	851 ml	900 ml
$1\frac{3}{4}$ pints	992 ml	1 litre

For quantities of $1\frac{3}{4}$ pints and over, litres and fractions of a litre have been used.

Solid		
Imperial	**Exact conversion**	**Recommended grams**
1 oz	28.35 g	25 g
2 oz	56.7 g	50 g
4 oz	113.4 g	100 g
8 oz	226.8 g	225 g
12 oz	340.2 g	325 g
14 oz	397.0 g	400 g
16 oz (1 lb)	453.6 g	450 g

1 kilogram (kg) equals 2.2 lb.

	Electricity		Gas Mark
	°C	°F	
Very cool	110	225	$\frac{1}{4}$
	120	250	$\frac{1}{2}$
Cool	140	275	1
	150	300	2
Moderate	160	325	3
	180	350	4
Moderately hot	190	375	5
	200	400	6
Hot	220	425	7
	230	450	8
Very hot	240	475	9

Sewing and home dressmaking

Materials
These are sold by length, which is calculated in metres, the width being calculated in centimetres.

Width
90cm replaces 35–36in
115cm replaces 44–45in
120cm replaces 48in
140cm replaces 54–56in
150cm replaces 60in

For converting imperial and metric fabric lengths, see chart on page 296.

Sewing machine needles

British	Metric
11	70
12	80
14	90
16	100

Machine stitches

stitches (in)	stitches (cm)
14	6
12	5
10	4
8	3

Crochet hooks

Crochet hooks in two ranges, one for wool and one for cotton used to be available. The International Standard Range (below) shows the new equivalents.

Metric hook	Old wool size	Metric hook	Old cotton size
7.00 (mm)	2	2.00 (mm)	$1\frac{1}{2}$
6.00	4	1.75	$2\frac{1}{2}$
5.50	5	1.50	$3\frac{1}{2}$
5.00	6	1.25	$4\frac{1}{2}$
4.50	7	1.00	$5\frac{1}{2}$
4.00	8	0.75	$6\frac{1}{2}$
3.50	9	0.60	7
3.00	10		
2.50	12		
2.00	14		

Knitting yarns

20g is almost $\frac{3}{4}$ oz
25g is not quite 1 oz
40g is not quite $1\frac{1}{2}$ oz
50g is almost $1\frac{3}{4}$ oz

Knitting needles

Old No.	New U.K. metric No.	U.S. No.
14	2 (mm)	00
13	$2\frac{1}{4}$	0
12	$2\frac{3}{4}$	1
11	3	2
10	$3\frac{1}{4}$	3
9	$3\frac{3}{4}$	4
8	4	5
7	$4\frac{1}{2}$	6
6	5	7
5	$5\frac{1}{2}$	8
4	6	9
3	$6\frac{1}{2}$	10
2	7	$10\frac{1}{2}$
1	$7\frac{1}{2}$	11
0	8	12
00	9	13
000	10	15

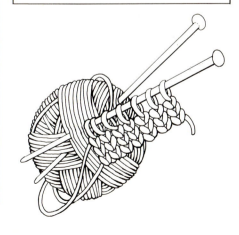

Quick conversions

Length

IMPERIAL TO METRIC

Inches to centimetres
Rough rule: multiply by 10, divide by 4.

Feet to metres
Rough rule: divide by 3 and subtract about a tenth of the result.

Yards to metres
Rough rule: subtract about a tenth.

Miles to kilometres
Rough rule: multiply by 8, divide by 5.

METRIC TO IMPERIAL

Centimetres to inches
Rough rule: divide by 10, multiply by 4.

Metres to feet
Rough rule: multiply by 3 and add about a tenth of the result.

Metres to yards
Rough rule: add about a tenth.

Kilometres to miles
Rough rule: divide by 8, multiply by 5.

Weight and capacity

IMPERIAL TO METRIC

Ounces to grammes
Rough rule: multiply by 30 and subtract about a twentieth from the result.

Pounds to kilogrammes
Rough rule: divide by 2 and subtract a tenth from the result.

Fluid ounces to millilitres
(same as ounces to grammes)

Pints (Imperial) to litres
Rough rule: multiply by $5\frac{1}{2}$ and divide by 10.

Gallons to litres
Rough rule: multiply by $4\frac{1}{4}$.

METRIC TO IMPERIAL

Grammes to ounces
Rough rule: add about a twentieth and divide the result by 30.

Kilogrammes to pounds
Rough rule: add a tenth and multiply the result by 2.

Millilitres to fluid ounces
(same as grammes to ounces)

Litres to pints (Imperial)
Rough rule: divide by $5\frac{1}{4}$ and multiply by 10.

Litres to gallons
Rough rule: divide by $4\frac{1}{2}$.

INDEX

H

Hall, cloakroom in, 47
Hammer, 75, 91
Handyman's knife, 75
Hat sizes, 300
Hay fever, 133
Health, family, 125–46
  first aid, 147–68
  general care and hygiene, 126–30
  inoculation and immunisation,
    130–31
  insurance, 226
  symptoms and treatment of
    illness, 132–46
Heart failure, 161–2
  external heart massage, 162
  symptoms, 161–2
Heat exhaustion, 162
Heat stroke, 162–3
Heating, 59–63
  bathroom, 45–6, 120
  central, 59–62
  water, 62–3
  see also Insulation
Herbs:
  cooking with, 265–6
  freezing, 265
Hessian wallcovering, 33
Highlighter clip light, 30
Hire purchase, 222
Histamine, 133
Holidays:
  care of house plants, 21
  emptying and turning off fridge
    before, 114
  precautions against burglars, 117
Holland blinds, 7
Holloway Chewing Gum Remover,
  105
Home decoration, 6–41
  blinds, 7–8
  carpets, 8–11
  colour schemes, 11–12
  curtains, 12–13
  cushions, 14
  floor coverings, 14–18
  furniture, 18–20
  indoor plants, 20–22
  lighting, 22–3
  mirrors, 24
  painting, 24–30
  pictures, 30
  room planning, 30–31
  rugs, 31–2
  wallpapering, 32–41
Home improvement grants, 66–7
  intermediate and special grants,
    66–7
  repair grants, 67
Home improvements, 42–73
  attic conversions, 42–4
  basement conversions, 44–5

bathrooms, 45–6
bedrooms, 46
cloakrooms, 47–8
cupboards, 48–9
damp problems, 49–52
dimmer switches, 52–3
doors, 53–4
double glazing, 54–6
exterior decorating, 56
extractor fans, 57
flooring, 57–9
heating, 59–63
insulation, 63–6
shelving, 67–70
showers, 70–72
tiling, 72–3
Home nursing, 145
Home valeting, 175–6
  dinner jackets and trousers, 175
  raincoats, 175–6
  suits and overcoats, 175
  women's skirts and dresses, 176
Horsefly bites, 152
Household basic, bulk buying, 218
Household insurance, 226–7
  building, 226
  contents, 226
Hydrochloric acid, 101
Hydrogen peroxide, 189
Hygiene, 130
  see also Cleaning
Hypothermia, 163
  in babies, 163
  in old people, 163

I

Ice cream stains, 105, 186
Illnesses, 132–46
  allergies, 133
  boils, 133–4
  bronchitis, 134–5
  bugs and body parasites, 135–7
  colds, 137
  contagious diseases, 137–41
  convulsions, 143
  coughs, 141
  cramp, 141–2
  ear disorders, 142–3
  fever, 143
  first aid, 147–68
  food poisoning, 143–4
  gastric disorders, 144–5
  home nursing, 145
  inoculations and
    immunisations, 130–31
  travel sickness, 145–6
  worms, 146
  see also First aid
Immersion heater, 62
Immunisation, 130–31
  contra-indications, 131
  triple vaccine programme, 130–31

whooping cough, 131
Imperial measurements/
  conversions, 291–304
Income tax, 225
  covenants and, 221
  relief and assurances, 212
  self-employed, 225
  tax return forms, 225
Indian fabric bedspreads, 191
Indian muslin, washing, 181
Indian rugs, 31
Inertia switches, 117
Ink stains, 105, 186
Inoculation, 130–31
Insecticides, 126, 129, 130
Insects:
  ants, 126–7
  bed bugs, 135
  bee and wasp stings, 152
  bites, 135, 151–2
  body parasites, 135–7
  cockroaches, 127
  fleas, 135
  flies and mosquitoes, 129–30
  lice, 136–7
  removing from ear, 158
Insulating blinds, 7
Insulating board or softboard, 65
Insulation, 62–6
  condensation and, 50
  draught-proofing, 63
  floors, 65–6
  loft, 63–5
  walls, 65
Insurance (policies), 225–7
  all risks, 226
  building, 226
  contents, 226
  difference between assurance
    and, 211
  freezer, 243
  health, 226
  household, 226
  indemnity, 226
  medical, 217
  new for old, 226
  personal, 226–7
  removers, 206, 209
  travel, 226
  unusual, 226–7
Interlining, curtain, 12, 195–6
Iodine, 288
Iron mould and rust stains, 187
Ironing and pressing, 176–8
  aids, 177
  care of irons, 176
  dampness and dryness, 178
  dry irons, 176
  steam irons, 176
  suits and overcoats, 175
  symbols, 178
Ironwork, rust and corrosion, 94